Table of Contents

READING COMPREHENSION

Try This! *(Using context clues)* 12

Moon Walk *(Finding the main idea)* 13

ABC *(Finding the main idea)* 14

Call the Police! *(Finding the main idea)* 15

Rachel's Recipe *(Reading for details)* 16

Rodeo Clowns *(Reading for details)* 17

Gorillas *(Reading for details)* 18

Fun at the Farm *(Real or fantasy)* 19

Grandma Hugfuzzy *(Real or fantasy)* 20

The Change Game *(Real or fantasy)* 21

The Rescue *(Sequencing)* 22

New Kid in School *(Sequencing)* 23

A Pencil Sandwich? *(Sequencing)* 24

Secret Message *(Following directions)* 25

Rainy Day Fun *(Following directions)* 26

Our Flag *(Following directions)* 27

After School at Jake's House *(Drawing
   conclusions)* 28

?ti si tahW *(Drawing conclusions)* 29

They Could Do Better *(Drawing
   conclusions)* 30

Miss Maple *(Visualizing)* 31

Sentence Shapes *(Visualizing)* 32

Curious Creature *(Making inferences)* 33

Figure It Out *(Making inferences)* 34

Summer Vacation *(Sorting and classifying)* . . .35

Which One Doesn't Belong? *(Sorting
   and classifying)* 36

My Favorites *(Sorting and classifying)* 37

Will He Be All Right? *(Making predictions)* . . .38

What Will Happen Next? *(Making
   predictions)* 39

Wishes Come True *(Making predictions)* 40

Zoo Reports *(Comparing and contrasting)* 41

The Contest *(Comparing and contrasting)* 42

The Accident *(Comparing and contrasting)* . . .43

What Is Cotton? *(Developing vocabulary)* 44

Busy as a Bee *(Developing vocabulary)* 45

Sioux Life *(Developing vocabulary)* 46

Chain Reaction *(Identifying
   cause and effect)* 47

An American Volcano *(Identifying
   cause and effect)* 48

My Favorite Dentist *(Analyzing characters)* . .49

What a Kid! *(Analyzing characters)* 50

Lunch Lady *(Analyzing characters)* 51

Limericks *(Appreciating literature)* 52

A Tall Tale *(Appreciating literature)* 53

A Play *(Appreciating literature)* 54

TESTS: READING

Reading Skills Practice Test 1 57

Reading Skills Practice Test 2 61

Reading Skills Practice Test 3 65

Reading Skills Practice Test 4 69

Reading Skills Practice Test 5 73

Reading Skills Practice Test 6 77

Reading Skills Practice Test 7 81

Reading Skills Practice Test 8 85

Reading Skills Practice Test 9 89

Reading Skills Practice Test 10 93

Reading Skills Practice Test 11 97

CONTEMPORARY MANUSCRIPT

Aa 102
Bb 103
Cc 104
Dd 105
Ee 106
Ff 107
Gg 108
Hh 109
Ii 110
Jj 111
Kk 112
Ll 113
Mm 114
Nn 115
Oo 116
Pp 117
Qq 118
Rr 119
Ss 120
Tt 121
Uu 122
Vv 123
Ww 124
Xx 125
Yy 126
Zz 127
A–Z 128
a–z 129
1–5 130
6–10 131
Color Words 132
More Color Words 133
Number Words .134
More Number Words 135

Shapes 136
Days of the Week 137
Months 138
Special Days 140
Careers From A to Z 142
The Planets 145
Keep Up the Good Work! 146

GRAMMAR

Telling Sentences and Questions 148
Exclamations and Commands 151
Types of Sentences; Capital I 154
Common Nouns .157
Capitalize Names and Places 160
Verbs 163
Simple Sentences 166
Past-Tense Verbs 169
Pronouns 172
Types of Sentences 175
Word Order 178
Plural Nouns 181
Adjectives 184
Verb *to be* 187
Irregular Verbs *go, do* 190
Quotation Marks 193
Contractions With *not* 196
Subject/Verb Agreement 199
More About Subject/Verb
    Agreement 202
Verbs *have, has, has* 205

WRITING

You're Sharp! *(Capitalizing sentence beginnings)* 210

Stick With It *(Capitalizing sentence beginnings)* 211

A Whale of a Sentence *(Punctuating statements)* 212

That Sounds Fishy to Me *(Writing statements)* ...213

Ask Mother Goose *(Punctuating questions)* 214

Ask the Wolf *(Writing questions)* 215

Is Your Head in the Clouds? *(Punctuating statements and questions)* 216

Sunny Sentences *(Capitalizing/punctuating statements and questions)* 217

Camp Fiddlestick *(Writing statements and questions)* 218

A Happy Camper *(Proofreading statements and questions)* 219

A Day at the Beach *(Punctuating exclamations)* 220

Seashore Sentences *(Writing statements, questions, and exclamations)* 221

Building Blocks *(Building sentences)* 222

Keep Building! *(Building sentences)* 223

Get Your Ticket! *(Building sentences)* 224

Slide Show *(Building sentences)* 225

Mystery Bags *(Brainstorming descriptive words)* 226

Country Roads *(Writing descriptive words)* 227

It's in the Bag *(Adding descriptive words)* 228

City Streets *(Writing descriptive sentences)* 229

Football Frenzy *(Expanding sentences)* 230

Take Me Out to the Ball Game *(Expanding sentences)* 231

Cake and Ice Cream *(Combining sentences)* 232

Salt and Pepper *(Combining sentences)* 233

Great Gardening Tips *(Combining sentences)* 234

Growing Sentences *(Combining sentences)* 235

The Sky's the Limit *(Using commas in a series)* ...236

Up, Up, and Away *(Using commas in a series)* 237

Out of This World *(Proofreading)* 238

Smart About Saturn *(Proofreading)* 239

Banana-Rama *(Choosing the correct verb)* 240

An Apple a Day *(Choosing the correct verb)* 241

Stories of Nature *(Completing a sequenced story)* 242

Nestled in a Nest *(Writing a sequenced story)* ...243

Stories on Parade *(Writing the middle and end of stories)* 244

An Original Story *(Writing the beginning, middle, and end of a story)* 245

Once Upon a Time *(Mapping a story: The setting)* 246

All Kinds of Characters *(Mapping a story: The characters)* 247

That's a Problem! *(Mapping a story: The problem)* 248

Good Solution! *(Mapping a story: The solution)* 249

The Mighty Knight *(Writing a story from a map)* 250

A Story Fit for a King *(Mapping and writing a story)* 251

The Father of Our Country *(Proofreading)* 252

Presidential Pen Pals *(Writing a friendly letter)* ..253

MAPS

Looking at a Map 256

A Globe and Earth 258

A World Map 260

A Compass Rose 262

Using Directions 264

Map Symbols 266

Using Map Symbols 268

Distance 270

A Map Grid 272

Using a Map Grid 274

The United States 276

Looking at a State 278

A City Map 280

Small Places ... Large Places 282

Landforms 284

Bodies of Water 286

Using a Landform Map 288

A Road Map 290

A Resource Map 292

North America 294

Map Review 1 296

Map Review 2 297

Thinking About Maps 298

Glossary 299

ADDITION & SUBTRACTION

Spell It Out *(Adding to 10)* 302

Beautiful Bouquets *(Subtracting from 10)* 303

Crazy Creatures *(Adding/subtracting through 18)* 304

Can You See It? *(Adding/subtracting through 18)* 305

Scarecrow Sam *(Adding 1-digit and 2-digit numbers without regrouping)* 306

You've Got Mail *(Adding 1-digit and 2-digit numbers without regrouping)* 307

Counting on Good Manners *(Adding 2-digit numbers without regrouping)* 308

Just the Same *(Adding 2-digit numbers without regrouping)* 309

Planet Earth *(Adding 2-digit numbers without regrouping)* 310

Let Freedom Ring *(Adding 2-digit numbers without regrouping)* 311

Detective Work *(Subtracting 1-digit numbers)* ...312

Chirp, Chirp! *(Subtracting 1-digit numbers)* 313

Winter Is Coming *(Subtracting 1-digit numbers)* ..314

Baseball Puzzle *(Subtracting 1-digit numbers)* 315

Bubble Yum! *(Subtracting 2-digit numbers without regrouping)* 316

Super Star *(Subtracting 2-digit numbers without regrouping)* 317

Moving West *(Subtracting 2-digit numbers without regrouping)* 318

High Flying *(Subtracting 2-digit numbers without regrouping)* 319

Weather Drops *(Subtracting 2-digit numbers without regrouping)* 320

Animal Families *(Subtracting 2-digit numbers without regrouping)* 321

Triple the Fun *(Adding three addends)* 322

A Great Catch *(Regrouping review— ones to tens)* 323

Kaleidoscope Math *(Adding with and without regrouping)* 324

Zoo Animals *(Adding 1-digit and 2-digit numbers with regrouping)* 325

Don't Forget Your Keys *(Adding 1-digit and 2-digit numbers with regrouping)* 326

Scholastic Professional Books

Treasure of a Book *(Adding 2-digit numbers with regrouping)* 327

How Do We Get There? *(Adding 2-digit numbers with regrouping—multiple addends)* 328

Crossdigit Wiz *(Adding—multiple addends)* 329

Carnival Fun *(Adding 2-digit numbers with regrouping—multiple addends)* 330

Crack the Numbers *(Regrouping review—tens to ones)* 331

Digging Up Bones *(Subtracting 2-digit numbers with regrouping)* 332

First, Next, Last *(Subtracting 2-digit numbers with regrouping)* 333

Purdy Bird *(Subtracting 2-digit numbers with regrouping)* 334

Grandma's Quilt *(Subtracting 2-digit numbers with regrouping)* 335

All Tied Up *(Subtracting 2-digit numbers with regrouping)* 336

Teenie Tiny Babies *(Adding/subtracting 2-digit numbers with regrouping)* 337

Day by Day *(Adding/subtracting 2-digit numbers with regrouping)* 338

Pizza Vote *(Adding/subtracting 2-digit numbers with regrouping)* 339

Tool Time *(Adding/subtracting 2-digit numbers with regrouping)* 340

Powerful Presidents *(Adding 3-digit numbers without regrouping)* 341

Hundreds of Pumpkins *(Regrouping review—tens to hundreds)* 342

Through the Tunnels *(Adding 3-digit numbers with regrouping)* 343

Tricky Twins *(Adding 2-digit and 3-digit numbers with regrouping)* 344

Eager Leader *(Missing addends)* 345

Sandwich Shop *(Adding/subtracting 3-digit numbers with regrouping—using money)* 346

Easy as 1, 2, 3 *(Adding 3-digit numbers with regrouping—multiple addends)* 347

Count Down *(Regrouping review—hundreds to tens)* 348

The Sun's Family *(Subtracting 3-digit numbers without regrouping)* 349

A Place in Space *(Subtracting 3-digit numbers with regrouping)* 350

Tricky Zero *(Subtracting 3-digit numbers with zero)* 351

Treasures Under the Sea *(Adding/subtracting 3-digit numbers with regrouping)* 352

Follow the Trees *(Adding/subtracting 3-digit numbers with regrouping)* 353

School Supplies *(Adding/subtracting 3-digit numbers with regrouping)* 354

Movie Madness *(Adding/subtracting 3-digit numbers with regrouping)* 355

Animal Facts *(Adding/subtracting 3-digit numbers with regrouping)* 356

Very Special Helpers *(Adding/subtracting 3-digit numbers with regrouping)* 357

Vacation Time *(Adding 3-digit numbers with regrouping—using money)* 358

Bull's-eye *(Adding/subtracting 3-digit numbers with regrouping)* 359

Grid Math *(Adding/subtracting 3-digit numbers with regrouping—using a grid)* 360

Perfect Punt *(Adding/subtracting 3-digit numbers with regrouping)* 361

Tic-Tac-Toe *(Adding/subtracting 3-digit numbers with regrouping)* 362

MATH

Lone Donor (Missing numbers, counting) 365

Mystery Critter (Counting) 366

Order Recorder (Missing numbers, counting) 367

Missing Bone (Odd and even numbers) 368

Patterns for the Mail Carrier (Odd and even numbers) 369

Presidents' Day Problem (Ordinal numbers) 370

Amused Chooser (Greater than, less than, equal to) 371

Riddle Fun (Place Value) 372

Pattern Learner (Identifying patterns) 373

Shape Tricks (Combining shapes) 374

Picking Out Patterns (Identifying patterns) .. 375

Shape Study (Identifying shapes) 376

Shape Gaper (Identifying shapes) 377

Rocket Riddle (Fact families) 378

Wise Owls (Fact families) 379

Jack's Beanstalk (Multiplication picture problems) 380

Candy Boxes (Introducing division) 381

Creature Categories (Sorting and grouping) 382

Coin-Toss Addition (Writing simple equations) 383

Clear Reader (Writing simple equations) 384

Time to Get Up (Solving story and picture problems) 385

Pizza Party (Sorting and grouping) 386

Prime Timer (Telling time) 387

Just Snacks (Comparing coins and amounts) 388

Money Matters (Comparing coins and amounts) 390

Best Estimator (Comparing lengths) 391

December Weather (Reading tables) 392

Measuring Perimeter (Introducing perimeter) 393

Night-Light (Ordered pairs) 394

Great Graphing (Reading and creating simple graphs) 395

Fruit Graph (Reading and creating simple graphs) 396

Chester's Cakes and Pies (Identifying parts of a whole) 397

Part Timer (Identifying parts of a whole).... 398

Fraction Fun (Identifying parts of a whole) .. 399

Fun With Fractions (Finding parts of a whole or grouping) 400

More Fun With Fractions (Finding parts of a whole or grouping) 401

Answer Key 402

Scholastic Professional Books

"Nothing succeeds like success."

Alexandre Dumas the Elder, 1854

Dear Parent,

Congratulations on choosing this excellent educational resource for your child. Scholastic has long been a leader in educational publishing—creating quality educational materials for use in school and at home for nearly a century.

As a partner in your child's academic success, you'll want to get the most out of the learning experience offered in this book. To help your child learn at home, try following these helpful hints:

✤ Provide a comfortable place to work.

✤ Have frequent work sessions, but keep them short.

✤ Praise your child's successes and encourage his or her efforts.
   Offer positive help when a child makes a mistake.

✤ Display your child's work and share his or her progress with family and friends.

In this workbook you'll find hundreds of practice pages that keep kids challenged and excited as they strengthen their skills across the classroom curriculum.

The workbook is divided into eight sections: Reading Comprehension; Reading Tests; Contemporary Manuscript; Grammar; Writing; Maps; Addition & Subtraction; and Math. You and your child should feel free to move through the pages in any way you wish.

The table of contents lists the activities and the skills practiced. And a complete answer key in the back will help you gauge your child's progress.

Take the lead and help your child succeed with the *Scholastic Success With: 2nd Grade Workbook!*

The activities in this workbook reinforce age-appropriate skills and will help your child meet the following standards established as goals by leading educators.

Mathematics

★ Uses a variety of strategies when problem-solving

★ Understands and applies number concepts

★ Uses basic and advanced procedures while performing computation

★ Understands and applies concepts of measurement

★ Understands and applies concepts of geometry

Writing

★ Understands and uses the writing process

★ Uses grammatical and mechanical conventions in written compositions

Reading

★ Understands and uses the general skills and strategies of the reading process

★ Can read and understand a variety of literary texts

★ Can understand and interpret a variety of informational texts

Geography

★ Understands the characteristics and uses of maps and globes

★ Knows the location of places, geographic features, and patterns of the environment

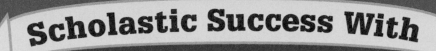

Scholastic Success With

READING COMPREHENSION

Try This!

*When you are reading, do you get stuck on words that you don't know? Does not knowing a word make it hard to understand what you are reading? This idea can help you. Use **context clues** to figure out what the word is. That means think about the other words in the sentence. What clues do they give? Then ask yourself what other word would make sense there.*

What do you think the underlined word means in each sentence below? Circle the meaning that makes sense. Then rewrite each sentence using the meaning instead of the underlined word.

1. **My domino has two white pips, and yours has five.**

   baby dogs   (spots)   long metal tubes

   My domino has two white spots and your has five.

2. **A gray fulmar flew by the cruise ship.**

   lizard   swordfish   (seabird)

   A gray seabird flew by the cruise ship.

3. **The queen had a beautiful necklace made of jasper.**

   (a green stone)   yellow pudding   wet snow

   The queen had a beautiful necklace made of a green stone.

4. **My sister is the best flutist in the high school band.**

   waitress   runner   [flute player]

   My sister is the best flute player the high school band.

Write a meaning for this nonsense word: zeebit. Use it in a sentence on another piece of paper. See if a friend can guess the meaning of your word by looking at the clues in the sentence.

Moon Walk

 *The **main idea** tells what the whole story is about.*

Neil Armstrong was an astronaut. He made history on July 20, 1969. He was the first man to walk on the moon! When he stepped on the moon, he said, "That's one small step for (a) man, one giant leap for mankind." Millions of people were watching this amazing event on TV. It was an awesome thing to look up at the moon that night and know that a man was walking around on it! For years, people had wondered if there would be moon creatures living there. But the only things Armstrong found were moon rocks and moon dust.

Draw a line connecting the correct star words that tell the main idea of the story. Begin at Earth. Some star words will not be used.

moon

uncle   dance   walk

to

river   on

cold   uncle

the

Armstrong   man

was   frog

hat

Neil

the   candy

plate

first

Write a short story with this title: "My Trip to the Moon." Underline the main idea of the story.

ABC

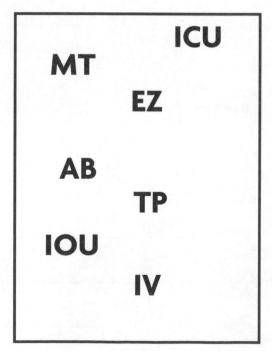

The **main idea** of a story tells what the whole story is about.

When you were in kindergarten, or maybe before that, you learned your ABCs. Letters are the building blocks for words. Words are the building blocks for sentences. We use sentences to communicate our thoughts and feelings. Each letter of the alphabet has at least one sound. Some letters have more than one sound. There are 26 letters in our alphabet. Many of our letters came from alphabets made many years ago in foreign countries. In fact, the word *alphabet* comes from two words, *alpha* and *beta*, which are the first two letters in the Greek alphabet!

Underline the title that describes the main idea of this story.

Playing With Blocks　　　**All About Our Alphabet**　　**The Greek Language**

Now let's play a game using the alphabet. Read each clue below. Draw a line to the letters that sound like the correct answer.

1. I borrowed some money from your piggy bank. _____ fifty cents.

2. This math is not hard. It's _____.

3. What did the blind man say to the doctor who made him see again? _____

4. What insect makes honey? _____

5. What does a Native American sleep in? _____

6. I drank all my milk. Now my glass is _____.

7. What kind of plant is that? _____

> **ICU**
>
> **MT**
>
> **EZ**
>
> **AB**
>
> **TP**
>
> **IOU**
>
> **IV**

Call the Police!

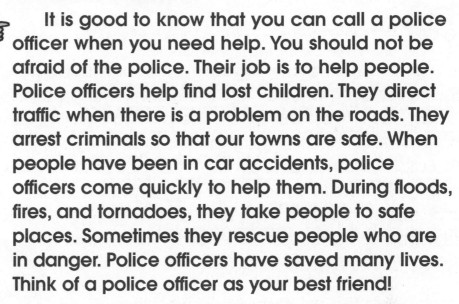

It is good to know that you can call a police officer when you need help. You should not be afraid of the police. Their job is to help people. Police officers help find lost children. They direct traffic when there is a problem on the roads. They arrest criminals so that our towns are safe. When people have been in car accidents, police officers come quickly to help them. During floods, fires, and tornadoes, they take people to safe places. Sometimes they rescue people who are in danger. Police officers have saved many lives. Think of a police officer as your best friend!

What do you think the main idea of this story is? To find out, read the letters that are connected in the puzzle. Write the letters in order beside the matching shapes.

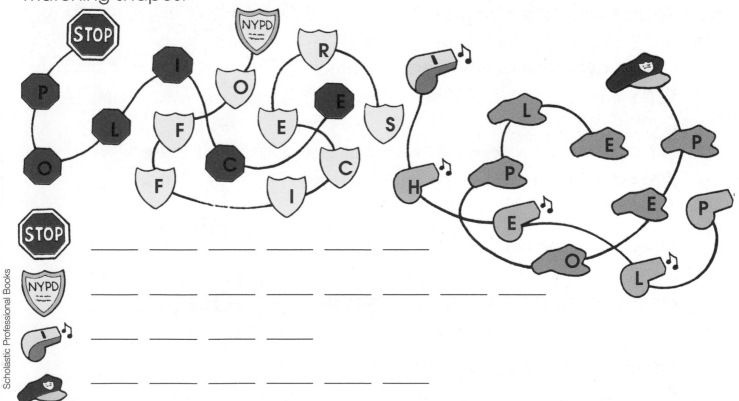

Write a letter to your town's police officers. Make sure the letter's main idea is to thank them for keeping your town safe. Ask an adult to mail it for you.

Rachel's Recipe

 Details *are parts of a story. Details help you understand what the story is about.*

On Saturday, Rachel got up early. Her mom was still asleep, so Rachel made her own breakfast. She put some peanut butter in a bowl. She mixed it with a little honey. Then she stirred in some oatmeal, bran flakes, and raisins. It tasted yummy! When Mom got up, she said, "Oh! You made granola!"

Follow the directions below.

- **Circle the word that tells who the main character is.**

- **Underline the word that tells what day Rachel made breakfast.**

- **Put a box around the word that tells what dish Rachel put the peanut butter in.**

- **Put a star by each of the four words that tell what she mixed with the peanut butter.**

- **Put a dotted line under the word that describes how it tasted.**

- **Put two lines under the word that tells what Mom called the food.**

Now find each of the nine words in the puzzle below and circle it. The words go across and down.

```
B R A N F L A K E S M H N C L
O A T M E A L B K E Q O J W I
W R A I S I N S G R A N O L A
L G S A T U R D A Y P E R D R
G R A C H E L Y U M M Y F A H
```

 On another sheet of paper, draw your favorite breakfast. Then write the steps to prepare it.

Rodeo Clowns

Details *are parts of a story. Details help you understand what the story is about.*

Have you ever been to a rodeo or seen one on TV? If so, you probably saw some rodeo clowns. Like clowns at a circus, they entertain the audience by doing funny tricks to make people laugh. But the main job of rodeo clowns is to protect the cowboys from the bulls. They try to catch the bull's attention long enough to allow the cowboy to escape from the arena without getting hurt. Bulls are quite fast, and they make sudden moves, so it is hard to get away from them. Angry bulls use their horns as weapons. Rodeo clowns sometimes jump in a barrel while the bull pushes it around. Other times they wave their arms or yell to keep the bull away from the cowboy. They make it look like a funny game, but it is really a very dangerous job.

Circle the letter under true or false to show your answer.

True	False		
B	Z	1.	Rodeo clowns do funny tricks.
R	U	2.	Rodeo clowns work at the circus.
L	M	3.	Rodeo clowns help protect the cowboys.
A	L	4.	Rodeo clowns distract the goats while the cowboy gets away.
R	X	5.	Rodeo clowns are brave.
I	V	6.	Bulls can make sudden moves.
F	D	7.	Bulls use their tails as weapons.
P	E	8.	Sometimes rodeo clowns jump in a cardboard box while the bull pushes it around.
R	W	9.	Sometimes rodeo clowns yell and wave their arms to distract the bulls.
S	C	10.	Rodeo clowns have a very dangerous job.

To find out who likes rodeo clowns, write the letters you circled in order.

_____ _____ _____ _____ _____ _____ _____ _____ _____ _____

Gorillas

Details *are parts of a story. Details help you understand what the story is about.*

Gorillas are the largest apes. They live in the rain forests of Africa. Every morning, they wake up and eat a breakfast of leaves, fruit, and bark. During most of the day, the adult gorillas take naps. Meanwhile, young gorillas play. They wrestle and chase each other. They swing on vines. When the adults wake up, everyone eats again. When there is danger, gorillas stand up on their hind legs, scream, and beat their chests. Every night before it gets dark, the gorillas build a new nest to sleep in. They break off leafy branches to make their beds, either on the ground or in the trees. Baby gorillas snuggle up to their mothers to sleep.

Find the answers to the puzzle in the story. Write the answers in the squares with the matching numbers.

Across

1. During the day, adult gorillas _____.

3. Gorillas eat leaves, bark, and _____.

5. The largest apes are _____.

7. In danger, gorillas beat their _____.

8. Young gorillas swing on _____.

Down

2. The continent where gorillas live is _____.

4. When young gorillas play, they _____ and chase each other.

6. Baby gorillas snuggle up to their mothers to _____.

On another piece of paper, write two things gorillas do that people also do.

Scholastic Professional Books

Fun at the Farm

 *Story events that can really happen are **real**. Story events that are make-believe are **fantasy**.*

Read each sentence below. If it could be real, circle the picture. If it is make-believe, put an X on the picture.

  Dairy cows give milk.

 The farmer planted pizza and hamburgers.

 The pig said,"Let's go to the dance tonight!"

 The mouse ate the dinner table.

  The hay was stacked in the barn.

 The chickens laid golden eggs.

 The green tractor ran out of gas.

  The newborn calf walked with wobbly legs.

 The goat and the sheep got married by the big tree.

  Two crickets sang "Mary Had a Little Lamb."

  Horses sat on the couch and watched TV.

 Rain made the roads muddy.

 Four little ducks swam in the pond.

 The farmer's wife baked a pumpkin pie.

 On another sheet of paper, write one make-believe sentence about the farmer's house and one real sentence about it.

Grandma Hugfuzzy

Grandma Hugfuzzy lived all alone in the country. She loved to sit on the porch and watch the animals. Every day, she put food out for the rabbits and raccoons. She fed the birds with scraps of bread. She put corn out for the deer. One terrible, awful, dreadful day, Grandma Hugfuzzy's house burned down. Poor Grandma! She had nowhere to go and no one to help her. She spent the night in an old barn on a bed of hay, crying herself to sleep. During the night, the animals came to her rescue. Nine black bears chopped down some trees. A herd of deer carried the wood on their antlers. Dozens of raccoons and squirrels worked all night building a log cabin for Grandma. Birds flew above the house nailing on the roof. When morning came, Grandma Hugfuzzy was amazed to see what her animal friends had done! She threw a big party for them that lasted ten years!

Write a red *R* on things that are real. Write a purple *F* on things that are fantasy.

a woman feeding animals

deer that carry lumber

a grandmother living alone

sleeping on hay in a barn

animals building a log cabin

Home Sweet Home

WELCOME

a house burning down

bears chopping down trees

birds that can nail on a roof

crying that her house burned

a party that lasted ten years

The first part of this story could be real. Draw a big orange star at the place where the story changes to fantasy.

Scholastic Professional Books

The Change Game

Each sentence below is make-believe. Change it!
Rewrite the sentence so that it is real.
Study the example.

The broom carried the dog to the moon.

The broom was kept in the closet.

1. **The newborn baby was bigger than a house.**

   _____

2. **The walls were painted with gooey green slime.**

   _____

3. **The Queen of England turned into a frog.**

   _____

Now change and do it the other way! Each sentence below is real.
Change it so that it is fantasy. Study the example.

The moon is made of rocks and ice.

The moon is made of green cheese.

4. **The black spider crawled across the floor.**

   _____

5. **The deep-sea diver saw a whale and five dolphins.**

   _____

6. **My pizza has pepperoni and olives on it.**

   _____

 On another piece of paper, draw a picture about one of your fantasy sentences.

The Rescue

 Sequencing *means putting the events in a story in the order that they happened.*

Mia's black cat climbed to the top of a telephone pole and couldn't get down. "Come down, Spooky!" cried Mia. Mia thought hard. What could she do? She went across the street to ask Mr. Carson for help. He was a firefighter before he retired. "What's the matter, Mia?" asked Mr. Carson when he saw Mia's tears. "My cat is up on that pole, and I can't get her down!" Mr. Carson hugged Mia and said, "I'll call my buddies at the fire station. They will come and help." A few minutes later, Mia saw the fire truck coming. The firefighters parked near the pole and raised a long ladder to the top. A firefighter climbed the ladder and reached out for Spooky. Just then, Spooky jumped to a nearby tree limb, climbed down the tree, and ran into the backyard. Mia said, "Spooky! You naughty cat!" Mr. Carson and the firefighters laughed and laughed.

Read the sentences on the ladder. Number them in the order that they happen in the story.

Mia asked Mr. Carson for help.

Mr. Carson called his firefighter friends.

The firefighters laughed.

A firefighter climbed the ladder.

Mia begged Spooky to come down.

Spooky jumped to a tree and climbed down.

The fire truck came.

Mia scolded Spooky.

New Kid in School

When they finished moving, Mom took Shelby to meet her new teacher. The teacher said, "Welcome to our school, Shelby. Let me tell you what we do in our second-grade class. We start the day with reading and writing. After that, we do math. Then we go out to recess. Just before lunch, we have social studies. We eat lunch at 11:00. Then we have story time. After story time, we have science. Then comes learning centers, where you can work on the computer, play a game, or read a book. Next, we have spelling. Finally, we go to music and art classes for the last hour of the day. Here is a schedule for you to take home. I'll see you tomorrow, Shelby!"

Fill in the blanks with the missing words or time.

Second-Grade Class Schedule

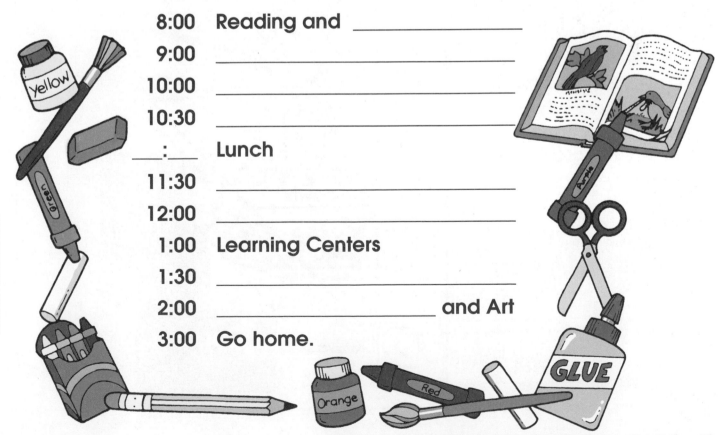

8:00   Reading and _____

9:00   _____

10:00   _____

10:30   _____

___:___ Lunch

11:30   _____

12:00   _____

1:00   Learning Centers

1:30   _____

2:00   _____ and Art

3:00   Go home.

A Pencil Sandwich?

How does the lead get inside a wooden pencil? Pencils are made out of strips of wood cut from cedar trees. Then grooves are cut in the strips. Graphite is laid into the grooves. (We call it lead, but it is really graphite.) Then another strip of wood is glued on top of the first one, making a pencil sandwich! The wood is rounded in rows on the top strip of wood and the bottom strip. Then the pencils are cut apart and painted. An eraser is added on the end and held in place by a metal ring. When you buy a pencil, you sharpen it, and then you are ready to write.

Look at the pictures. Number them in the order that they happen in the story.

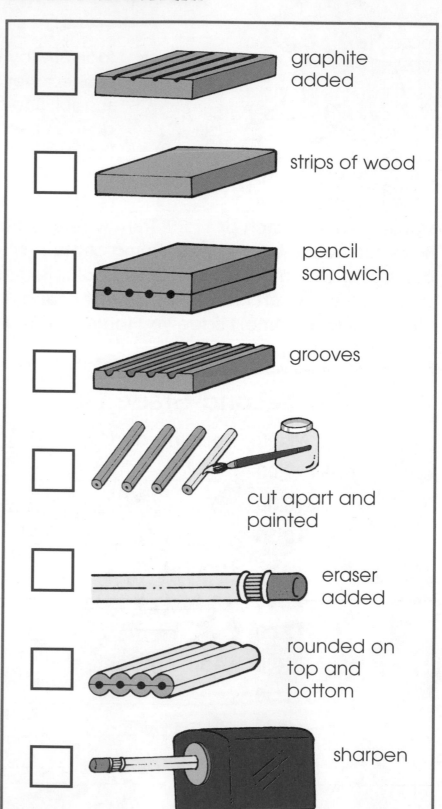

□ graphite added

□ strips of wood

□ pencil sandwich

□ grooves

□ cut apart and painted

□ eraser added

□ rounded on top and bottom

□ sharpen

 Use a pencil to practice writing the alphabet, uppercase and lowercase.

Scholastic Professional Books

leaf

Secret Message

Follow the directions in each shape. Write the answer in the shape that matches it. If you follow directions carefully, you will discover a secret message!

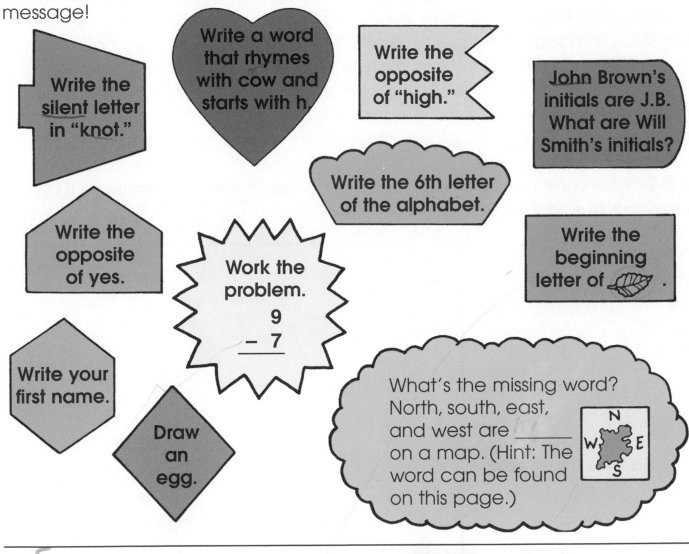

Write the <u>silent letter</u> in "knot."

Write a word that rhymes with cow and starts with h.

Write the opposite of "high."

John Brown's initials are J.B. What are Will Smith's initials?

Write the 6th letter of the alphabet.

Write the opposite of yes.

Work the problem.
9
− 7

Write the beginning letter of .

Write your first name.

Draw an egg.

What's the missing word? North, south, east, and west are _____ on a map. (Hint: The word can be found on this page.)

Trenton

K *no* *w.s*

how hart

−2

b

O

f

low

directions

 Write step-by-step directions that tell how to make a peanut butter and jelly sandwich.

Rainy Day Fun

One rainy afternoon, Sharon and I decided to play grocery store. We went to the garage and set up four empty boxes for our shelves. Mom let us have all the canned food from the pantry to play with. We wrote prices on little strips of paper and taped them to the cans. We used Dad's calculator for our cash register. We set our cash register on the old table in the garage. Then we got some play money out of a game in my closet. Sharon made signs that said, "Green Beans: 3 cans for $1.00" and things like that. There were lots of brown paper bags in the kitchen, so we took some to sack the groceries. When our cousins came over, we gave them some play money and let them be the customers. Then we traded places. Who cares if it rains when you are having so much fun?

Follow the directions to illustrate the story.

1. Draw a table and four empty boxes.

2. Draw cans in all the empty boxes.

3. Draw three signs on the wall telling what is being sold.

4. Draw Sharon by the table.

5. Draw some play money in Sharon's hand.

6. Draw two paper sacks under the table.

Write the directions from your house to a another place in your neighborhood. Follow the directions to see if they are correct.

Scholastic Professional Books

Our Flag

I pledge allegiance to the flag of the United States of America and to the Republic for which it stands, one nation under God, indivisible, with liberty and justice for all.

Follow the directions given in each of the following sentences.

1. **There is one star for every state in the nation. Count the stars. Write the number in the star.** *(star: 50)*

2. **Write the name of your state.** _Verginia_

3. **Color the area around the stars blue. The stars should be white, so do not color them.**

4. **Write the total number of stripes.** _13_

5. **Seven stripes are red. Beginning with the top stripe, color it and every other stripe red. The six stripes in between should be white, so do not color them.**

6. **Write these letters in reverse to make two words that tell another name for the flag.**   D L O   Y R O L G
   OlO   _GlOxr_

7. **Draw a box around every word in the Pledge of Allegiance that has more than six letters.**

💡 **Design a flag with four stars and three stripes for a make-believe country. Draw and color it.**

After School at Jake's House

*You are **drawing conclusions** when you use your own thoughts to answer the question, "How could that have happened?"*

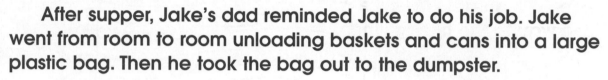

Jake had a lot of homework to do. It was three pages long. He added and subtracted until his hand got tired of writing.

1. What kind of homework did Jake have?

   spelling   math   reading

   What clues told you the answer? Underline them in the story.

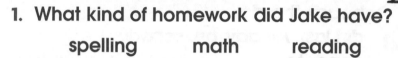

After supper, Jake's dad reminded Jake to do his job. Jake went from room to room unloading baskets and cans into a large plastic bag. Then he took the bag out to the dumpster.

2. What was Jake's job?

   washing dishes   making the bed   taking out the trash

   What clues told you the answer? Underline them in the story.

Now Jake could have some free time. He decided to play "Star Monsters." He turned on the TV and put a cartridge in the player. He watched the monsters fighting on the TV screen while his fingers pushed buttons to make them move.

3. What was Jake doing?

   playing a video game   watching the news   playing with toys

   What clues told you the answer? Underline them in the story.

Jake was tired. He put on his pajamas, brushed his teeth, and crawled under the covers.

4. What was Jake doing?

   waking up   getting ready for school   going to bed

   What clues told you the answer? Underline them in the story.

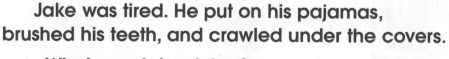

Scholastic Professional Books

?ti si tahW

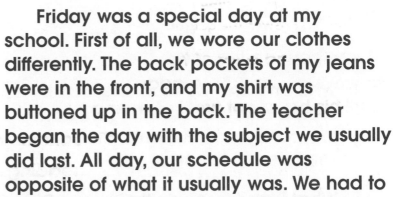

Friday was a special day at my school. First of all, we wore our clothes differently. The back pockets of my jeans were in the front, and my shirt was buttoned up in the back. The teacher began the day with the subject we usually did last. All day, our schedule was opposite of what it usually was. We had to write our name backwards on our papers. At lunch time, we ate dessert first, then our meals! When we went out to recess, we had to walk backward all the way to the playground. Then we had backward relay races. Some people fell down. Everyone was giggling! When it was time to go home, we sang "Good Morning to You."

1. What special day was it? Circle one.

   Valentine's Day   Grandparent's Day   Backward Day

2. Connect the dots in backward ABC order to find out how the principal looked that day.

3. If the math assignment was to count by 5's to 50, how would the children have written it that day? Write the numbers.

Make up a spelling word list with ten words. Then write them the way the children would have written them on this special day.

They Could Do Better

Read each story below. Choose your answers from the bubble-gum machine. Write them on the lines.

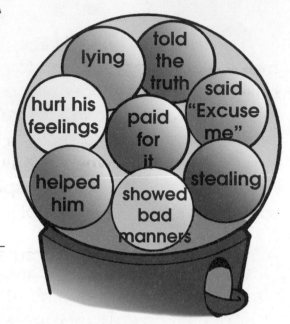

Bubble-gum machine contains: lying, told the truth, hurt his feelings, said "Excuse me", paid for it, helped him, showed bad manners, stealing

1. When no one was looking, James took a piece of bubble gum from the candy counter and chewed it. Then he left the store.

   What was James doing? _____

   What should he have done?

   _____

2. Dad's boss, Mr. Hill, came for dinner. Zach burped during the meal. He laughed. His dad looked angry.

   What did Zach do wrong? _____

   What should he have done? _____

3. While Mom was gone, Ashley played with matches. When Mom came home, she sniffed the air and said, "Ashley, did you light   some matches?" Ashley said, "No, Mom, I didn't."

   What was Ashley doing? _____

   What should she have done? _____

4. Becky and Cindy saw a boy trip and fall down. Becky pointed at   him and told Cindy to look. Then they laughed. The boy looked   away sadly.

   What did Becky and Cindy do? _____

   What should they have done? _____

On a piece of paper, write the name of a person in your class who has good manners. Explain why you came to that conclusion.

Scholastic Professional Books

Miss Maple

   I am a sugar tree. I live in Vermont. In the summer, my green leaves make a cool, shady place for people to rest. Every fall, my leaves turn brilliant colors of yellow, red, and orange. Some people think it looks like my leaves are on fire! In the winter, my leaves are all gone. I stretch my empty arms out to the falling snow. In the spring, little flowers appear along with my new leaves. That's when the sweet sap inside me begins to rise. People drill holes in my trunk and put a spout in me to drain the sap. Then they boil the sap and make maple syrup!

Add to and color each picture the way it is described in the story.

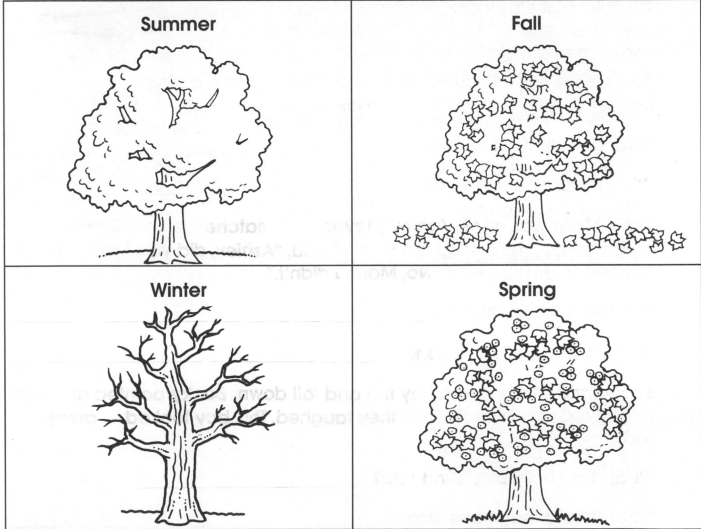

Summer

Fall

Winter

Spring

 Do you like maple syrup? Draw a picture of the kind of food that you would put maple syrup on.

Sentence Shapes

Let's have some fun reading and writing sentences! Look at the sentence below. It is shaped like what it is telling about.

Yahoo! I love rollercoasters. They are so much fun! They tickle my tummy!

Now it is your turn! Read each sentence below. Think about what it means. On another piece of paper, rewrite each sentence in the shape that shows what it is telling about. The shapes at the bottom of the page may help you.

1. I wonder if this box has my birthday gift in it.

2. I will send a valentine to someone that I love.

3. Columbus believed that Earth was round.

4. If you see someone without a smile, give them one of yours.

5. Jets taxi down the runway, then fly into the air.

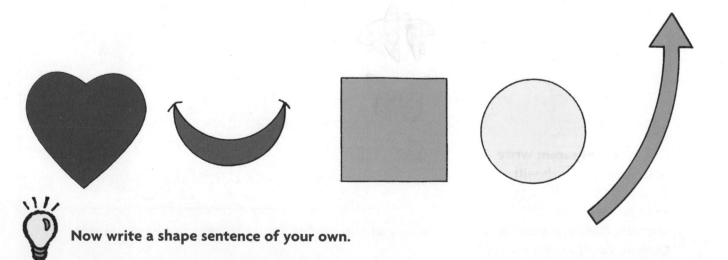

Now write a shape sentence of your own.

Scholastic Professional Books

Curious Creature

Use story details to help you make decisions about what has happened in the story.

Zolak boarded his spaceship and blasted off from the planet Vartog. He was on a special mission to learn about earthlings. His spaceship landed gently in a desert. Zolak walked around looking for earthlings, but all he could see were rocks and sand. Then he looked down and saw a dark creature lying down right next to him. In fact, the creature's feet were touching Zolak's feet. Zolak was scared and tried to run away, but everywhere he went, the creature followed him. At noon, Zolak realized that the creature had shrunk to a very small size but was still right next to his feet. However, during the afternoon, the dark creature grew longer and longer! Then the strangest thing happened. Night came and the dark creature completely disappeared!

1. Who do you think the dark creature was? _____

2. Was the dark creature an earthling?   yes   no

3. Do you think Zolak will give a true report about the earthlings when he returns to Vartog?   yes   no

   Why or why not?

   _____

4. Draw a line to match the object to its correct shadow.

 On a piece of paper, write the story you think will appear in Vartog newspapers under the headline "Zolak Discovers a Curious Creature on Earth?"

Figure It Out

Read each sentence. Then color the numbered space in the picture that matches the number of the correct answer.

He rode his bike?
Who rode it?
  1. a boy
  2. a girl

Let's throw snowballs!
What time of year is it?
  3. summer
  4. winter

Run, John, run!
What sport is John in?
  5. swimming
  6. track

Please bait my hook.
What am I doing?
  7. fishing
  8. playing baseball

Breakfast is ready!
What time is it?
  9. night
  10. morning

I'm so thirsty.
What will I do?
  11. drink something
  12. eat something

Sorry! I broke it.
What could it be?
  13. a stuffed animal
  14. a crystal vase

He's a professor.
What is he?
  15. an adult
  16. a baby

It won't fit in the car.
What is it?
  17. a football
  18. a swing set

Look at the dark cloud.
Where should you look?
  19. down
  20. up

The lamb lost its mother.
Who is its mother?
  21. a sheep
  22. a horse

She wore a red hat.
Who wore it?
  23. a man
  24. a woman

I see a thousand stars.
What time is it?
  25. noon
  26. night

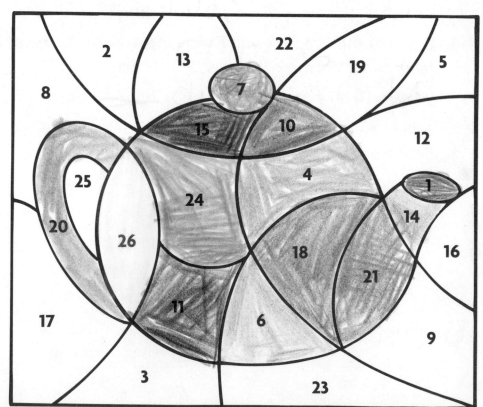

Riddle: What begins with T, ends with T, and has T in it? Find it in the puzzle.

Summer Vacation

 Grouping like things together helps you see how parts of a story are connected and makes the story easier to understand.

Last summer, Dad, Mom, Tim, and Tara went to the beach in Florida. They swam, fished, built sandcastles, and went sailing. Mom brought a picnic lunch. She spread a blanket on the sand and set out ham sandwiches, potato chips, apples, and cookies. She brought lemonade in the cooler. Later, Tim and Tara walked along the beach and saw a crab walking sideways. A stray dog was barking at it. A starfish had washed up on the beach, too. Tim threw bread crumbs up in the air to feed a flock of seagulls. Then the family went back to the hotel, and Tim and Tara played video games until bedtime.

Use the story to find the answers. Fill in the blanks.

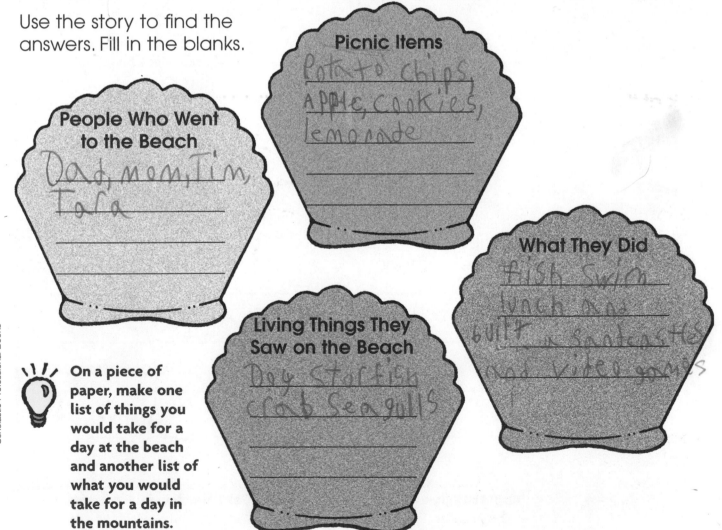

Picnic Items
Potato chips,
Apple, cookies,
lemonade

People Who Went to the Beach
Dad, mom, Tim
Tara

Living Things They Saw on the Beach
Dog Starfish
crab Seagulls

What They Did
Fish swim
lunch and
built a sandcastles
and video games

On a piece of paper, make one list of things you would take for a day at the beach and another list of what you would take for a day in the mountains.

Which One Doesn't Belong?

Look for similarities when grouping items.

Read each list. Cross out the word that doesn't belong. Then choose a word from the kite that belongs with each list and write it in the blank.

1. grouchy   mad   ~~cheerful~~   fussy   *angry*

2. north   ~~away~~   east   south   *west*

3. ~~goat~~   blue jay   robin   eagle   *parakeet*

4. juice   milk   tea   ~~mud~~   *lemonade*

5. hand   ~~toy~~   foot   head   *arm*

6. David   Bob   Ronald   ~~Sarah~~   *George*

7. ~~spinach~~   cake   cookies   pie   *pudding*

8. glue   ~~bicycle~~   pencils   scissors   *crayons*

9. penny   nickel   quarter   ~~marble~~   *dime*

Kite words: arm, dime, George, pudding, lemonade, parakeet, crayons, angry, west

Now read these categories. In each box, write the number from the above list that matches the category.

Birds *3*	Desserts *7*	*1* Bad Feelings
Boys' Names *6*	Money *9*	*8* School Supplies
Directions *2*	Body Parts *5*	*4* Drinks

Write a list of five things that go with this category: Things That Are Hot.

Scholastic Professional Books

My Favorites

This page is all about you! Read the categories and write your own answers.

My Favorite TV Shows	My Favorite Foods	My Favorite Sports
_____	_____	_____
_____	_____	_____
_____	_____	_____

Draw two of your favorite people here and write their names.

Favorite Color

_____

Favorite Holiday

_____

Favorite Song

_____

Favorite Movie

_____

Favorite School Subject

_____

Favorite Thing to Do After School

_____

Favorite Thing to Do With My Family

_____

 Trade pages with friends and read what they wrote. You might get to know them a little better!

Will He Be All Right?

Use story details to guess what will happen next.

Father Eagle said to his young son, "Today is a very special day. You will fly for the first time." Baby Eagle was afraid. He said, "But Father, I don't know how. What should I do?" His father laid a strong wing on his little shoulder and said, "You will know." They stood at the edge of a very high cliff. Far below were huge rocks and a canyon. "Ride the wind, my son!" said Father Eagle, and he gently pushed his son off the cliff. Baby Eagle yelled, "Help! Help!" and wildly flapped his wings. All of a sudden something wonderful happened!

Help!

He got hurt.

He fell on the rocks.

He broke his wing on a tree limb.

He learned to fly.

1. What do you think happened next? Color the rock that tells the most likely answer.

2. Why did you choose that answer? Find the sentence in the story that gives you a hint that the story has a happy ending. Write it here.

Something wonderfull happened

Unscramble the words and write the answer: **ODPRU** **AARDFI**

Proud afraid

3. How do you think Baby Eagle felt at first when he was pushed off the cliff? Scared

4. How do you think Father Eagle felt at the end of the story? Proud

Scholastic Professional Books

What Will Happen Next?   *out*

Read each story. Write your answer on the blanks.

1. The baseball game was tied 6-6 at the bottom of the ninth inning with bases loaded. The home team batter hit a high fly ball deep into right field. The outfielder caught the ball but then dropped it. What will happen next?

   the players will run

2. Latoya decided to bake some brownies. She put them in the oven and went outside and jumped in the pool. She swam for a long time. She forgot all about the brownies. What will happen next?

   burnt

3. Mrs. Lopez ran over a big nail. It stuck in the tire. Air began to seep out. What will happen next?

   flat

4. The wind began to blow. Dark clouds drifted in. Lightning cracked, and thunder roared. What will happen next?

   rain

5. One day Greg left his toy truck on the stairs. Mom came down the stairs carrying a laundry basket, piled high with dirty towels. She stepped on Greg's truck. What will happen next?

   She will fall

6. Dad and Sam went fishing. They rowed the boat to the middle of the lake. Then they hit a rock that made a hole in the boat. Water started rushing in it. What will happen next?

   The boat will sink

Choose one of the stories above and draw a picture of what happens next.

Scholastic Professional Books

Wishes Come True

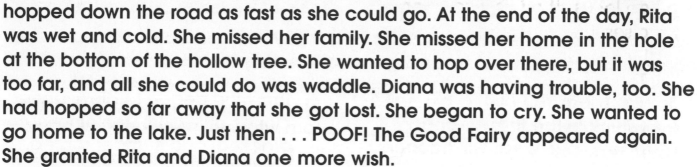

Once upon a time Rita Rabbit was complaining to Diana Duck. "You always have fun, swimming around in the lake. I wish I was a duck. You're lucky." Diana Duck said, "Oh, really? Well, I wish I was a rabbit! You can hop so fast and go so far. I think you're lucky!" Just then the Good Fairy appeared and said, "You are both lucky! I will grant you each your wish." All of a sudden Rita Rabbit became a duck! She waddled to the lake and went for a swim. Diana Duck became a rabbit and hopped down the road as fast as she could go. At the end of the day, Rita was wet and cold. She missed her family. She missed her home in the hole at the bottom of the hollow tree. She wanted to hop over there, but it was too far, and all she could do was waddle. Diana was having trouble, too. She had hopped so far away that she got lost. She began to cry. She wanted to go home to the lake. Just then . . . POOF! The Good Fairy appeared again. She granted Rita and Diana one more wish.

Draw what you think happened when Rita got her second wish.

Draw what you think happened when Diana got her second wish.

 If you had a wish, what would it be? On a piece of paper, draw a picture of what might happen if your wish came true.

Zoo Reports

Compare *means to look for things that are the same.*
Contrast *means to look for things that are different.*

The second-grade class went to the zoo for a field trip. The next day, the teacher asked the children to write a report about what they learned. Read the two reports below.

Ryan

What I Learned at the Zoo

I learned about the giant tortoise. It was so big that the guide let us sit on its back. Some tortoises live to be over 100 years old! That's older than my grandpa!

The slowest-moving mammal is the three-toed sloth. It hangs from trees and eats fruit. Some sloths sleep more than 20 hours a day. What a lazy animal!

I thought the albino alligator was really cool. It wasn't green. It was completely white all over. It was born that way.

Jessica

What I Learned at the Zoo

The tallest animal on earth is the giraffe. It eats leaves from the tops of the trees. Giraffes come from Africa.

I learned about an albino alligator. It was white instead of green. The guide told us that it was born without the coloring of other alligators.

I saw an owl sleeping in a tree. Owls sleep in the daytime and hunt at night. When they sleep, they don't fall out of the tree because they have sharp claws that lock onto the branch.

Ryan and Jessica each wrote about three animals. Write the names of the animals they wrote about in the correct circles. In the center where both circles overlap, write the name of the animal that they both wrote about.

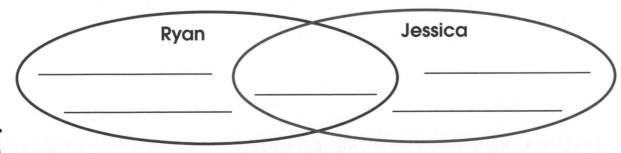

Ryan   Jessica

Write three facts about a zoo animal. If you need help, use a dictionary or encyclopedia.

The Contest

The Super Grocery Store held a contest. Whoever could guess the correct number of jelly beans in the big jar would win a prize. There were exactly 372 jelly beans. Two people guessed the right answer. They were Joey Jumpjolly and Harry Honkhorn. Since there were two winners, both of them were given a $20 gift certificate. Joey Jumpjolly decided to spend his prize money on his favorite foods. He bought vanilla ice cream, animal cookies, angel food cake, and a chocolate candy bar. Harry Honkhorn had a different idea. He used his money to buy bacon, eggs, cereal, and waffles.

How are Joey and Harry alike? How are they different? To find out, work the puzzle below. Cross out all the Q's, V's, Z's, and X's. Next cross out all the numbers 1–9. Then cross out every question mark. What is left? Write the words in order in the blanks at the bottom of the page.

3	?	5	Q	B	O	T	H	9	9	7	X	H	A	D	6	2
T	W	E	N	T	Y	X	Q	8	D	O	L	L	A	R	S	7
X	V	5	Z	T	O	4	?	Q	S	P	E	N	D	3	2	1
?	Q	J	O	E	Y	3	B	O	U	G	H	T	Z	V	7	6
Z	9	X	S	W	E	E	T	S	4	?	V	H	A	R	R	Y
7	?	V	Z	V	B	O	U	G	H	T	8	9	X	V	3	7
B	R	E	A	K	F	A	S	T	4	?	V	F	O	O	D	X

_____ _____ _____ _____

_____ _____ _____ . _____

_____ . _____

_____ .

On a piece of paper, make a list of what you would buy at a grocery store. Are your choices more like Joey's or Harry's?

The Accident

Kendra and her mom left their house on Oak Street to go to school. Kendra put on her safety belt. About that same time, Lacey and her mom left their house on Maple Street. On the way to school, Lacey bounced up and down on the seat watching her pigtails fly up and down in the mirror. She had forgotten to wear her safety belt. Both moms turned into the school parking lot at the same time, and they crashed into each other! Kendra was not hurt. Her safety belt kept her in her seat. But, Lacey fell forward and bumped her head HARD! She cried and cried. She had to go to the hospital and get an X ray. Lacey got well in a day or two, but she learned an important lesson!

Draw a ☺ in the correct column.

	Kendra	Lacey	both
driven to school by Mom			
wore a safety belt			
didn't wear a safety belt			
lives on Maple Street			
was in a wreck			
bumped her head			
got an X ray			
lives on Oak Street			
bounced up and down in the car			
didn't get hurt			
learned a lesson			

 Write a sentence telling why it is important to wear a safety belt.

What Is Cotton?

Cotton is a very useful plant. Farmers plant cotton in the spring. The plants grow and make white <u>flowers</u>. When a flower falls off, a <u>boll</u> grows in its place. The boll is the seed pod, which looks kind of like a walnut. When the boll dries, it splits open. Inside is the fluffy, white cotton. Farmers take the cotton to a <u>gin</u>. Machines at the gin take the cotton out of the bolls. The cotton is pressed into wrapped bundles called <u>bales</u>. The bales are sent to cotton mills where the cotton is spun into <u>yarn</u>. The yarn is woven into <u>fabric</u>, or cloth. Then it is made into clothes, sheets, curtains, towels, and many other things.

Draw a line from the word to its picture. The story will help you.

flowers •   • bales

boll •   • yarn

gin •   • fabric

Color the things below that could be made from cotton. Put an X on things that are not made of cotton.

 Draw and color the clothes that you are wearing today. Put an X on the ones made of cotton.

Busy as a Bee

Bees are hardworking insects. They live together in a nest called a <u>hive</u>. There is one <u>queen bee</u> in each hive. She is the largest bee. There are hundreds of <u>worker bees</u>. The worker bees fly from flower to flower gathering a sweet liquid called <u>nectar</u>. They make honey from the nectar and store it in little rooms in the hive. Each little room is a <u>cell</u>. Many cells in a row make a <u>honeycomb</u>. When a bear or a person tries to steal the honey, the bees swarm, flying around in large groups. Each bee has a <u>stinger</u> to protect it from its enemies. A person who is a <u>beekeeper</u> makes wooden hives for bees, then sells the honey when the bees finish making it.

Look at the picture below. Use each underlined word in the story to label the pictures.

On a piece of paper, make a list of five other insects. You may need an encyclopedia to help you.

Sioux Life

Many years ago, the Sioux tribes lived on the grasslands, called the
<u>plains</u>. They killed bison for meat. Some called these animals <u>buffalo</u>. The
Sioux cut the meat in strips and dried it in the sun to make <u>jerky</u>. Buffalo
hides were used to make <u>tepees</u>. The hides were wrapped
around long poles, making tall tents. The tepees could be
taken down and moved around from place to place to
follow the buffalo herds. <u>Canoes</u> were used for traveling
down a river or crossing a lake. The Sioux made
<u>buckskin clothing</u> out of deer hides. Sometimes
they decorated their clothes with colorful beads.
A group of Sioux living together was called a tribe.
The leader of the tribe was called the <u>chief</u>. The
chief often wore a long <u>headdress</u> of eagle feathers.

Draw a line from each word to the picture that matches it.

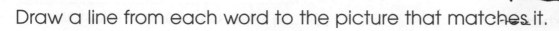

- plains
- buffalo
- jerky
- tepee
- canoe
- buckskin clothing
- chief
- headdress

Circle the things below that the Sioux tribes might have had. Put an X on the
things they didn't have.

Chain Reaction

 *In a story, there is usually a reason something happens.
This is the **cause**. What happened as a result is the **effect**.*

It was a long way to Aunt Ruth's house. Terry
and Mary Beth started getting a little bit too loud
in the back seat, so Dad said, "Girls, settle
down. Be quiet and read your books." They knew
Dad meant business. Just then, Mary Beth saw a
bee flying around in the car. Her eyes got big, and she ducked her head,
swatting the bee away. Terry looked at her, and Mary Beth loudly whispered,
"BEEEE!" Terry wanted to scream, but she knew Dad would get mad. "What
are you two doing back there?" Dad asked. Just then, the bee landed on
Dad's bald head. Mary Beth knew she had to save him from getting stung, so
she whopped Dad on the head with her book. Dad jerked the steering
wheel, and the car ran off the road and through a fence. The cows that were
in the field ran away. Later, a police officer gave Dad a ticket for reckless
driving.

Draw a line to match the cause to the effect.

The girls got too loud, so	which let the cows out.
The girls saw a bee land on Dad's bald head, so	Dad said to be quiet.
The car ran off the road and through a fence	Mary Beth whopped Dad on the head with a book.

Keep the chain going! Write what happened next because Dad got a ticket.

An American Volcano

Mount Saint Helens is an active volcano in the state of Washington. In 1980, this volcano erupted, spewing hot lava into the air. Explosions caused a huge cloud of dust. This gray dust filled the air and settled on houses and cars many miles away. The thick dust made it hard for people and animals to breathe. The explosions flattened trees on the side of the mountain. The hot rocks caused forest fires. The snow that was on the mountain melted quickly, causing floods and mud slides. Mount Saint Helens still erupts from time to time but not as badly as it did in 1980.

Read each phrase below. Write the number of each phrase in the explosion of the volcano that correctly completes the sentence.

1. **Mount Saint Helens erupted,**

2. **The thick ash made it hard**

3. **The explosions**

4. **The hot rocks caused**

5. **Melting snow caused**

6. **Because Mount Saint Helens is an active volcano,**

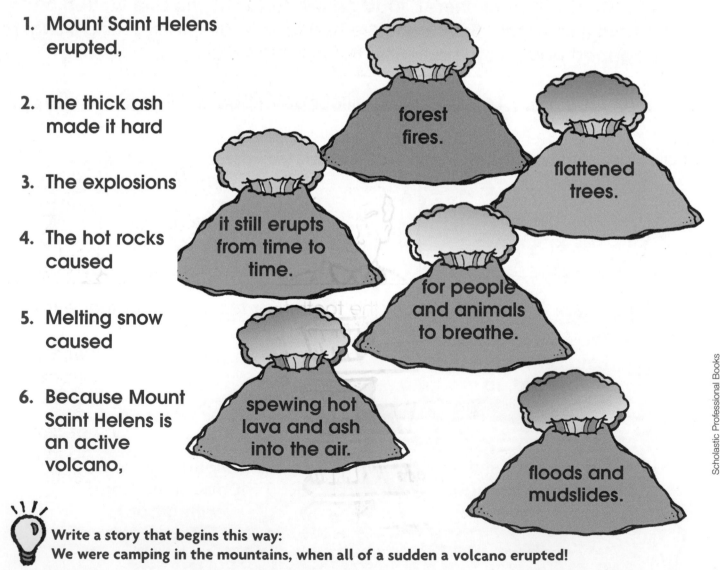

forest fires.

flattened trees.

it still erupts from time to time.

for people and animals to breathe.

spewing hot lava and ash into the air.

floods and mudslides.

Write a story that begins this way:
We were camping in the mountains, when all of a sudden a volcano erupted!

Scholastic Professional Books

My Favorite Dentist

> A **character** is a person or animal in a story. To understand a character better, you should pay attention to the details a story often gives about the character.

    Some kids are scared to go to the dentist, but not me. I have a funny dentist. His name is Dr. Smileyface. I don't think that's his real name, but that's what he tells all the kids who come to see him. He has a cool waiting room. It has video games and a big toy box. Dr. Smileyface always wears funny hats. Sometimes he has his face painted. He asks funny questions like "Are you married yet?" and "Do you eat flowers to make your breath smell so sweet?" That makes me laugh. One time, he told me this joke, "What has lots of teeth but never goes to the dentist? A comb!" When I laughed, he pulled my tooth. It didn't hurt at all! He also teaches me how to take care of my teeth because he says he doesn't want me to get a cavity the size of the Grand Canyon. Before I go home, he always gives me a surprise. Last time I went, he gave me a rubber spider to scare my mom with!

Color the pictures that could be Dr. Smileyface. Put an X on the pictures that could not not be him.

1.	2.	3.	4.	5.

Draw a line from the toothbrush to the tooth that makes the sentence true.

6. Dr. Smileyface makes

7. The child who wrote this story

8. Dr. Smileyface teaches kids

9. Dr. Smileyface sends kids home

how to take care of their teeth.

his patients laugh.

with a surprise.

is not afraid to go to the dentist.

Scholastic Professional Books

What a Kid!

Tad is a very special boy. He is confined to a wheelchair. He was born with a disease that made him unable to walk. Some boys would be sad or angry about that, but not Tad. Instead, he looks for ways to make people happy. He called the Green Oaks School for the Blind and asked if he could volunteer. They said, "Sure!" Tad went to the school and quickly made friends. Every day, he reads books to the children. He plays games with them. Sometimes he helps them do their schoolwork. The children at the school nicknamed him Lucky because they feel so lucky to have him as a friend. That makes Tad very happy!

- If Tad is confined to a wheelchair, write an H in Box 1 and Box 9. If not, write a J in both boxes.

- If Tad feels sorry for himself, write a U in Box 2 and Box 10. If he doesn't, write a E in both boxes.

- If Tad looks for ways to make people happy, write an L in Box 3. If he doesn't, write a B.

- If Tad volunteers at the River Oak School for the Blind, write a Z in Box 4. If that is not correct, write a P.

- If Tad reads to the blind children, write an N in Box 5. If not, write a V.

- If Tad plays games with the blind children, write a G in Box 6. If not, write a D.

- If Tad helps them with their homework, write an O in Box 7. If not, write an R.

- If the children nicknamed Tad "Grumpy," write a K in Box 8. If not, write a T.

- If Tad is a happy person, write an R in Box 11. If not, write a C.

This is the story of Helen Keller.

Tad's secret of happiness is

					I						

Scholastic Professional Books

The writing assignment in Ms. Daniels' class was to write about someone you admire. Read what one student wrote.

Lunch Lady

by Karen Jackson

I don't know her name. She is one of the workers in our school cafeteria. I just call her Lunch Lady. She's my friend. There are several nice ladies in the cafeteria, but the Lunch Lady is the nicest of all. Every day she smiles at me when I go through the line. She says things like, "Hi Karen! Are you having a good day?" Lunch Lady always remembers that I like chicken nuggets the best. Whenever that is what is being served, she hands me the chicken nuggets and says, "Look, your favorite!" One day, I tripped and dropped my tray. Food went all over the floor. I was so embarrassed, but Lunch Lady came to my rescue. She helped me pick up the mess, and she told me, "Don't worry about it. It's okay." That made me feel better. Another time, I was at the shoe store with my mom, and I saw Lunch Lady. She gave me a big hug. The reason I admire Lunch Lady is because she is friendly and kind.

Read each sentence. Find the words that are wrong and cross them out. Then above them write the correct word or words that make the sentence true.

1. Karen wrote about Lunch Man.

2. Karen's favorite ~~food is hot dogs.~~

3. Lunch Lady frowns when Karen comes through the line.

4. When Karen dropped her tray, Miss Daniels helped her.

5. One time, Karen saw the Lunch Lady at the hardware store.

6. Karen admires Lunch Lady because she is friendly and mean.

 Write a paragraph about someone you admire.

Scholastic Professional Books

Limericks

 A **limerick** is a poem that has five lines in it. It is usually funny and has a special order of rhyming words. The first two lines rhyme. Then the next two lines rhyme. Then the last line rhymes with the first two lines. Read the limerick below.

There once was a fellow named Jed

Who spent too much time in his bed.

He slept for so long

That something went wrong,

His hair grew long on his head.

In the limerick above, draw a red circle around the three words that rhyme. Draw a green box around the two words that rhyme.

Help finish the limerick below by filling in the blanks with a word from the Word Bank.

Word Bank
class   lazy   pass   crazy   Daisy

There once was a student named ___ ___ ___ ___ ___

Who wouldn't work because she was ___ ___ ___ ___

She slept during ___ ___ ___ ___ ___.

No way she could ___ ___ ___ ___.

Her poor teacher finally went ___ ___ ___ ___ ___.

 Work with a partner and write a limerick. It helps to start with three rhyming words and two other rhyming words, then make up the sentences.

A Tall Tale

 A **tall tale** is a story about a superhuman hero. The story is funny because everything is exaggerated. That means it is much bigger and better than real life. Read the tall tale below. Use a yellow crayon or marker to highlight each thing that is exaggerated.

Paul Bunyan

Paul Bunyan was a mighty man. He was so big, he had to use wagon wheels for buttons. Paul was a lumberjack. He owned a blue ox named Babe. Paul and Babe were so big that their tracks made 10,000 lakes in the state of Minnesota.

Paul worked with seven axmen. They were so big that they were six feet tall sitting down. All of them were named Elmer. So when Paul called "Elmer!" they all came running.

The year of the two winters, it got so cold that when the axmen would speak, their words froze in midair. When it thawed in the spring, there was a terrible chatter for weeks.

One time Paul caught two giant mosquitoes and used them to drill holes in maple trees.

Paul Bunyan had a purple cow named Lucy. In the year of two winters, it got so cold that Lucy's milk turned to ice cream before it hit the pail.

The End

 Choose two funny sentences above and copy them on another piece of paper. Then draw a picture about each one.

Scholastic Professional Books

A Play

A **play** is a story written as a script. Actors read the script, then memorize their lines, so they can pretend to be the characters in the story. Read the play below. The words in parentheses tell the actors what to do.

A Bad Idea

(Megan and Kyle are talking before class starts.)

Megan: Hey, Kyle, are you ready for the big test today? I studied that list of words and the definitions for two hours last night.

Kyle: Oh, brother! I didn't study at all. I just wrote all the answers on the palm of my hand, see?

Megan: Kyle! You can't do that! That's cheating!

Kyle: Hey, don't worry. I won't get caught. Mrs. King will never know. *(Teacher passes out the tests.)*

Mrs. King: Okay, no more talking. Everyone keep your eyes on your own paper, and cover your answers with a cover sheet. You may begin. *(Kyle looks at his hand when the teacher isn't looking.)*

Joe: *(raising his hand)* Mrs. King, may I get a drink? I have the hiccups.

Mrs. King: Yes, you may.

Kyle: *(raising his hand)* Mrs. King, may I get a drink, too?

Mrs. King: Kyle, what is that on your hand? I think you better come to my desk.

Kyle: *(looks over at Megan)* Oh no . . .

Megan: Busted!

Use markers or crayons to follow each direction.

1. The words in parentheses are called *stage directions*. Underline all the stage directions with a blue line.

2. Highlight Megan's words in pink.

3. Highlight Kyle's words in yellow.

4. Highlight Mrs. King's words in green.

5. Highlight Joe's words in orange.

TESTS: READING

Name _____

Reading Skills Practice Test 1

A. Phonic Analysis: Consonants

Look at each picture.
Write the missing letter or letters on the blank line.

Sample _____**at**	**1.** _____**indow**	**2.** _____**eese**
3. _____**ip**	**4.** _____**og**	**5.** _____**amp**
6. ha_____	**7.** tee_____	**8.** tru_____

B. Dictation

Write the word after your teacher says it.

Sample _____

1. _____

2. _____

3. _____

C. Vocabulary: Picture-Word Match

Fill in the bubble next to the word that names each picture.

Sample	1.	2.
○ girl ○ gift ○ giraffe	○ life ○ leaf ○ leak	○ ball ○ barn ○ bull
3. ○ main ○ mine ○ moon	**4.** ○ box ○ boy ○ boil	**5.** ○ mice ○ mound ○ mouse

D. High-Frequency Word Match

Fill in the bubble next to the word your teacher says out loud.

Sample	1.	2.
○ the ○ this ○ thick	○ of ○ over ○ or	○ fun ○ from ○ fresh
3. ○ has ○ had ○ have	**4.** ○ when ○ where ○ which	**5.** ○ throw ○ through ○ thing

E. Grammar, Usage, and Mechanics

Read each sentence. Fill in the bubble next to the word or words that best fit in the blank.

Sample _____ ran up the hill.

- ○ he
- ○ He
- ○ He's

1. Did you take that book _____

- ○ home.
- ○ home
- ○ home?

2. We _____ outside all day.

- ○ plays
- ○ played
- ○ playing

3. _____ is our teacher this year.

- ○ mrs smith
- ○ Mrs Smith
- ○ Mrs. Smith

4. _____ is in my class.

- ○ Maria
- ○ maria
- ○ MARIA

5. I _____ have any homework last week.

- ○ didnt
- ○ didnt'
- ○ didn't

F. Story Comprehension

Read the story. Then answer each question.
Fill in the bubble next to the best answer.

Frogs lay their eggs in ponds. The eggs grow. Slowly, they turn into tadpoles. The tadpoles grow and change. They become frogs.

The frogs hop. They can hop onto land. They can even hop onto rocks in the pond. Frogs stay near the pond. There they can get water. They can also catch bugs to eat.

1. Where do frogs lay their eggs?
- O on lily pads
- O in ponds
- O under rocks

2. What is a good title (name) for this story?
- O Farm Animals
- O Kittens Play
- O Frogs

3. What does a tadpole become?
- O a fish
- O a frog
- O an egg

4. What do frogs eat?
- O rocks
- O bugs
- O hay

Reading Skills Practice Test 2

A. Phonic Analysis: Consonants
Look at each picture.
Write the missing letter or letters on the blank line.

Sample	1.	2.
_____ar	_____ock	_____ain
3.	**4.**	**5.**
ne _____	_____at	fi _____

B. Phonic Analysis: Vowels
Look at each picture.
Write the missing letter or letters on the blank line.

Sample	1.	2.
ch _____se	br _____m	c _____t
3.	**4.**	**5.**
m _____se	thr _____	b _____k _____

C. Dictation
Write the word after your teacher says it.

Sample

_____   _____

- - - - - - - - - - - - -   - - - - - - - - - - - - -

_____   1. _____

_____   _____

- - - - - - - - - - - - -   - - - - - - - - - - - - -

2. _____   3. _____

D. High-Frequency Word Match
Fill in the bubble next to the word your teacher says out loud.

Sample	**1.**	**2.**
O when O where O which	O over O of O off	O every O vest O very
3.	**4.**	**5.**
O knew O know O knot	O cook O coat O could	O some O something O summer

Scholastic Professional Books

E. Grammar, Usage, and Mechanics

Read each sentence. Fill in the bubble next to the word or words that best fit in the blank.

Sample _____ plays in the park.
- O   he
- O   He
- O   He's

1. Did you see that _____
- O   star.
- O   star
- O   star?

2. We _____ in the yard.
- O   runs
- O   run
- O   running

3. _____ is my neighbor.
- O   mr smith
- O   Mr Smith
- O   Mr. Smith

4. She moved to _____
- O   New York.
- O   new york.
- O   NEW YORK.

5. He _____ come to my house today.
- O   cant
- O   cant'
- O   can't

6. Watch _____
- O   out.
- O   out!
- O   out?

7. The dog _____ the cat.
- O   chased
- O   chasing
- O   chase

8. _____ is nice.
- O   dr hamilton
- O   Dr Hamilton
- O   Dr. Hamilton

9. We went to _____
- O   texas.
- O   TEXAS.
- O   Texas.

Scholastic Professional Books

Name _____

F. Story Comprehension

Read the story. Then answer
each question.
Fill in the bubble next to the
best answer.

> A whale is a very big animal. Whales live in the
> sea. Some whales swim with each other. They travel
> in large groups, called pods. They swim around,
> looking for food.
>
> Whales feed on sea life. Some whales eat plants.
> Other whales have teeth and can eat seals and
> small fish.
>
> Whales must stay wet all the time. However, they
> also must come to the top of the sea to breathe.
> When a whale leaps out of the water to catch a
> breath of air, it is an amazing sight.

1. What are pods?
- O whale food
- O groups of whales
- O sea animals

2. What is a good title
(name) for this story?
- O The Sea
- O Fish
- O Whales

3. What must all whales do?
- O eat seals and fish
- O spend time on land
- O stay wet

4. Why do whales sometimes
jump out of the water?
- O to warm up
- O to get air
- O to catch fish

Scholastic Professional Books

Reading Skills Practice Test 3

A. Phonic Analysis: Consonants

Look at each picture.
Write the missing letter or letters on the blank line.

Sample	1.	2.
_____ar	_____ed	_____ock
3.	**4.**	**5.**
_____apes	ha_____	too_____

B. Phonic Analysis: Vowels

Look at each picture.
Write the missing letter or letters on the line.

Sample	1.	2.
b_____t	h_____se	f_____t
3.	**4.**	**5.**
sp_____n	tr_____n	k_____t_____

C. Dictation
Write the word after your teacher says it.

Sample

_____

- -

_____

1. _____

- -

_____

_____

2. _____

- -

3. _____

D. High-Frequency Word Match
Fill in the bubble next to the word your teacher says out loud.

Sample	**1.**	**2.**
○ where ○ then ○ there	○ above ○ about ○ away	○ shall ○ ship ○ should
3.	**4.**	**5.**
○ those ○ this ○ though	○ know ○ knew ○ now	○ every ○ something ○ everything

E. Grammar, Usage, and Mechanics

Read each sentence. Fill in the bubble next to the word or words that best fit in the blank.

Sample _____ walk to school.
- O they
- O she
- O They

1. I _____ my bike in the park.
- O rides
- O ride
- O riding

2. Can you lift this _____
- O box?
- O box
- O box.

3. My friend's name is _____
- O peter Jones.
- O Peter Jones.
- O Peter Jones

4. We live in _____
- O maine.
- O Maine.
- O MAINE.

5. Be _____
- O careful!
- O careful.
- O careful?

6. I _____ want to play.
- O dont'
- O dont
- O don't

7. We _____ at his house.
- O playing
- O played
- O plays

8. _____ on her way home.
- O she's
- O She
- O She's

9. Our family doctor is _____.
- O dr. Smith
- O Dr. Smith
- O Dr Smith

F. Story Comprehension
Read the story. Then answer each question.
Fill in the bubble next to the best answer.

A tornado is a kind of wind storm. The winds can be very strong. A tornado is shaped like a funnel. Sometimes, a tornado is called a "twister."

Most tornadoes take place in April, May, or June. They usually happen on hot days.

A tornado does not last long. But it can wreck everything in its path! When a tornado comes, the safest place to be is below ground. That's why people often go to their basements before a tornado comes.

1. What is a good title (name) for this story?

○ Storms
○ Tornadoes
○ Wind

2. What is a twister?

○ a basement
○ a tornado
○ a hard rain

3. When do tornadoes usually happen?

○ only in June
○ in winter
○ on hot days

4. Why do people go to their basements before a tornado comes?

○ to be safe
○ to watch the storm
○ to play games

Scholastic Professional Books

Reading Skills Practice Test 4

A. Phonic Analysis: Consonants

Look at each picture.
Write the missing letter or letters on the blank line.

Sample	1.	2.
_____oom	_____ag	_____oon
3.	4.	5.
_____ake	ri_____	tru_____

B. Phonic Analysis: Vowels

Look at each picture.
Write the missing letter or letters on the line.

Sample	1.	2.
b_____k_____	c_____t	c_____k_____
3.	4.	5.
l_____f	r_____n	c_____ch

C. Phonemic Awareness

Write the number of syllables in each word your teacher says out loud.

Sample _____   1. _____   2. _____

3. _____   4. _____   5. _____

D. High-Frequency Word Match

Fill in the bubble next to the word your teacher says out loud.

Sample	**1.**	**2.**
O when O how O who	O after O afraid O often	O skate O school O shore
3.	**4.**	**5.**
O between O because O beneath	O might O mice O mitten	O knew O now O know

E. Grammar, Usage, and Mechanics

Read each sentence. Fill in the bubble next to
the word or words that best complete each sentence.

Sample _____ walk to school.
- ○ She
- ○ We
- ○ they

1. The boys _____ their pictures.
- ○ colors
- ○ coloring
- ○ color

2. Yesterday, I _____ with my friend.
- ○ played
- ○ play
- ○ plays

3. What is in your _____
- ○ bag?
- ○ bag.
- ○ bag

4. Look _____
- ○ out
- ○ out!
- ○ out?

5. My dog _____ run.
- ○ won't
- ○ wont
- ○ wont'

6. _____ going to the fair.
- ○ She
- ○ shes'
- ○ She's

7. My mother _____ me a new coat next week.
- ○ will buy
- ○ buy
- ○ bought

8. I went on a trip to _____
- ○ florida.
- ○ FLORIDA
- ○ Florida.

9. _____ gave me a checkup.
- ○ dr. Lee
- ○ Dr. Lee
- ○ Dr Lee

F. Story Comprehension

Read the story. Then answer each question.
Fill in the bubble next to the best answer.

Tigers are the world's biggest cats. Most tigers are bigger than lions. A tiger's body can be as long as a car. A tiger can even weigh as much as two adult people!

Tigers are good hunters. Why? They are good at jumping. They are fast. They can see well in the dark. When tigers hunt at night, they surprise other animals. A tiger's favorite foods are deer and wild pigs. They also eat other animals, like monkeys, buffalo, and goats.

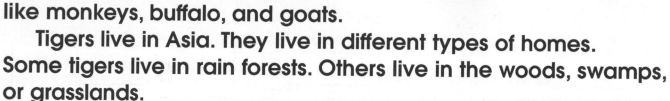

Tigers live in Asia. They live in different types of homes. Some tigers live in rain forests. Others live in the woods, swamps, or grasslands.

1. What is a good title (name) for this story?
- ○ Animals
- ○ Cats
- ○ Tigers

2. What animals do tigers often eat?
- ○ deer and wild pigs
- ○ pigs and dogs
- ○ birds and lions

3. Where do tigers live?
- ○ Africa
- ○ Mexico
- ○ Asia

4. Write a sentence telling why tigers are good hunters.

_____

_____

_____

Reading Skills Practice Test 5

A. Phonic Analysis: Consonants

Look at each picture.
Write the missing letter or letters on the blank line.

Sample	1.	2.
_____ee	_____air	_____ane
3.	**4.**	**5.**
_____ake	ne_____	fi_____

B. Phonic Analysis: Vowels

Look at each picture.
Write the missing letter or letters on the blank line.

Sample	1.	2.
b_____by	h_____se	g_____t
3.	**4.**	**5.**
z_____bra	sp_____der	b_____k

C. Dictation

Write the word after your teacher says it.

Sample

_____   _____

- - - - - - - - - - - - - - - - -   - - - - - - - - - - - - - - - - -

_____   1._____

_____   _____

- - - - - - - - - - - - - - - - -   - - - - - - - - - - - - - - - - -

2._____   3._____

D. High-Frequency Word Match

Fill in the bubble next to the word your teacher says out loud.

Sample	**1.**	**2.**
O when O why O which	O over O or O off	O every O vest O very
3.	**4.**	**5.**
O knew O know O knot	O will O weed O would	O tugging O together O teacher

Scholastic Professional Books

E. Grammar, Usage, and Mechanics

Read each sentence. Fill in the bubble next to the word or words that best fit in the blank.

Sample _____ ran in the park.
- ○ she
- ○ She
- ○ She's

1. Did you read that _____
- ○ book.
- ○ Book.
- ○ book?

2. We _____ in the lake.
- ○ swims
- ○ swam
- ○ swimming

3. _____ is my dentist.
- ○ dr bell
- ○ Dr Bell
- ○ Dr. Bell

4. She lives in _____
- ○ Centerville.
- ○ centerville.
- ○ CENTERVILLE.

5. He _____ be at the soccer game.
- ○ wont
- ○ wont'
- ○ won't

6. Watch _____
- ○ out.
- ○ out!
- ○ out?

7. The rabbit _____ to the carrot.
- ○ hoped
- ○ hopping
- ○ hopped

8. _____ drove the school bus.
- ○ mrs campbell
- ○ Mrs Campbell
- ○ Mrs. Campbell

9. We took a trip to _____
- ○ new york.
- ○ NEW YORK.
- ○ New York.

10. I _____ go to the park.
- ○ couldnt
- ○ couldn't
- ○ couldnt'

F. Story Comprehension

Read the story. Then answer each question.
Fill in the bubble next to the best answer.

Many animals have claws.
Claws are like your fingernails.
Animal claws can be long or short.
Most claws are very sharp.

Claws have many uses. Birds
have claws called talons. These
claws help them to hold on to
things and to catch their food.

Bears have claws on their large paws. They use their claws to
get food and to climb up trees. Cats have claws that help them
to climb and hold on to things. Cats like to scratch with their
claws. Scratching keeps their claws sharp.

1. What are talons?
- O cat claws
- O bird claws
- O bear claws

2. What is a good title
(name) for this story?
- O Birds
- O Climbing
- O Claws

3. How do animals use
claws?
- O to hold on to things
- O to write in the sand
- O to swim in the ocean

4. Which animal has claws?
- O fish
- O bear
- O snake

Reading Skills Practice Test 6

A. Phonic Analysis: Consonants

Look at each picture.
Write the missing letter or letters on the blank line.

Sample	1.	2.
_____ar	_____apes	_____ide
3.	4.	5.
_____anch	ha_____	clo_____

B. Phonic Analysis: Vowels

Look at each picture.
Write the missing letter or letters on the line.

Sample	1.	2.
k_____t_____	b_____t	sn_____k_____
3.	4.	5.
p_____r	r_____nbow	cl_____d

C. Phonemic Awareness

Write the number of syllables in each word your teacher says out loud.

Sample _____   **1.** _____   **2.** _____

3. _____   **4.** _____   **5.** _____

D. Grammar, Usage, and Mechanics

Read each sentence. Fill in the bubble next to the word or words that best complete each sentence.

Sample _____ rides a horse.
- ○ she
- ○ She
- ○ We

1. The children _____ soccer.
- ○ play
- ○ plays
- ○ playing

2. Last night, we _____ a great movie.
- ○ watch
- ○ watching
- ○ watched

3. Which story is _____
- ○ yours!
- ○ yours.
- ○ yours?

4. That frog _____ jump.
- ○ wont
- ○ wont'
- ○ won't

5. _____ going to the zoo.
- ○ He's
- ○ He
- ○ Hes'

6. My book _____ in the mail tomorrow.
- ○ came
- ○ come
- ○ will come

7. _____ read a story to us.
- ○ ms. Jones
- ○ Ms Jones
- ○ Ms. Jones

E. Story Comprehension

Read the story. Then answer each question.
Fill in the bubble next to the best answer.

A baby elephant grows up with its family, or *herd*. A herd is made up of mothers, sisters, cousins, and aunts.

The herd takes care of the *calf*, or baby elephant, in many ways. A mother stands over her calf to keep it safe from danger and the hot sun. An aunt helps the calf keep up when the herd is walking. When an enemy is near, the adult elephants stand in front of the calf. Then, the oldest female fans out her ears to look big and angry. The herd doesn't want anything to happen to the calf.

1. What is a good title (name) for this story?

○ Mother Elephants

○ Elephant Herds

○ Adult Elephants

2. What is a calf?

○ a baby elephant

○ the oldest elephant

○ an elephant family

3. When an elephant fans out its ears, it looks _____.

○ big and funny

○ small and angry

○ big and angry

4. Write a sentence telling one way the herd helps the baby.

_____

_____

_____

F. Story Comprehension

Read the story. Then answer each question.
Fill in the bubble next to the best answer.

Chinese New Year is the most important Chinese holiday. It celebrates the end of one year and the beginning of a new year. The holiday falls in January or February and lasts for 15 days.

People do many things to get ready for Chinese New Year. They clean and decorate their homes. They buy flowers and new clothes.

When the holiday starts, people visit with family and friends. They gather for a big feast. They also go to parades, where they see dancers, drummers, and colorful dragons.

1. What is a good title (name) for this story?
- O Dragons
- O China
- O Chinese New Year

2. Chinese New Year lasts for how long?
- O 24 days
- O 15 days
- O one year

3. People get ready for the holiday by _____.
- O cleaning their homes
- O dancing
- O going to parades

4. Write a sentence telling some ways that people celebrate Chinese New Year. _____

_____

_____

Reading Skills Practice Test 7

A. Phonic Analysis: Consonants

Look at each picture.
Write the missing letter or letters on the blank line.

Sample	1.	2.
_____ider	wat_____	_____an
3.	**4.**	**5.**
_____ant	lo_____	bo_____

B. Phonic Analysis: Vowels

Look at each picture.
Write the missing letter or letters on the line.

Sample	1.	2.
bab_____		_____ron
3.	**4.**	**5.**
st_____v_____	r_____ler	b_____

C. Phonemic Awareness

Write the number of syllables in each word your teacher says out loud.

Sample _____   **1.** _____   **2.** _____

3. _____   **4.** _____   **5.** _____

D. Grammar, Usage, and Mechanics

Read each sentence. Fill in the bubble next to the word or words that best complete each sentence.

Sample _____ live in a city.
- O they
- O They
- O He

1. The farm animals _____ grain.
- O eating
- O eats
- O eat

2. Today, we will _____ the dog a bath.
- O gived
- O giving
- O give

3. Ouch! A bee stung _____
- O Me.
- O me?
- O me!

4. I _____ swim in the deep water yet.
- O cant
- O can't
- O cant'

5. _____ going to the library.
- O She's
- O Shes
- O Shes'

6. My aunt _____ me to the movies tomorrow.
- O take
- O took
- O will take

7. _____ fixed my bike.
- O Mr. Smith
- O mr. Smith
- O Mr Smith

E. Story Comprehension

Read the story. Then answer each question.
Fill in the bubble next to the best answer.

Kwanzaa is a holiday celebrated by many people who have African ancestors. The word ancestors means family who lived before you — like your great, great, great grandparents. Kwanzaa celebrates families and sticking together. It always lasts for seven days, beginning on December 26th and ending on January 1st.

People do many things to celebrate Kwanzaa. They dress in special clothes and decorate their homes with fruits and vegetables. Families and friends get together for big meals. Children get gifts, like books and toys.

One of the most important parts of Kwanzaa is lighting candles in the kinara. The kinara is a special candleholder with seven candles. People who celebrate Kwanzaa light one candle each night.

1. What is a good title (name) for this story?
- O Kwanzaa
- O Children Get Gifts
- O Ancestors

2. Kwanzaa lasts for how many days?
- O 1
- O 7
- O 26

3. A kinara is a
- O kind of clothing
- O kind of food
- O kind of candleholder

4. Write a sentence telling some ways that people celebrate Kwanzaa.

_____

_____

F. Reading a Graph

Look at the graph. Then answer each question. Fill in the bubble next to the best answer.

Lost Teeth
Hardy School, Grade 2

Number of Teeth Lost

7 🦷	😀	😀				
6 🦷	😀	😀	😀	😀		
5 🦷						
4 🦷	😀	😀	😀	😀	😀	😀
3 🦷	😀	😀	😀	😀		
2 🦷	😀	😀	😀			
1 🦷	😀					

😀 equals one student.

---

1. What is this graph about?
O which students like teeth
O Hardy School
O how many teeth students have lost

2. How many students have lost six teeth?
O 2 students
O 3 students
O 4 students

3. What's the largest number of teeth that any student has lost?
O 4
O 7
O 20

4. How many students have lost five teeth?
O 0
O 1
O 2

Reading Skills Practice Test 8

A. Phonic Analysis: Consonants
Look at each picture.
Write the missing letter or letters on the blank line.

Sample _____ar	1. _____ale	2. _____ower
3. **3** _____ree	4. de_____	5. _____ebra

B. Phonic Analysis: Vowels
Look at each picture.
Write the missing letters on the blank line.

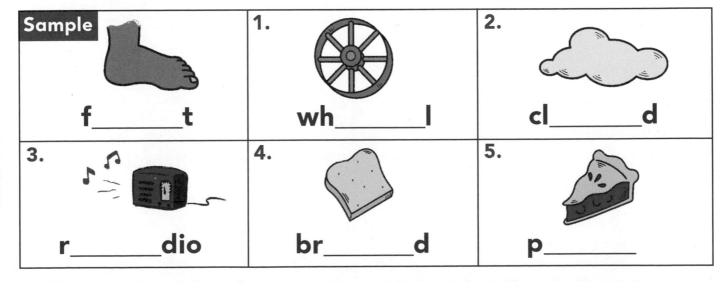

Sample f____t	1. wh____l	2. cl____d
3. r_____dio	4. br_____d	5. p_____

C. Grammar, Usage, and Mechanics

Read each sentence. Fill in the bubble next to the word or words that best fit in the blank.

Sample _____ go to the park.
- ○ we
- ○ We
- ○ We've

1. Can she run in the _____
- ○ race.
- ○ race
- ○ race?

2. They _____ baseball.
- ○ play
- ○ plays
- ○ playing

3. _____ is my teacher.
- ○ mrs miller
- ○ Mrs Miller
- ○ Mrs. Miller

4. She went on a trip to _____.
- ○ boston
- ○ Boston
- ○ BOSTON

5. He _____ drive the car.
- ○ couldnt
- ○ couldnt'
- ○ couldn't

6. _____ There is a fire!
- ○ Help.
- ○ Help!
- ○ Help?

7. My aunt lives in _____.
- ○ Dallas, Texas
- ○ dallas, texas
- ○ Dallas Texas

8. _____ eat out," said Mom.
- ○ let's
- ○ Let's
- ○ "Let's

9. The children can _____ around the track.
- ○ ran
- ○ runs
- ○ run

D. Story Comprehension

Read the story. Then answer each question.
Fill in the bubble next to the best answer.

We get many useful things from trees. Wood comes from trees. The wood can be used to make houses, desks, and chairs. Rubber comes from trees. Rubber is used to make balls and boots. We also get fruit and nuts from trees. Birds and other animals like these tree treats, too.

Trees can be helpful. Some medicines are made from tree bark. These medicines help sick people get well. Trees also give us shade on a sunny day. Many animals make their homes in trees. Birds build nests on tree branches. Owls, foxes, and other animals can live in tree holes.

1. What is a good title (name) for this story?

- ◯ Growing Trees
- ◯ Animals and Trees
- ◯ Trees Are Important

2. What do people <u>and</u> animals use from trees?

- ◯ desks
- ◯ food
- ◯ rubber

3. What animal can make its home in a tree?

- ◯ the fox
- ◯ the horse
- ◯ the elephant

4. What other thing might you make from a tree?

- ◯ a car
- ◯ a baseball bat
- ◯ a computer

E. Reading a Graph

Look at the graph. Then answer each question.
Fill in the bubble next to the best answer.

Favorite Sports
Mrs. Smith's Class, Grade 2

number of students	baseball	football	soccer	gymnastics	skating
10			▓		
9			▓		
8			▓	▓	
7			▓	▓	
6			▓	▓	
5	▓		▓	▓	▓
4	▓		▓	▓	▓
3	▓		▓	▓	▓
2	▓	▓	▓	▓	▓
1	▓	▓	▓	▓	▓

1. What is this graph about?
- O soccer and basketball
- O what sports kids like best
- O Mrs. Green's class

2. Which sport is liked by the most students?
- O soccer
- O skating
- O gymnastics

3. How many students like baseball best?
- O 2
- O 5
- O 7

4. Which 2 sports are liked by the same number of students?
- O baseball and soccer
- O gymnastics and soccer
- O skating and baseball

Reading Skills Practice Test 9

A. Phonic Analysis: Consonants

Look at each picture.
Write the missing letter or letters on the blank line.

Sample	1.	2.
_____arn	_____eese	fi_____
3.	**4.**	**5.**
te_____	_____ush	_____own

B. Phonic Analysis: Vowels

Look at each picture.
Write the missing letter or letters on the line.

Sample	1.	2.
m_____n	h_____se	f_____t
3.	**4.**	**5.**
p_____r	f_____y	c_____n

C. Grammar, Usage, and Mechanics

Read each sentence. Fill in the bubble next to the word or words that best fit in the blank.

Sample

_____ race down the hill.
- ○ We
- ○ we
- ○ She

1. May I go to the _____
   - ○ store.
   - ○ store?
   - ○ Store?

2. _____ plays football every day.
   - ○ he
   - ○ He
   - ○ They

3. I saw _____ at the park.
   - ○ Mrs Walker
   - ○ mrs. walker
   - ○ Mrs. Walker

4. I will visit my uncle in _____
   - ○ March.
   - ○ march.
   - ○ MARCH.

5. _____ You hit the ball hard.
   - ○ Wow
   - ○ Wow!
   - ○ Wow.

6. I _____ run as fast as Sam.
   - ○ cant
   - ○ cant'
   - ○ can't

7. _____ on my way," said Jane.
   - ○ I'm
   - ○ "Im
   - ○ "I'm

8. Yesterday, we _____ our bikes.
   - ○ ride
   - ○ rode
   - ○ riding

9. We will soon move to _____
   - ○ Kansas.
   - ○ Kansas
   - ○ kansas.

D. Story Comprehension

Read the story. Then answer each question.
Fill in the bubble next to the best answer.

Most people go to sleep at night. So do many animals. But a few animals sleep most of the day. Then they stay up all night. These animals can use their senses to get around in the dark.

Owls, skunks, and moths all stay up at night. The owl has very large eyes that can see in the dark. Both the skunk and the moth have a very strong sense of smell. They can smell other animals from very far away.

Why do some animals stay up all night? Sometimes, it's because nighttime is the best time to hunt. In hot places, animals can stay cooler at night. There are many reasons animals come out at night.

1. What is a good title (name) for this story?
- O Owls
- O Night Animals
- O Sleep

2. What do both skunks and moths have?
- O large eyes
- O a strong sense of smell
- O a bad smell

3. The owl's large eyes help it to
- O see in the dark.
- O see in the daytime.
- O sleep very well.

4. What might be another reason to stay up at night?
- O to get a suntan
- O to grow food
- O to hide from other animals

E. Reading a Graph

Look at the graph. Then answer each question.
Fill in the bubble next to the best answer.

STUDENTS' FAVORITE COLORS
Park School, Grade 2

COLORS	NUMBER OF STUDENTS

red — 6

blue — 9

yellow — 4

green — 6

1 2 3 4 5 6 7 8 9 10

NUMBER OF STUDENTS

---

1. What is this graph about?
- ○ how colors are made
- ○ what colors students like best
- ○ South School, Grade 2

2. How many students like red the best?
- ○ 7
- ○ 4
- ○ 6

3. Which two colors are liked by the same number of students?
- ○ red and blue
- ○ red and green
- ○ blue and green

4. How many more students like the color blue better than the color green?
- ○ 2
- ○ 3
- ○ 4

Reading Skills Practice Test 10

A. Word-Match Dictation

Fill in the bubble next to each word that fits
in the sentence your teacher says out loud.

Sample	1.	2.
○ two	○ deer	○ we're
○ too	○ dear	○ were
○ to	○ den	○ where
3. ○ knife	**4.** ○ sent	**5.** ○ there
○ night	○ scent	○ they're
○ knight	○ cent	○ their

B. Synonyms

Fill in the bubble next to the word that means the **same** as the
bold word.

Sample	1.	2.
	○ small	○ sad	○ funny
big	○ large	**happy** ○ shy	**fast** ○ quick
	○ skinny	○ glad	○ slow
3.	○ respond	**4.** ○ scared	**5.** ○ furious
answer	○ ask	**brave** ○ proud	**mad** ○ smart
	○ tell	○ fearless	○ laugh

C. Antonyms

Fill in the bubble next to the word that means the **opposite** of the
bold word.

Sample	1.	2.
	○ school	○ young	○ cold
day	○ time	**old** ○ age	**hot** ○ warm
	○ night	○ long	○ strange
3.	○ nice	**4.** ○ high	**5.** ○ weak
clean	○ dirty	**tall** ○ smooth	**strong** ○ powerful
	○ run	○ short	○ wild

D. Grammar, Usage, and Mechanics

Read each sentence. Fill in the bubble next to the word or words that best fit in the blank.

Sample

The boy walked _____
- ○ home
- ○ home.
- ○ home,

1. Where do you _____
- ○ live!
- ○ live
- ○ live?

2. Maria and I play _____
- ○ soccer.
- ○ soccer?
- ○ soccer

3. Our teacher is _____
- ○ mr. lee.
- ○ Mr. Lee.
- ○ mr. Lee.

4. We will _____ a movie tomorrow.
- ○ watch
- ○ watched
- ○ watches

5. Trish turned 8 years old on _____
- ○ February, 22. 2000
- ○ February 22, 2000.
- ○ February 22. 2000

6. _____ is in the South.
- ○ Texas
- ○ texas
- ○ TEXAS

7. Yesterday, my mom _____ me with my homework.
- ○ helped
- ○ helps
- ○ helping

8. Owls _____ sleep at night.
- ○ don't
- ○ dont'
- ○ dono't

9. Jake is _____ than Ed.
- ○ more tall
- ○ taller
- ○ tallest

10. Is this _____ book?
- ○ them
- ○ us
- ○ your

11. We went for a ride in _____ car.
- ○ Mike's
- ○ mike's
- ○ Mike

E. Story and Graph Comprehension

Read the story and look at the graph. Then answer each question. Fill in the bubble next to the best answer.

Watch out for tornadoes in spring! A tornado, or a twister, is a dangerous storm. Tornadoes form when air begins to spin under a thundercloud. The air whirls around very fast. It twists so fast that it can lift up a car or a tree.

Mr. Smith's second-grade class researched how many tornadoes hit their county in the last five years. Look at the graph to see what they found out.

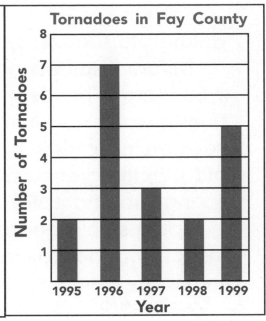

Tornadoes in Fay County

1. What is another name for a tornado?
   - ○ cloud
   - ○ hurricane
   - ○ twister

2. When do you think most tornadoes take place?
   - ○ spring
   - ○ summer
   - ○ winter

3. In which year did the most tornadoes hit Fay County?
   - ○ 1995
   - ○ 1996
   - ○ 1997

4. How many more tornadoes were there in 1999 than in 1998?
   - ○ 3
   - ○ 4
   - ○ 5

F. Story Comprehension

Read the story. Then answer each question.
Fill in the bubble next to the best answer.

Spiders are carnivores. That means that they eat other animals to survive. Spiders eat insects.

Different spiders have different ways to catch insects. A web weaver builds sticky webs to trap insects. A wandering hunter walks about in search of something to eat. When it sees an insect, it jumps on top of its prey. A tube dweller hides in the ground and waits for insects to come by. Then it springs up and catches its tasty meal.

Spiders help people by eating insects. How? Spiders eat insects that destroy farmers' crops. Spiders also eat insects that carry diseases. So if you see a spider, let it be!

1. What is a good title (name) for this story?
   O Wonderful Webs
   O Insects Everywhere
   O Hungry Spiders

2. A **carnivore** is an animal that eats other _____ .
   O animals
   O insects
   O plants

3. How do spiders help people?
   O They hide when people are near.
   O They don't eat animals.
   O They eat insects that destroy crops.

4. Write a sentence telling one or more ways a spider can catch its food.

_____

_____

Reading Skills Practice Test 11

A. Word-Match Dictation

Fill in the bubble next to each word that fits in the sentence your teacher says out loud. Write the missing letters on the line.

Sample	**1.**	**2.**
○ one	○ said	○ mad
○ won	○ sad	○ made
○ win	○ sand	○ mud
3.	**4.**	**5.**
○ pull	○ tore	○ hear
○ pill	○ tear	○ here
○ pail	○ tire	○ hair

B. SYNONYMS

Fill in the bubble next to the word that means the **same** as the **bold** word.

Sample middle	**1.** child	**2.** shut
○ center	○ kid	○ open
○ side	○ adult	○ lock
○ front	○ smiled	○ close
3. look	**4.** says	**5.** done
○ hear	○ tells	○ completed
○ see	○ yells	○ behind
○ taste	○ plays	○ good

C. ANTONYMS

Fill in the bubble next to the word that means the **opposite** of the **bold** word.

Sample many	**1.** yours	**2.** long
○ few	○ that	○ tall
○ a lot	○ mine	○ big
○ money	○ those	○ short
3. quiet	**4.** grow	**5.** more
○ loud	○ rise	○ better
○ shy	○ shrink	○ big
○ silent	○ flower	○ less

D. Grammar, Usage, and Mechanics

Read each sentence. Fill in the bubble next to the word or words that best fit in the blank.

Sample

It is time for _____
- ○ bed
- ○ bed.
- ○ bed,

1. Did you brush your _____
- ○ teeth?
- ○ teeth.
- ○ teeth

2. Pam and I played with _____
- ○ blocks
- ○ blocks.
- ○ Blocks.

3. School is over at _____
- ○ Three O'clock.
- ○ three o'clock
- ○ three o'clock.

4. Today I will ____ piano.
- ○ practice
- ○ practices
- ○ practicing

5. What _____ you want for your birthday?
- ○ does
- ○ do
- ○ Do

6. _____ is where the President lives.
- ○ Washington
- ○ washington
- ○ WASHINGTON

7. Will you _____ me on the swing?
- ○ pushed
- ○ pushing
- ○ push

8. I am ____ reading this book.
- ○ finish
- ○ finished
- ○ Finish

9. ____ can ride a horse.
- ○ She
- ○ she
- ○ she's

10. Jack's brother will turn 5 on _____.
- ○ October 28, 2002
- ○ october 28, 2002
- ○ October 29. 2002

11. _____ cat has kittens.
- ○ Tim's
- ○ Tims
- ○ tim's

E. Story Comprehension

Read the story. Then answer each question.
Fill in the bubble next to the best answer.

When you were born, you had 300 bones in your body! Why so many? They do many different jobs. Bones in your back, arms, and legs allow you to stand up and move around. Other bones protect your insides. Your skull, for example, is like a hard helmet for your brain. Your ribs protect your heart and lungs.

Did you know that bones are alive? They are made of hard stuff and tiny living cells, so small you need a microscope to see them. The living cells help your bones grow as you get older. If you break a bone, the living cells help heal it.

1. When you were born, you had _____ bones.
   O 100
   O 200
   O 300

2. Your skull protects your _____.
   O brain
   O arms
   O legs

3. What is in your bones that can help heal them?
   O ribs
   O microscope
   O living cells

4. A good title for this story is:
   O Babies
   O Legs
   O Your Bones

F. Story Comprehension

Read the story. Then answer each question.
Fill in the bubble next to the best answer.

> When astronauts go to work in space, they are too far away to come home each night. They have to live in space for a short time to do their work. But life in space is different from life on earth! The main reason is that there is less *gravity*. Gravity is the invisible force that holds everything—even you—to the earth. With less gravity, astronauts' feet don't stay on the ground, so they float instead of walk. It feels a bit like swimming. At night, astronauts sleep in sleeping bags strapped to the walls so they don't float around. To eat without pots and pans flying, astronauts have special foods like dried scrambled eggs. To get clean, astronauts rub soap and water on their bodies and sponge it off. That's because a shower would spray all over.

1. Why do astronauts have to live in space to do their work?
- ◯ They are lost.
- ◯ They are too far away to come home each night.
- ◯ They are floating.

2. The force that holds you to the earth is called _____.
- ◯ gravity
- ◯ astronaut
- ◯ eggs

3. One thing an astronaut has to do in space is:
- ◯ sleep in a sleeping bag strapped to the walls.
- ◯ eat candy.
- ◯ watch TV.

4. Write a sentence telling something about life in space.

_____

_____

Scholastic Professional Books

Aa

Trace and write.

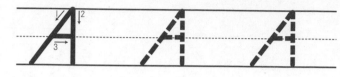

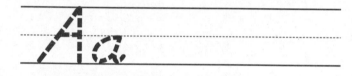

Artist Anthony

asks for answers.

Name ______________________________

Bb

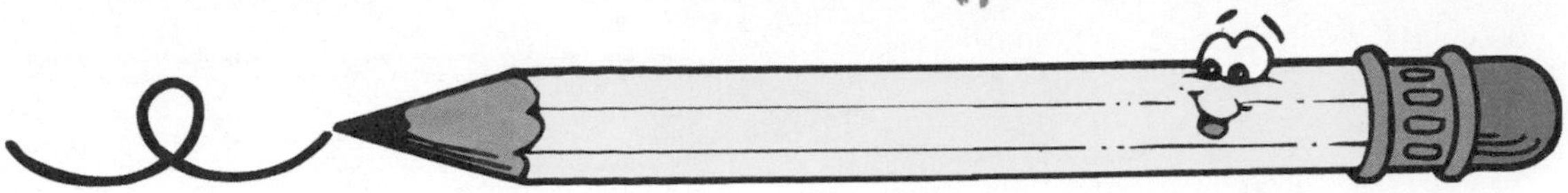

Trace and write.

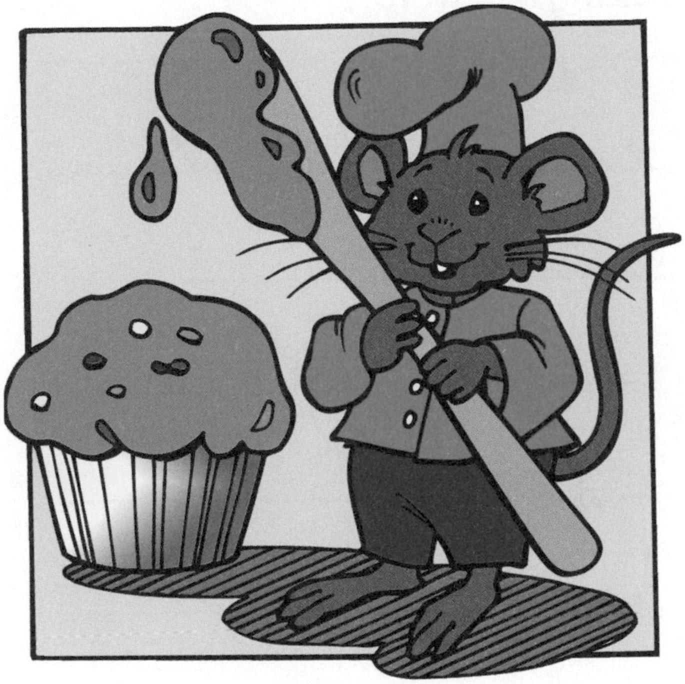

B B B

b b b b

Bb

Baker Bobby

buys biscuits.

Cc

Trace and write.

C   C   C   C

c   c   c   c

Cc

Cowboy Christopher

catches coyotes.

Dd

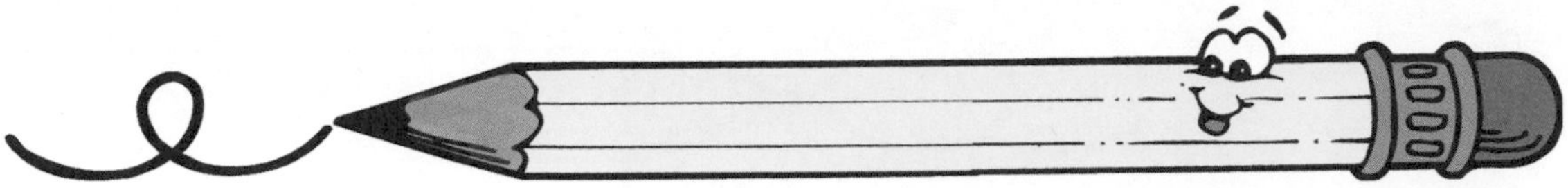

Trace and write.

D D D D

d d d d

Dd

Dancer Deandra

dances with ducks.

Name _____

Ee

Trace and write.

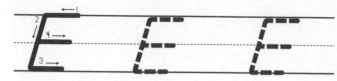

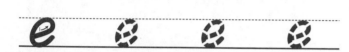

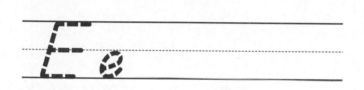

Engineer Eduardo

enjoys eating.

Ff

Trace and write.

F F F F

f f f f

Ff

Firefighter Freda

feels fearless.

Gg

Trace and write.

G G G

g g g g

Gg

Gardener Gloria

grows greens.

Hh

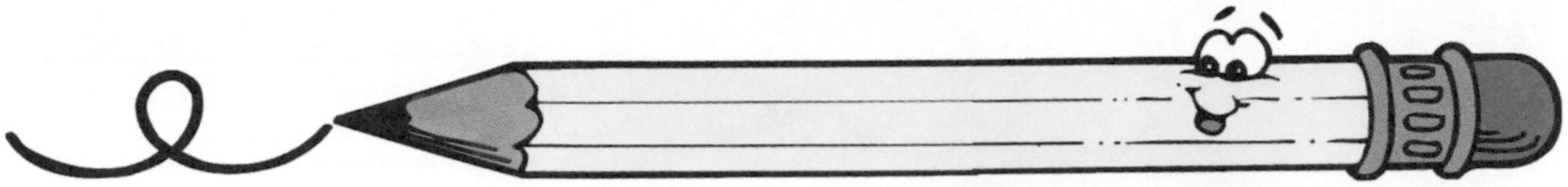

Trace and write.

H H H H

h h h h

Hh

Handyman Harry

helps Hazel Hippo.

Name _____  Ii

Ii

Trace and write.

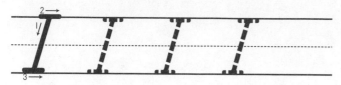

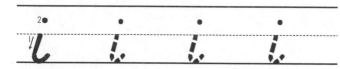

Ii

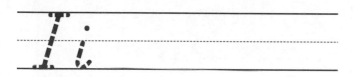

Inspector Irving

is investigating.

Jj

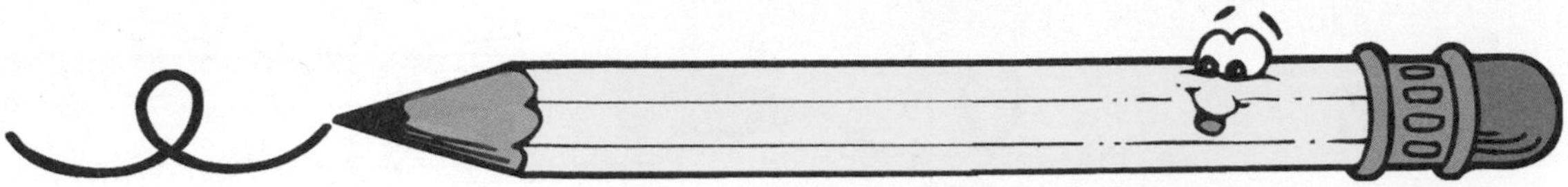

Trace and write.

J J J J

j j j j j

Jj

Juggler Jeannie

jumps joyfully.

Name _____

Kk

Trace and write.

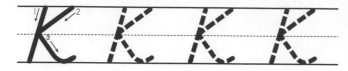

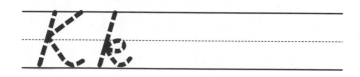

King Kevin kisses

kind kittens.

Name ______________________________

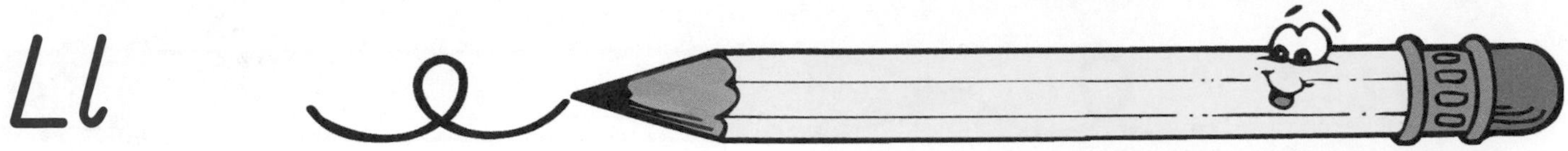
Ll

Trace and write.

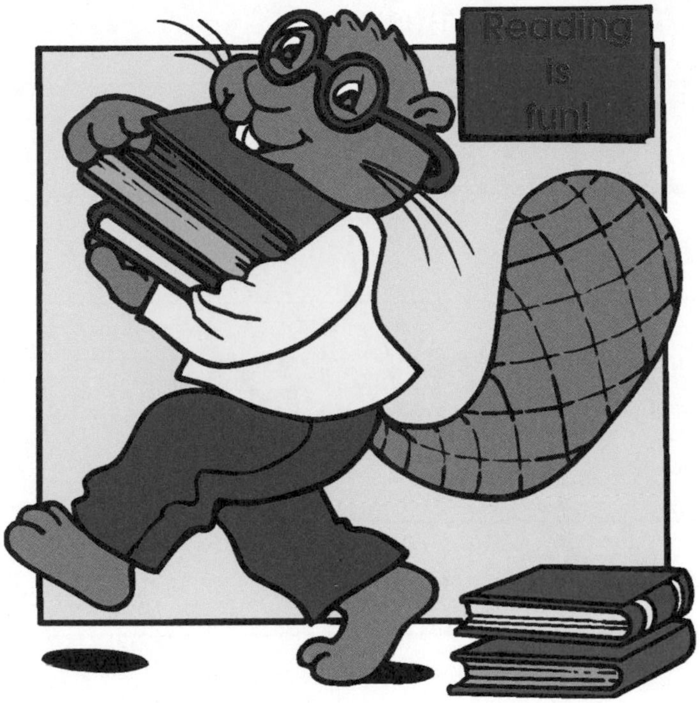
Reading is fun!

L L L L

l l l l

L l

Librarian Louis

loves listening.

Trace and write.

M M M

m m m

Mm

Musician Matt

makes merry.

Nn

Trace and write.

N N N N

n n n n

Nn

Nurse Nancy

needs new patients.

Oo

Trace and write.

O   O   O   O

O   O   O   O

Oo

Optometrist Oliver

owns one octopus.

Scholastic Professional Books

Pp

Trace and write.

P P P P

P p p p

Pp

Postman Paul

piles packages.

Qq

Trace and write.

Q Q Q Q

q q q q

Qq

Queen Quiana

quilts quietly.

Rr

Trace and write.

R R R R

r r r r

Rr

Racer Rowena rides

rapidly to Rome.

Ss

Trace and write.

S S S S

s s s s

Ss

Sailor Susanna

sings sea songs.

Tt

Trace and write.

T T T T T

t t t t t

Tt

Teacher Tatiana

tells tall tales.

Uu

Trace and write.

U u u

u u u u

U u

You're out!

Umpire Ulysses

upset Ursula.

Vv

Trace and write.

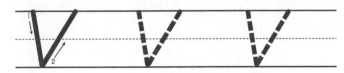

Veterinarian Vince visited Vermont.

Ww

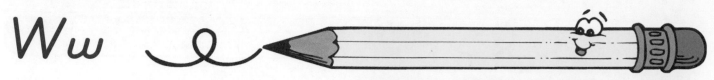

Trace and write.

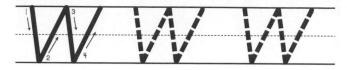

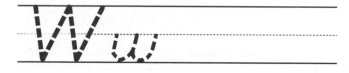

Weatherman Wes

went west.

Xx

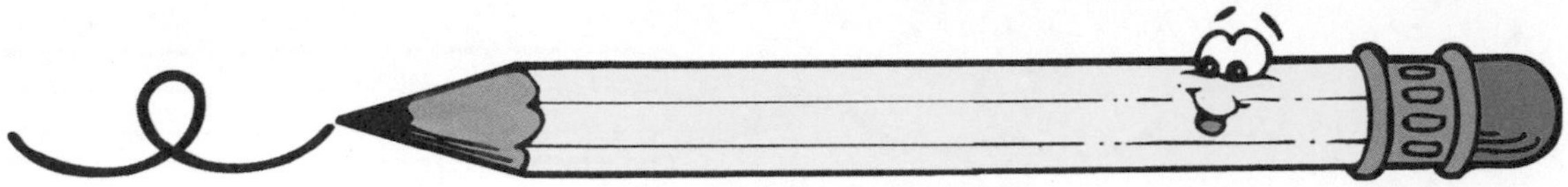

Trace and write.

X X X X X

X x x x x

Xx

Explorer Xenia

is excited.

Y y

Trace and write.

Y Y Y Y

y y y y

Y y

Yachtsman Yves

yodels loudly.

Zz

Trace and write.

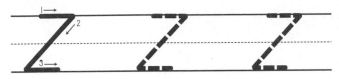

Zena Zeke

zooms to the zoo.

A–Z

Trace and write.

A B C D E F G H I

J K L M N O P Q R

S T U V W X Y Z

Scholastic Professional Books

a–z

Trace and write.

a   b   c   d   e

f   g   h   i   j   k

l   m   n   o   p

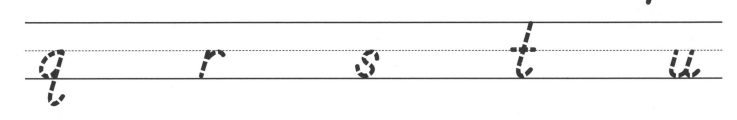

q   r   s   t   u

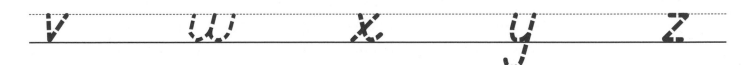

v   w   x   y   z

abcd

1–5

Trace and write.

1

2

3

4

5

1 1

2 2

3 3

4 4

5 5

Scholastic Professional Books

6-10

Trace and write.

6   6

7   7

8   8

9   9

10 10

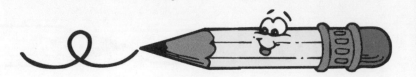

Color Words

Trace and write.

red

yellow

blue

green

orange

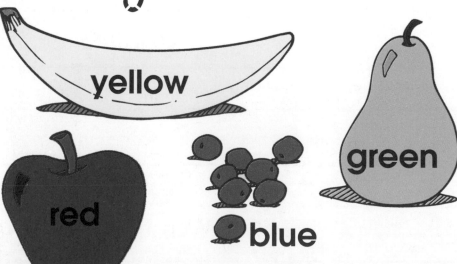

yellow

red

blue

green

orange

More Color Words

Trace and write.

purple _____

brown _____

black _____

white _____

pink _____

pink

purple

white

brown

black

Number Words

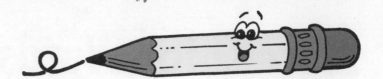

Trace and write.

1 one

2 two

3 three

4 four

5 five

More Number Words

Trace and write.

6 six

7 seven

8 eight

9 nine

10 ten

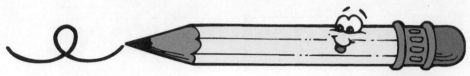

Shapes

Trace and write.

oval

heart

circle

square

triangle

diamond

rectangle

Scholastic Professional Books

Days of the Week

Trace and write.

Sunday

Monday

Tuesday

Wednesday

Thursday

Friday

Saturday

Months

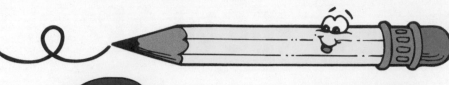

Trace and write.

January

February

March

April

May

June

Months

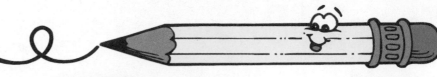

Trace and write.

July

August

September

October

November

December

Special Days

Write each
special day.

New Year's Day

Valentine's Day

Presidents' Day

St. Patrick's Day

Mother's Day

Father's Day

Fourth of July

Special Days

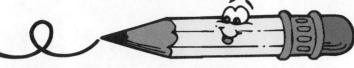

Write each
special day.

Labor Day

Halloween

Veterans Day

Thanksgiving

Hannukah

Christmas

Kwanzaa

Careers From A to Z

Write the career names on the lines below.

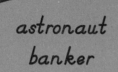

astronaut   chef   inspector
banker   doctor   engineer   grocer   janitor
                     firefighter   hotel worker

Careers From A to Z

Write the career names on the lines below.

knitter   musician   professor   senator

lawyer   nurse   quilter   teacher

optometrist   reporter

Name _____

Careers From A to Z

Write the career names on the lines below.

umpire   X-ray technician

veterinarian   yoga instructor

weatherman   zookeeper

The Planets

Write the names of the planets.

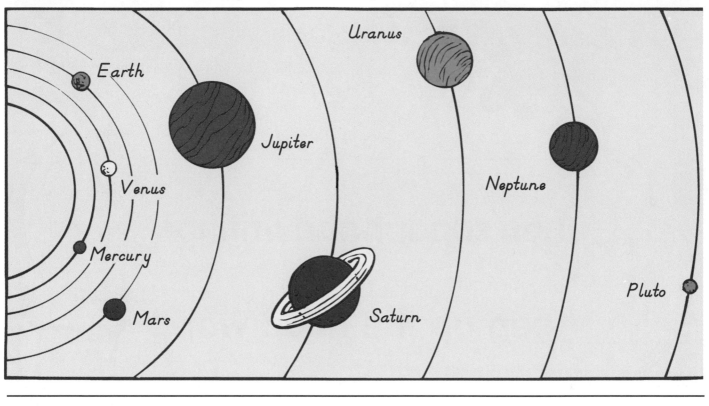

_____

- -

_____

_____

- -

_____

_____

- -

_____

_____

- -

_____

has super handwriting!

Keep up the good work!

_____
signed

_____
date

Scholastic Success With

GRAMMAR

Telling Sentences and Questions

A **telling sentence** tells something. It begins with a capital letter and ends with a period.
A **question** asks something. It begins with a capital letter and ends with a question mark.

Read each sentence. Write T on the line if the sentence is a telling sentence. Write Q on the line if it is a question.

1 I took my pet to see the vet.   _____

2 Was your pet sick?   _____

3 What did the vet do?   _____

4 The vet checked my pet.   _____

5 The vet said my pet had a cold.   _____

The order of the words in a sentence can change its meaning.
Write T next to the sentence that is a telling sentence.
Write Q next to the sentence that is a question.

6 Is your pet well now?   _____

7 Now your pet is well.   _____

Telling Sentences and Questions

*A **telling sentence** tells something. It begins with a capital letter and ends with a period.*
*A **question** asks something. It begins with a capital letter and ends with a question mark.*

Underline the capital letter that begins each sentence. Add a period (.)
if it is a telling sentence. Add a question mark (?) if it is a question.

1 The vet is nice _____

2 She helped my dog _____

3 Did she see your cat _____

4 Is the cat well now _____

5 My cat feels better _____

The order of the words in a sentence can change its meaning.
Change the word order in the telling sentence to make it a
question. Write the question.

6 He will take the cat home.

_____

Telling Sentences and Questions

Look at the underlined part of each sentence. If it is written correctly, fill in the last bubble. If not, fill in the bubble next to the correct answer.

1 The <u>girl</u> likes dogs.
- ◯ the girl
- ◯ Girl the
- ◯ correct as is

2 <u>the vet</u> helps sick pets.
- ◯ the Vet
- ◯ The vet
- ◯ correct as is

3 The boy likes <u>cats?</u>
- ◯ cats.
- ◯ cats
- ◯ correct as is

4 Is the vet <u>nice?</u>
- ◯ nice
- ◯ nice.
- ◯ correct as is

5 <u>do you</u> have a pet?
- ◯ Do You
- ◯ Do you
- ◯ correct as is

6 <u>Is when</u> the vet open?
- ◯ When is
- ◯ when Is
- ◯ correct as is

7 <u>he has</u> a bird.
- ◯ Has he
- ◯ He has
- ◯ correct as is

8 My dog likes <u>the vet?</u>
- ◯ The vet.
- ◯ the vet.
- ◯ correct as is

9 Who has a <u>goldfish.</u>
- ◯ goldfish?
- ◯ goldfish
- ◯ correct as is

10 <u>will you</u> see the vet again?
- ◯ Will you
- ◯ You
- ◯ correct as is

Exclamations and Commands

 An **exclamation** shows strong feelings, such as excitement, surprise, or fear. It begins with a capital letter and ends with an exclamation mark (!).

A **command** makes a request or tells someone to do something. It ends with a period or an exclamation mark.

Read each sentence. Write E if the sentence is an exclamation. Write C if the sentence is a command.

1 Ruby copies Angela! _____

2 Look at their dresses. _____

3 They're exactly the same! _____

4 Angela is mad! _____

5 Look at Ruby! _____

6 Show Angela how Ruby hops. _____

Write each sentence correctly.

Exclamation ▷ be yourself

7 _____

Command ▷ don't copy other people

8 _____

Exclamations and Commands

*An **exclamation** shows strong feelings, such as excitement, surprise, or fear. It begins with a capital letter and ends with an exclamation mark (!).*

*A **command** makes a request or tells someone to do something. It ends with a period or an exclamation mark.*

Read each exclamation. Use words from the box to tell what strong feeling it shows.

> excitement   fear   anger   surprise

1 I lost my jacket. I'll be so cold! _____

2 Look what I have! _____

3 I didn't know you had my jacket! _____

4 Give it to me now! _____

Look at the picture.

5 Circle the command that goes with the picture.

Please don't be upset!   Wear your new hat.

6 Write another command for the picture.

_____

7 Write an exclamation for the picture.

_____

Scholastic Professional Books

Exclamations and Commands

Read each exclamation. If it is written correctly, fill in the last bubble.
If not, fill in the bubble next to the correct way to write it.

1 You are a great hopper

○ you are a great hopper!

○ you are a great hopper.

○ You are a great hopper!

○ correct as is

2 the picture looks beautiful.

○ The picture looks beautiful!

○ The picture looks beautiful

○ the picture looks beautiful!

○ correct as is

3 i can paint, too!

○ i can paint, too

○ I can paint, too!

○ I can paint, too

○ correct as is

4 I did it!

○ i did it!

○ I did it

○ i did it

○ correct as is

Read each command. If it is written correctly, fill in the last bubble.
If not, fill in the bubble next to the correct way to write it.

5 teach me how to hop.

○ teach me how to hop

○ Teach me how to hop

○ Teach me how to hop.

○ correct as is

6 Hop backward like this

○ Hop backward like this.

○ hop backward like this

○ hop backward like this!

○ correct as is

Types of Sentences; Capital I

 A **telling sentence** *begins with a capital letter and ends with a period. A question begins with a capital letter and ends with a question mark. An* **exclamation** *begins with a capital letter and ends with an exclamation mark. A* **command** *begins with a capital letter and ends with a period. The word* **I** *is always capitalized in a sentence.*

Read each sentence. Circle the beginning letter, end punctuation, and the word I in each sentence.

1 I sail my boat in the lake.

2 May I have a turn?

3 I am so happy!

4 Can Kiku and I play?

5 Bill and I fly the kite.

Write each sentence in the correct box.

Telling Sentences

_____

_____

Questions

_____

_____

Exclamation _____

Types of Sentences; Capital I

*A **telling sentence** begins with a capital letter and ends with a period. A **question** begins with a capital letter and ends with a question mark. An **exclamation** begins with a capital letter and ends with an exclamation mark. A **command** begins with a capital letter and ends with a period. The word **I** is always capitalized in a sentence.*

Decide if each sentence is a telling sentence, a question, an exclamation,or a command. Write T, Q, E, or C on the lines.

1 My sister and I went to the lake. _____

2 Come see this. _____

3 I saw three little sailboats. _____

4 Put the boat in the water. _____

5 Did I have a good time? _____

6 You bet! I loved it! _____

7 Can I go again soon? _____

What would you do at the lake? Use the word I and your own ideas to finish the sentences.

8 At the lake _____ saw _____ .

9 _____ can _____ .

10 My friend and _____ liked _____ best.

Types of Sentences; Capital I

Read each sentence. If it is written correctly, fill in the last bubble. If not, fill in the bubble next to the correct way to write it.

1 i have fun with my bike.

- ◯ I have fun with my bike.
- ◯ I have fun with my bike
- ◯ i have fun with my bike
- ◯ correct as is

2 can I ride to the beach

- ◯ Can I ride to the beach
- ◯ Can I ride to the beach?
- ◯ Can i ride to the beach?
- ◯ correct as is

3 i find a pretty shell

- ◯ I find a pretty shell
- ◯ i find a pretty shell.
- ◯ I find a pretty shell.
- ◯ correct as is

4 Jill and I see a crab.

- ◯ Jill and I see a crab
- ◯ Jill and i see a crab.
- ◯ Jill and i see a crab
- ◯ correct as is

5 get the shovel

- ◯ Get the shovel
- ◯ Get the shovel.
- ◯ get the shovel.
- ◯ correct as is

6 what a mess I made

- ◯ What a mess I made!
- ◯ What a mess I made
- ◯ what a mess I made!
- ◯ correct as is

Common Nouns

 Common nouns *name people, places, or things.*

Read each sentence. Circle the common nouns.

1 The boy made a boat.

2 The brothers went to the park.

3 A girl was with her grandmother.

4 Two boats crashed in the lake.

5 Friends used a needle and thread to fix the sail.

Write the common nouns you circled under the correct heading below.

People	Places	Things
_____	_____	_____
_____	_____	_____
_____		_____
_____		_____
_____		_____

Common Nouns

Common nouns *name people, places, or things.*

Help sort the cards. Some of the words are nouns. Some are not.
Circle the nouns.

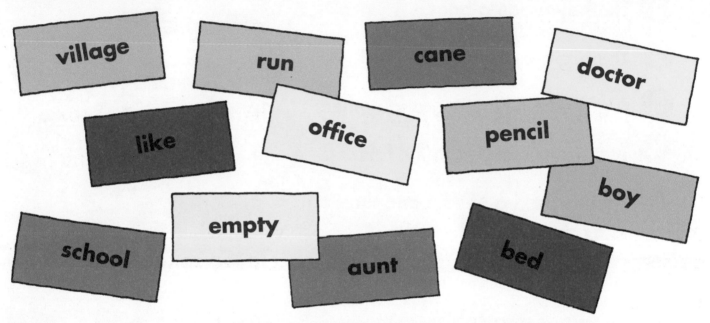

village   run   cane   doctor

like   office   pencil   boy

school   empty   aunt   bed

Write each noun you circled under the correct heading.

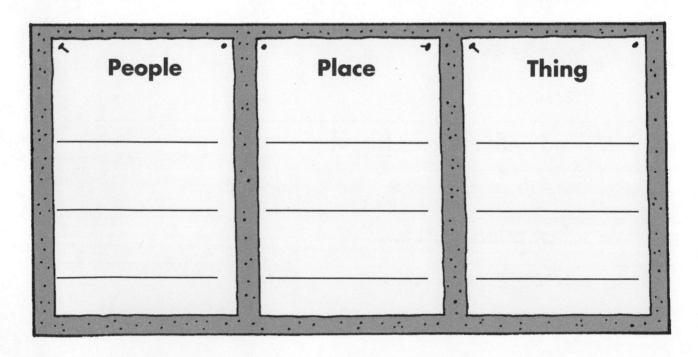

People	Place	Thing

Common Nouns

Look at the underlined word in each sentence. If it is a common noun, fill in the bubble next to yes. If it is not a common noun, fill in the bubble next to no.

1 Our class <u>went</u> on a trip.

○ yes   ○ no

2 We went to the <u>city</u>.

○ yes   ○ no

3 The buildings were <u>tall</u>.

○ yes   ○ no

4 There were many <u>cars</u>.

○ yes   ○ no

A common noun is underlined in each sentence. Tell if it names a person, place or thing. Fill in the bubble next to the correct answer.

5 We went into a big <u>room</u>.

○ person   ○ place   ○ thing

6 Our <u>teacher</u> led us.

○ person   ○ place   ○ thing

7 I walked with my best <u>friend</u>.

○ person   ○ place   ○ thing

8 We sat at a long <u>table</u>.

○ person   ○ place   ○ thing

Capitalize Names and Places

Special names of people and places always begin with capital letters. They are called **proper nouns**.

Read each sentence. Circle the proper noun.

1 George Ancona is a photographer.

2 He was born in Mexico.

3 His family called him Jorgito.

4 They lived in Coney Island.

5 Now he travels to Honduras to take pictures.

6 Tio Mario worked in a sign shop.

Write the proper nouns you circled under the correct heading below.

People   **Places**

_____   _____

_____   _____

_____   _____

Capitalize Names and Places

Special names of people and places always begin with capital letters. They are called **proper nouns**.

Read the postcard. Find the proper nouns. Write them correctly on the lines below.

Dear sue,

It's very hot here in california. We visited the city of los angeles. Then we swam in the pacific ocean. I miss you.

Love,

tonya

sue wong
11 shore road
austin, texas 78728

1 _____   **2** _____

3 _____   **4** _____

5 _____   **6** _____

7 _____   **8** _____

Write a sentence with a proper noun. Underline the capital letter or letters in the proper noun. Then write whether it names a person or a place.

_____

_____

Capitalize Names and Places

A proper noun is underlined in each sentence. Does it name a person or a place? Fill in the bubble next to the correct answer.

1 <u>Betty</u> is a photographer.
○ person   ○ place

2 She goes to <u>Florida</u> to take pictures.
○ person   ○ place

3 She meets her older brother <u>Peter</u>.
○ person   ○ place

4 She takes his picture in a city called <u>Miami</u>.
○ person   ○ place

Read each sentence. Find the proper noun. Fill in the bubble next to the word that is a proper noun.

5 Their friend is Emilio.
○ friend   ○ Emilio
○ Their   ○ is

6 They all went to Orlando.
○ Orlando   ○ all
○ They   ○ went

7 They visited Disney World there.
○ They
○ there
○ visited
○ Disney World

8 They walked down Main Street in the park.
○ park
○ walked
○ They
○ Main Street

Verbs

 *A **verb** is an action word. It tells what someone or something is doing.*

Read each sentence. Write the action verb in the telling part of the sentence.

1 Ronald runs to the field. _____

2 Michael wears a batting helmet. _____

3 He smacks the ball hard. _____

4 Ronald holds the wrong end of the bat. _____

5 He misses the ball. _____

6 Ronald waits in left field. _____

7 He writes G for great. _____

8 Ronald's father helps him. _____

Write a sentence about the picture. Use an action verb and circle it.

_____

_____

Verbs

> A **verb** is an action word. It tells what someone or something is doing.

Draw a line to match each sentence with an action verb. Then write the action verbs on the lines to finish the sentences.

1 Moms and dads _____ the game.   throws

2 The pitcher _____ the ball.   opens

3 Ronald _____ his eyes.   watch

4 The team _____ for Ronald.   cheers

5 Ronald _____ the ball past the pitcher.   runs

6 He _____ to first base.   hits

7 Someone _____, "Go Ronald go!"   eat

8 The kids _____ ice cream after the game.   yells

Verbs

Look at the underlined word in each sentence. Fill in the correct bubble to tell whether or not it is an action verb.

1 The dog <u>runs</u> down the road.
- ◯ action verb
- ◯ not an action verb

2 The girl chases the <u>dog</u>.
- ◯ action verb
- ◯ not an action verb

3 The dog finds a <u>bone</u>.
- ◯ action verb
- ◯ not an action verb

4 The <u>sun</u> sets.
- ◯ action verb
- ◯ not an action verb

5 Rain <u>falls</u> from the sky.
- ◯ action verb
- ◯ not an action verb

6 The girl <u>splashes</u> water.
- ◯ action verb
- ◯ not an action verb

7 The dog hides <u>under</u> a bush.
- ◯ action verb
- ◯ not an action verb

8 The girl <u>finds</u> the dog.
- ◯ action verb
- ◯ not an action verb

9 The sun <u>shines</u>.
- ◯ action verb
- ◯ not an action verb

10 The girl sees a <u>rainbow</u>.
- ◯ action verb
- ◯ not an action verb

Simple Sentences

*A **simple sentence** has a naming part and a telling part. It tells a complete thought.*

Read each group of words. Put an X next to it if it is a complete thought. Circle the naming part and underline the telling part in each sentence.

1 One day thirsty _____

2 Crow could not get a drink. _____

3 The water rose. _____

4 The old mouse _____

5 Put the bell _____

6 One mouse had a plan. _____

Write a simple sentence about the picture below.
Circle the naming part and underline the telling part.

_____

Simple Sentences

 *A **simple sentence** has a naming part and a telling part. It tells a complete thought.*

Circle the sentence in each pair. Then underline the naming part of the sentence.

1 (a)   Lin likes to play soccer.

(b)   likes to play soccer

2 (a)   Her friends

(b)   Her friends watch her play.

3 (a)   They cheer for Lin.

(b)   They cheer for

4 (a)   Her mom goes to all of her games.

(b)   goes to all of her games

5 (a)   The coach is very proud of Lin.

(b)   The coach is

Simple Sentences

Read each sentence. Fill in the bubble to tell if the underlined words are the naming or the telling part of the sentence. Some of the underlined words may not be the whole part.

1 The cat <u>was under the tree</u>.
- ○ naming part
- ○ telling part
- ○ not the whole part

2 <u>A bird</u> saw the cat.
- ○ naming part
- ○ telling part
- ○ not the whole part

3 The bird <u>flew</u> away.
- ○ naming part
- ○ telling part
- ○ not the whole part

4 <u>Then, the</u> cat walked away.
- ○ naming part
- ○ telling part
- ○ not the whole part

Fill in the bubble to choose a naming or telling part that makes a sentence.

5 The bird ____.
- ○ in the tall tree
- ○ saw the cat go away
- ○ flying very fast in the sky

6 ____ came back to the tree.
- ○ Deep in the woods
- ○ The large and pretty
- ○ Then the bird

7 ____ saw the bird.
- ○ After a minute, the cat
- ○ Running across the grass
- ○ The cat was watching

8 So the cat ____.
- ○ walking to the tree
- ○ under the tree
- ○ walked back, too

Scholastic Professional Books

Past-Tense Verbs

 Some verbs add -ed to tell about actions that happened in the past.

Find the past-tense verb in each sentence. Write it on the line.

1 Last spring, Daisy planted a garden. _____

2 Floyd watered the garden. _____

3 Together they weeded their garden. _____

4 One day they discovered a big carrot. _____

Read each sentence. If the sentence has a past-tense verb, write it on the line. If the sentence does not have a past-tense verb, leave the line blank.

5 They like to eat carrots. _____

6 They pulled on the carrot. _____

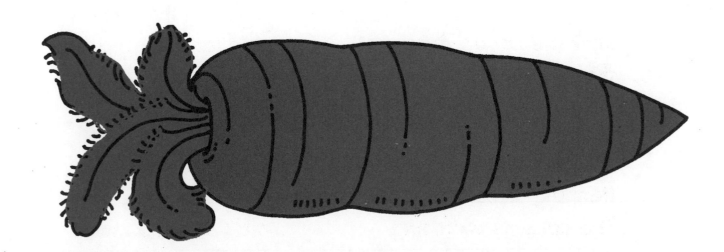

Past-Tense Verbs

 *Some verbs add **-ed** to tell about actions that happened in the past.*

Read the first sentence in each pair. Change the underlined verb to tell about the past.

1 Today my dogs <u>push</u> open the back door.

Yesterday my dogs _____ open the back door.

2 Today they <u>splash</u> in the rain puddles.

Last night they _____ in the rain puddles.

3 Now they <u>roll</u> in the mud.

Last week they _____ in the mud.

4 Today I <u>follow</u> my dogs' footprints.

Last Sunday I _____ my dogs' footprints.

5 Now I <u>wash</u> my dogs from head to toe.

Earlier I _____ my dogs from head to toe.

Write a sentence using one of the verbs you wrote.

_____

_____

_____

Past-Tense Verbs

Read each sentence. Look at the underlined verb. If it is not correct, fill in the bubble next to the correct verb. If it is correct, fill in the last bubble.

1 Last Saturday I <u>visit</u> John in the country.
○ visited
○ correct as is

2 Two weeks ago we <u>watched</u> a sailboat race.
○ watch
○ correct as is

3 A week ago we <u>walked</u> to the top of a big hill.
○ walk
○ correct as is

4 Last week I <u>talk</u> to John on the phone.
○ talked
○ correct as is

5 Earlier I <u>ask</u> him to visit me in the city.
○ asked
○ correct as is

6 Friday morning his train <u>pulled</u> into the station.
○ pull
○ correct as is

7 Last night my dog <u>barked</u> when he saw John.
○ bark
○ correct as is

8 Yesterday I <u>show</u> John around the city.
○ showed
○ correct as is

Pronouns

 A **pronoun** *takes the place of the name of a person, place, or thing.*

Read each pair of sentences. Circle the pronoun in the second sentence of each pair. Then write what the pronoun stands for. The first one has been done for you.

1 Wendell did not like to clean his room.

(He) liked a messy room.   Wendell

2 Mother wanted Wendell to do some work.

She handed Wendell a broom.   _____

3 The pigs came into Wendell's room.

They helped Wendell clean the room.   _____

4 Wendell and the pigs played a board game.

Wendell and the pigs had fun playing it.   _____

5 The pigs and Wendell played for a long time.

They liked to play games.   _____

6 Wendell was sad to see his friends go.

He liked playing with the pigs.   _____

Pronouns

 A **pronoun** *takes the place of the name of a person, place, or thing.*

Read the story. Use the pronouns in the box to complete each sentence. The first one has been done for you.

they   he   she   it

Glenda was walking in the woods. At last ____she____

came to a house. _____ was empty. She opened the door

          1

and saw three chairs by the fireplace. _____ were all

                         2

different sizes. She sat down on the smallest one. _____

                                           3

was the perfect size for her. Soon _____ fell asleep.

                    4

When she woke up, three pigs were

standing over her. The father pig spoke. _____

                           5

asked Glenda if she would stay for dinner. "I would love to!"

said Glenda.

Pronouns

Read each sentence. Fill in the bubble next to the word or words that the underlined pronoun stands for.

1 <u>She</u> did not like the mess.
- ○ Wendell
- ○ The boy
- ○ The pigs
- ○ Mrs. Fultz

2 <u>He</u> did not like brooms.
- ○ The pigs
- ○ The boys
- ○ The boy
- ○ Mrs. Fultz

3 <u>It</u> was full of pigs.
- ○ The rooms
- ○ The house
- ○ The pigs
- ○ The door

4 <u>They</u> wanted to play.
- ○ The room
- ○ Wendell
- ○ The pigs
- ○ Mrs. Fultz

Read each sentence. Fill in the bubble next to the pronoun that can take the place of the underlined word or words.

5 <u>Wendell</u> waved good-bye to the pigs.
- ○ He
- ○ She
- ○ It
- ○ They

6 Wendell hoped <u>the pigs</u> would come back.
- ○ it
- ○ he
- ○ they
- ○ she

Scholastic Professional Books

Types of Sentences

 *A **telling sentence** tells something. A **question** asks something. An **exclamation** shows strong feelings. A **command** makes a request or gives a command.*

Read each sentence. Write it next to the correct heading.

What a big mango!   I like mangos.

Is that a banana?   Did you find the fruit?

Buy me an avocado.   Come over for dinner.

I want to eat dinner.   This tastes great!

Exclamation: _____

_____

Command: _____

_____

Question: _____

_____

Telling Sentence: _____

_____

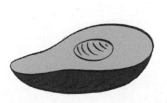  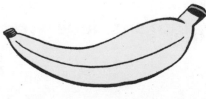

Types of Sentences

A **telling sentence** tells something. A **question** asks something. An **exclamation** shows strong feelings. A **command** makes a request or gives a command.

Read the following sentences. Write the correct end punctuation mark for each sentence. Then write the sentence type on the line to the right of each sentence. Write T for each telling sentence or statement, Q for each question, E for each exclamation, and C for each command.

1 We're going to the beach __   _____

2 Do you have your bathing suit __   _____

3 We will play in the sand __   _____

4 Pack the sunscreen __   _____

5 I love swimming __   _____

6 Take the beach chair __   _____

7 What time do we leave __   _____

8 Wow, that's a huge wave __   _____

Types of Sentences

Read each sentence. Fill in the bubble next to the correct type of sentence.

1 Give me that apple.

　○ telling　○ question　○ exclamation　○ command

2 What kind of fruit is this?

　○ telling　○ question　○ exclamation　○ command

3 What a great dinner!

　○ telling　○ question　○ exclamation　○ command

4 Buy this watermelon.

　○ telling　○ question　○ exclamation　○ command

5 This is the best watermelon!

　○ telling　○ question　○ exclamation　○ command

6 I would like to have another piece.

　○ telling　○ question　○ exclamation　○ command

7 Are those bananas ripe?

　○ telling　○ question　○ exclamation　○ command

8 A mango is smaller than a watermelon.

　○ telling　○ question　○ exclamation　○ command

Word Order

 Words in a sentence must be in an order that makes sense.

Read each group of words. Write the words in the correct order to make a statement. Begin each statement with a capital letter and end it with a period.

1 brothers two can live together

_____

2 Hungbu find will a home new

_____

3 will fix Mother the house

_____

Read each group of words. Write the words in the correct order to make a question. Begin each question with a capital letter and end it with a question mark.

4 clean Sister will house the

_____

5 help can the bird them

_____

Word Order

 Words in a sentence must be in an order that makes sense.

Write the words in the correct order to make a sentence. Then write if the sentence is a question or a statement.

1 find Will I some wood? _____

_____

2 must Each of help us. _____

_____

3 trees are the Where? _____

_____

Write each group of words in the correct order to make a statement. Then write them in the correct order to make a question. Add capital letters and end punctuation to your sentences.

4 your pumpkin is that _____

_____

5 help cut you can pumpkin the _____

_____

Word Order

Read each group of words. If the word order does not make sense, fill in the bubble next to the correct word order. If the words are in an order that makes sense, fill in the last bubble.

1 Dad made breakfast for eggs.
- ○ Made for breakfast Dad eggs.
- ○ Dad made breakfast eggs for.
- ○ Dad made eggs for breakfast.
- ○ correct as is

2 Open eggs four he cracked.
- ○ He cracked eggs open four.
- ○ He cracked open four eggs.
- ○ Four eggs cracked open he.
- ○ correct as is

3 Like do eggs you?
- ○ Eggs do you like?
- ○ Do you like eggs?
- ○ Do eggs like you?
- ○ correct as is

4 Help did you him?
- ○ Did help you him?
- ○ Did you help him?
- ○ Help you did him?
- ○ correct as is

5 With fork a beat eggs.
- ○ Beat eggs with a fork.
- ○ Eggs beat a fork with.
- ○ A fork beat with eggs.
- ○ correct as is

6 Do you want some toast?
- ○ Do you toast some want?
- ○ Do some toast want you?
- ○ You want do some toast?
- ○ correct as is

Scholastic Professional Books

Plural Nouns

 *Most nouns add **-s** to mean more than one. Nouns that end in **s, x, ch**, or **sh** add **-es** to mean more than one.*

Read the sentences. Underline the plural nouns. Circle the letter or letters that were added to mean more than one.

1 We have two accordions in our house.

2 Grandma has many brushes to fix her hair.

3 My grandfather has many clocks and watches.

4 A lot of flowers are in the boxes.

Write the nouns that add -s.

_____

Write the nouns that add -es.

_____

Plural Nouns

*Most nouns add **-s** to mean more than one. Nouns that end in **s**, **x**, **ch**, or **sh** add **-es** to mean more than one.*

Read each sentence. Add -s or -es to the noun at the end of the sentence to make it plural. Write it in the sentence.

1 Dad made five cheese _____. (sandwich)

2 He packed five _____ for the children. (lunch)

3 Lisa put fruit in all the _____. (lunchbox)

4 She packed some paper _____, **too.** (dish)

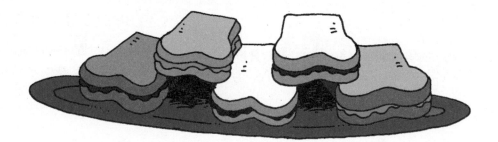

Write the plural for each noun on the line.

5 one box

two _____

6 one dress

two _____

7 one coat

two _____

8 one bench

two _____

Plural Nouns

Read each pair of nouns. If the plural noun is correct, fill in the last bubble. If it is not correct, fill in the bubble next to the correct plural noun.

1 sketch, sketchs
- ○ sketches
- ○ correct as is

2 tree, trees
- ○ treess
- ○ correct as is

3 fox, foxs
- ○ foxes
- ○ correct as is

4 paint, paints
- ○ paintes
- ○ correct as is

5 squirrel, squirrels
- ○ squirreles
- ○ correct as is

6 dress, dressees
- ○ dresses
- ○ correct as is

7 ball, balles
- ○ balls
- ○ correct as is

8 wish, wishes
- ○ wishs
- ○ correct as is

Adjectives

 An **adjective** describes a person, place, or thing. Color, size, and number words are adjectives.

Read each sentence. Underline the nouns. Write the adjective that tells about each noun.

1 The brown donkey carried the heavy

_____ _____

2 The striped cat chased two birds.

_____ _____

3 The little rooster crowed six times.

_____ _____

Write the adjectives from the sentences above.

4 Write the adjectives that tell what kind.

_____

5 Write the adjectives that tell how many.

_____

Scholastic Professional Books

Adjectives

*An **adjective** describes a person, place, or thing. Color, size, and number words are adjectives.*

Read each sentence. Find the adjective and the noun it describes. Circle the noun. Write the adjective on the line.

1 Peggy and Rosa went to the big zoo. _____

2 They looked up at the tall giraffe. _____

3 The giraffe looked down at the two girls. _____

4 The giraffe had brown spots. _____

Write adjectives from the sentences in the chart.

Color Word	Size Words	Number Word
_____	_____	_____
	_____	

Adjectives

Read each sentence. Fill in the bubble next to the word that is an adjective.

1 In the morning, Jenny put on red boots.

- ○ put
- ○ boots
- ○ red
- ○ on

2 She found a yellow hat in the closet.

- ○ She
- ○ hat
- ○ found
- ○ yellow

3 She opened her purple umbrella.

- ○ opened
- ○ She
- ○ umbrella
- ○ purple

4 Jenny walked past a big house.

- ○ big
- ○ house
- ○ walked
- ○ past

5 She waved to three friends.

- ○ waved
- ○ three
- ○ to
- ○ friends

6 A little puppy trotted behind her.

- ○ trotted
- ○ puppy
- ○ little
- ○ behind

7 She jumped over a huge puddle.

- ○ She
- ○ jumped
- ○ huge
- ○ puddle

8 Two birds took a drink of water.

- ○ birds
- ○ of
- ○ took
- ○ Two

Scholastic Professional Books

Verb *to be*

 Am, **is**, **are**, **was**, *and* **were** *are forms of the verb* **to be**. *These verbs show being instead of action.*

Read each sentence. Underline the verb. Write *past* if the sentence tells about the past. Write *now* if the sentence tells about the present.

1 The story is perfect.   _____

2 The producers are happy.   _____

3 The actors were funny.   _____

4 The movie studio is interested in the story.   _____

5 I am excited about the movie.   _____

6 I was sad at the end.   _____

Scholastic Professional Books

Verb *to be*

 Am, **is**, **are**, **was**, and **were** are forms of the verb **to be**. *These verbs show being instead of action.*

Choose a verb from the box to finish each sentence. There may be more than one right answer. Write *one* if the sentence tells about one. Write *more* if it tells about more than one.

| am | is | are | was | were |

1 The movie _____ long. _____

2 She _____ in the movie. _____

3 They _____ at the movie theater yesterday. _____

4 The producers _____ spending money now. _____

5 The director _____ not at work yesterday. _____

6 The actors _____ acting now. _____

Verb *to be*

Read each sentence. Fill in the bubble next to the words that correctly tell about the sentence.

1 The movie was very long.
- ○ past, more than one
- ○ present, more than one
- ○ past, one
- ○ present, one

2 The seats at the movies are high up.
- ○ past, more than one
- ○ present, more than one
- ○ past, one
- ○ present, one

3 The actors were all big stars.
- ○ past, more than one
- ○ present, more than one
- ○ past, one
- ○ present, one

4 The scenes were interesting.
- ○ past, more than one
- ○ present, more than one
- ○ past, one
- ○ present, one

5 The trees and flowers were so beautiful.
- ○ past, more than one
- ○ present, more than one
- ○ past, one
- ○ present, one

6 I am going to see the movie again.
- ○ past, more than one
- ○ present, more than one
- ○ past, one
- ○ present, one

Irregular Verbs *go, do*

Irregular verbs change their spelling when they tell about the past. **Did** *is the past form of* **do** *and* **does**. **Went** *is the past form of* **go** *and* **goes**.

Read each sentence. Write present if the underlined verb tells about action now. Write past if it tells about action in the past.

Present	Past
go, goes	went
do, does	did

1 Grace <u>goes</u> to the playground. _____

2 Some other children <u>go</u>, too. _____

3 Grace <u>does</u> a scene from a story. _____

4 The children <u>do</u> the scene with her. _____

5 Grace <u>went</u> into battle as Joan of Arc. _____

6 She <u>did</u> the part of Anansi the Spider, too. _____

7 In another part, Grace <u>went</u> inside a
   wooden horse. _____

8 She <u>did</u> many other parts. _____

Irregular Verbs *go, do*

Irregular verbs change their spelling when they tell about the past. **Did** *is the past form of* **do** *and* **does.** **Went** *is the past form of* **go** *and* **goes.**

Choose the correct word from the chart and write it on the line.

In the Present	In the Past
go, goes	went
do, does	did

1 Last week our family _____ to the art museum.

2 Pablo _____ there a lot.

3 His mother _____ the displays there now.

4 She _____ a new one yesterday.

5 _____ you want to join us tomorrow?

6 We want to _____ after lunch again.

Irregular Verbs *go, do*

Fill in the bubble next to the word that correctly completes the sentence.

1 Rose ____ to the ballet.
- ○ go
- ○ did
- ○ goes

2 Two dancers ____ a kick and a turn.
- ○ do
- ○ does
- ○ goes

3 Another dancer ____ a hop and a jump.
- ○ went
- ○ does
- ○ do

4 They ____ around in circles very fast.
- ○ goes
- ○ did
- ○ go

5 A girl ____ two big splits.
- ○ do
- ○ did
- ○ went

6 Then she ____ off stage.
- ○ go
- ○ did
- ○ went

7 Rose ____ home feeling very happy.
- ○ went
- ○ did
- ○ go

8 She ____ some of the steps, too.
- ○ do
- ○ did
- ○ goes

Scholastic Professional Books

Quotation Marks

Quotation marks *show the exact words someone says. They go before the speaker's first word. They also go after the speaker's last word and the end punctuation mark.*

Read each sentence. Underline the exact words the speaker says. Put the words in quotation marks. The first one is done for you.

1 Max said, "Let's go on a picnic."

2 Cori replied,   That's a great idea.

3 Andy asked,   What should we bring?

4 Max said with a laugh,   We should bring food.

5 Cori added,   Yes, let's bring lots and lots of food.

6 Andy giggled and said,   You're no help at all!

Finish the sentences below by writing what Max, Cori, and Andy might say next. Use quotation marks.

7 Max said, _____.

8 Cori asked, _____.

9 Andy answered, _____.

Quotation Marks

Quotation marks *show the exact words someone says. They go before the speaker's first word. They also go after the speaker's last word and the end punctuation mark.*

Read the sentences. Then put quotation marks where they belong. The first one has been done for you.

1 Jan cried, "It is raining!"

2 She asked, What will we do today?

3 Tomas answered, We could read.

4 Tomas whispered, Maybe the sun will come out soon.

5 Jan whined, But what will we do now?

6 Tomas said, Use your imagination!

Finish the sentence below. Use quotation marks to show what Jan asked.

Jan asked, _____

_____

Scholastic Professional Books

Quotation Marks

Fill in the bubble next to the correct way to write the sentence.

1

○ Let's make a sand castle, said Lenny.

○ "Let's make a sand castle, said Lenny.

○ "Let's make a sand castle," said Lenny.

2

○ Where's the pail and shovel?" asked Sonya.

○ "Where's the pail and shovel?" asked Sonya.

○ Where's the pail and shovel? asked Sonya

3

○ Sara said, "Maybe Otis can help."

○ Sara said, Maybe Otis can help."

○ Sara said, "Maybe Otis can help.

4

○ Do you want to dig? asked Lenny.

○ "Do you want to dig? asked Lenny.

○ "Do you want to dig?" asked Lenny.

5

○ Sonya shouted, Get some water!

○ Sonya shouted, "Get some water!

○ Sonya shouted, "Get some water!"

6

○ Look what we made! cried the children.

○ "Look what we made!" cried the children.

○ Look what we made!" cried the children.

Contractions With *not*

A **contraction** is two words made into one word. An apostrophe takes the place of the missing letter or letters. In a contraction, **not** becomes **n't**.

Read each sentence. Underline the contraction. Write the two words the contraction is made from.

1 The little old man and little old woman aren't ready.

are not

2 The Gingerbread Man doesn't want to be eaten.

does not

3 They can't catch him.

cannot

4 They couldn't run fast enough.

could not

5 He didn't come back.

did not

6 The Gingerbread Man isn't afraid of the fox.

is not

Draw a line to match each contraction to the two words it is made from.

7 hadn't   were not

8 don't   had not

9 weren't   do not

Scholastic Professional Books

Contractions With *not*

A **contraction** is two words made into one word. An apostrophe takes the place of the missing letter or letters. In a contraction, **not** becomes **n't**.

Read each sentence. Write a contraction for the underlined words.

 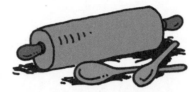 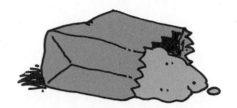

1 Cindy and Ed <u>could not</u> bake a cake.   *Couldn't*

2 There <u>was not</u> enough flour.   *Wasn't*

3 They <u>are not</u> happy.   *aren't*

4 They <u>cannot</u> surprise José.   *can't*

5 <u>Do not</u> give up.   *Don't*

6 They <u>did not</u> give up.
They made cupcakes!   *didn't*

Write a sentence using a contraction you wrote.

They aren't going to play.

_____

Contractions With *not*

Fill in the bubble next to the contraction that correctly completes the sentence.

1 Our players ____ as big as theirs.
- ○ doesn't
- ○ haven't
- ○ aren't

2 Our coach ____ worried.
- ○ isn't
- ○ didn't
- ○ can't

3 They ____ run as fast as we can.
- ○ weren't
- ○ can't
- ○ wasn't

4 Their runner ____ tag first base.
- ○ doesn't
- ○ haven't
- ○ isn't

5 Their hitters ____ hit the ball hard.
- ○ isn't
- ○ weren't
- ○ don't

6 Our hitters ____ miss any balls.
- ○ doesn't
- ○ didn't
- ○ aren't

7 The other players ____ catch our balls.
- ○ couldn't
- ○ haven't
- ○ isn't

8 They ____ ready for us.
- ○ don't
- ○ hadn't
- ○ weren't

Subject/Verb Agreement

*If the naming part of a sentence names one, add **-s** to the action word. If the naming part names more than one, do not add **-s** to the action word.*

Read each sentence. Underline the word in parentheses ( ) that correctly completes it. Write the word on the line.

1 Kim _____ a story about a monkey. (write, writes)

2 The monkey _____ his friend in the city.
(meet, meets)

3 The two friends _____ on the bus. (ride, rides)

4 The monkeys _____ for toys and presents.
(shop, shops)

5 The store _____ at 7 o'clock. (close, closes)

6 The monkeys _____ the time. (forget, forgets)

7 The owner _____ the door. (lock, locks)

8 The friends _____ on the window. (bang, bangs)

9 Many people _____ for help. (call, calls)

10 Finally the monkeys _____ the door open.
(hear, hears)

Scholastic Professional Books

Subject/Verb Agreement

*If the naming part of a sentence names one, add **-s** to the action word. If the naming part names more than one, do not add **-s** to the action word.*

Read each sentence. Circle the action word in parentheses ( ) that correctly completes the sentence.

1 Two baby llamas (play/plays) in the mountains.

2 One baby llama (hide/hides) under a bush.

3 The baby animals (chase/chases) flying leaves.

4 Soon the mother llama (call/calls) them.

5 The babies (run/runs) to her.

6 The two babies (stand/stands) next to their mother.

7 One baby (close/closes) its eyes.

8 The mother llama (nudge/nudges) the baby gently.

9 But the baby llama (sleep/sleeps).

10 Soon both baby llamas (sleep/sleeps).

Subject/Verb Agreement

Fill in the bubble next to the word that correctly completes the sentence.

1 Two friends ____ beautiful bead necklaces.
○ make   ○ makes

2 One girl ____ some pieces of string.
○ cut   ○ cuts

3 The girls ____ red, blue, and yellow beads.
○ use   ○ uses

4 The yellow beads ____ in the dark.
○ glow   ○ glows

5 The necklaces ____ from the rod.
○ hang   ○ hangs

6 The boys ____ a necklace for their mother.
○ buy   ○ buys

7 One boy ____ the short necklace with round beads.
○ pick   ○ picks

8 The other boy ____ the necklace with square beads.
○ pick   ○ picks

9 Two sisters ____ the same red necklace.
○ wear   ○ wears

10 The girls ____ all the necklaces.
○ sell   ○ sells

More About Subject/Verb Agreement

If the naming part of a sentence is a noun or pronoun that names one, the verb ends in **s**, *except for the pronouns* **I** *and* **you**. *If the naming part is a noun or pronoun that names more than one, the verb does not end in* **-s**.

Read each sentence. Circle the correct verb to complete it.

1 John and his family (camp, camps) in the woods.

2 Alice (like, likes) hiking the best.

3 John (walk, walks) ahead of everyone.

4 Mom and John (build, builds) a campfire.

5 Dad and Alice (cook, cooks) dinner over the fire.

6 Alice and Mom (crawl, crawls) into the tent.

Choose two of the verbs you circled. Write a sentence using each verb.

_____

_____

More About Subject/Verb Agreement

If the naming part of a sentence is a noun or pronoun that names one, the verb ends in **-s,** *except for the pronouns* **I** *and* **you.** *If the naming part is a noun or pronoun that names more than one, the verb does not end in* **-s.**

Choose the correct action word from the box to complete each sentence. Write it on the line.

play	run	dive	climb	throw
plays	runs	dives	climbs	throws

1 Mia _____ ball with her friends.

2 The children like to _____ together.

3 Juan _____ faster than I do.

4 We _____ on a track team.

5 Tom and Kara _____ into the pool.

6 Mary _____ without her goggles.

7 They _____ very tall trees.

8 Liz _____ steep mountains.

9 Juan and Mia _____ balls.

10 I _____ the ball to Juan.

She hops.

They hop..

More About Subject/Verb Agreement

Fill in the bubble next to the verb that correctly completes the sentence.

1 Bobby ____ a sandwich for lunch.

　○ bring 　○ brings

2 Maria ____ rice and black beans.

　○ like 　○ likes

3 Bobby and Maria ____ lunches.

　○ trade 　○ trades

4 The twins ____ fish sandwiches.

　○ eat 　○ eats

5 The children ____ milk with their lunches.

　○ drink 　○ drinks

6 They ____ fresh fruit for dessert.

　○ buy 　○ buys

7 Jill ____ for a ripe, yellow banana.

　○ ask 　○ asks

8 Aki ____ strawberries and blueberries.

　○ want 　○ wants

9 Nathan ____ grapes on his tray.

　○ put 　○ puts

10 Paulo and Sylvia ____ seats at the table.

　○ find 　○ finds

Scholastic Professional Books

Verbs *have, has, had*

The verb **have** *is irregular. Use* **have** *or* **has** *to tell about the present. Use* **had** *to tell about the past.*

Read each sentence. Write have, has, or had on the line in the sentence. Then write now or past on the line at the end to show if the sentence takes place now or in the past.

1 The man _____ many people
in his restaurant last week.

_____

2 He _____ good food in his kitchen.

_____

3 Now the restaurant _____ ten tables.

_____

4 The boy _____ time to help his
father today.

_____

5 The girl _____ time, too.

_____

6 The children _____ fun making
salads and setting the tables today.

_____

7 They _____ a good time together
in the restaurant.

_____

8 They _____ fun yesterday, too.

_____

Verbs *have, has, had*

The verb **have** *is irregular. Use* **have** *or* **has** *to tell about the present. Use* **had** *to tell about the past.*

Choose the correct word from the chart to complete each sentence.

In the Present	In the Past
have, has	had

1 Joe _____ new running shoes.

2 I _____ new shoes, too.

3 Last week we _____ old shoes.

4 I _____ a green shirt on.

5 Joe _____ a blue shirt on.

6 Yesterday we both _____ red shirts on.

7 Last year we _____ to walk to the park.

8 Now, I _____ skates.

9 Now, Joe _____ a bike.

Scholastic Professional Books

Verbs *have, has, had*

Read each sentence. If the underlined word is correct, fill in the last bubble. If not, fill in the bubble next to the correct word.

1 I <u>have</u> a pet bird.

  ○ has   ○ had   ○ correct as is

2 Now, she <u>had</u> big white wings.

  ○ has   ○ have   ○ correct as is

3 Before, she <u>has</u> little white wings.

  ○ have   ○ had   ○ correct as is

4 The baby bird <u>have</u> closed eyes when it was born.

  ○ has   ○ had   ○ correct as is

5 Now the baby bird <u>had</u> open eyes.

  ○ has   ○ have   ○ correct as is

6 The mother and baby birds <u>had</u> fun now.

  ○ has   ○ have   ○ correct as is

7 The baby bird <u>has</u> little wings now.

  ○ have   ○ had   ○ correct as is

8 It <u>had</u> even smaller wings when it was born.

  ○ has   ○ have   ○ correct as is

Scholastic Success With

WRITING

You're Sharp!

 A sentence begins with a **capital letter**.

Circle the words that show the correct way to begin each sentence.

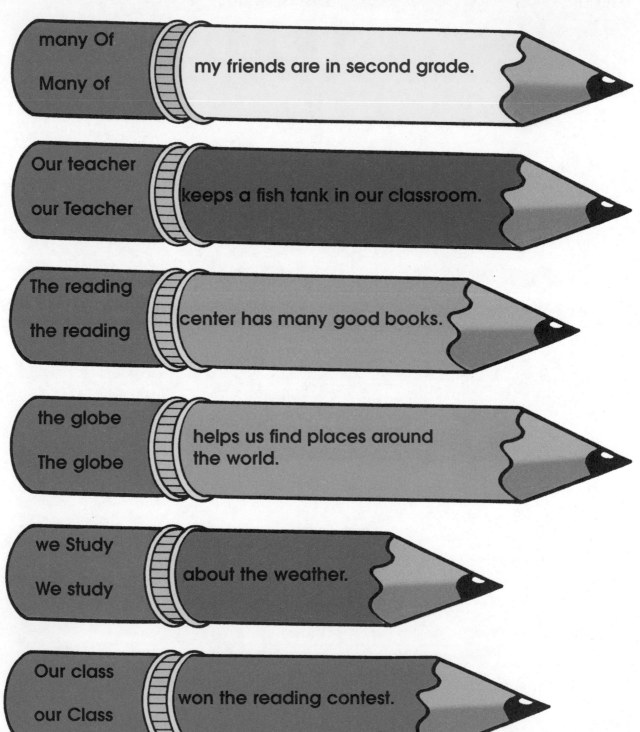

many Of
Many of — my friends are in second grade.

Our teacher
our Teacher — keeps a fish tank in our classroom.

The reading
the reading — center has many good books.

the globe
The globe — helps us find places around the world.

we Study
We study — about the weather.

Our class
our Class — won the reading contest.

Stick With It

A sentence begins with a **capital letter**.

Write the beginning words correctly to make a sentence.

1.
art class _____ begins at noon.

2.
today we _____ are making clay pots.

3.
first, we _____ form the clay into balls.

4.
the next _____ step is to make a hole in
the ball.

5.
my teacher _____ dries the pots.

6.
next week _____ we will paint the pots.

A Whale of a Sentence

 A **telling sentence** *ends with a* **period** *(.).*

Rewrite the sentences using capital letters and periods.

1. the blue whale is the largest animal in the world

_____

2. even dinosaurs were not as large as the blue whale

_____

3. blue whales are not part of the fish family

_____

4. the blue whale has no teeth

_____

5. blue whales eat tiny sea creatures

_____

6. blue whales have two blowholes

_____

 Scholastic Professional Books

That Sounds Fishy to Me

 *A **telling sentence** begins with a **capital letter** and ends with a **period**.*

Write a sentence about each fish. Remember to tell a complete idea.

swordfish

clownfish

eel

pufferfish

angelfish

sailfish

catfish

1. The swordfish has a long snout.
2. Sailfish have a long body.
3. I dont like catfish.
4. Pufferfish are fat.
5. Eels sting you.
6. Clownfish are very colorful.
7. I have never seen angelfish.

Ask Mother Goose

*A sentence that asks a question ends with a **question mark** (?).*
It often begins with one of these words.

Who . . .   Where . . .   Why . . .   Could . . .
What . . .   When . . .   Will . . .

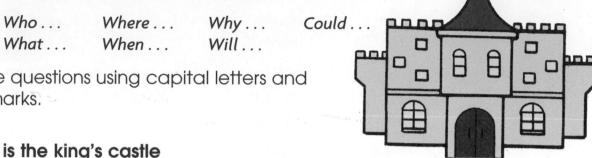

Rewrite the questions using capital letters and question marks.

1. where is the king's castle

_____

2. who helped Humpty Dumpty

_____

3. why did the cow jump over the moon

_____

4. will the frog become a prince

_____

5. could the three mice see

_____

Scholastic Professional Books

Ask the Wolf

 *An **asking sentence** begins with a **capital letter** and ends with a **question mark** (?).
It often begins with one of these words.*

How . . .	*Can . . .*	*Would . . .*
Did . . .	*Is . . .*	*Should . . .*

Imagine that you can meet the Big Bad Wolf. What questions would you ask him about Little Red Riding Hood and the Three Little Pigs? Use a different beginning word for each question you write.

1. How _____

2. Did _____

3. Can _____

1. Is _____

2. Should _____

3. Would _____

 Pretend that you are the Big Bad Wolf. Write a sentence on another piece of paper to answer each question above.

Is Your Head in the Clouds?

 *A **telling sentence** ends with a **period** (.).*
*An **asking sentence** ends with a **question mark** (?).*

Finish each sentence by putting a period or a question mark in
the cloud at the end.

1. Clouds can look like cotton balls, feathers, or blankets

2. Do you know what makes a cloud form in the sky

3. Have you ever seen dark clouds on rainy days

4. Dark clouds may bring thunderstorms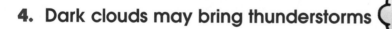

5. Can you imagine pictures in the clouds

6. White clouds drift across the blue sky

7. Why don't we see clouds every day

8. Rain, snow, sleet, and hail may fall from clouds

 **Find two telling sentences and two questions in one of your favorite books. Write them on
another piece of paper.**

Scholastic Professional Books

Name _____

Sunny Sentences

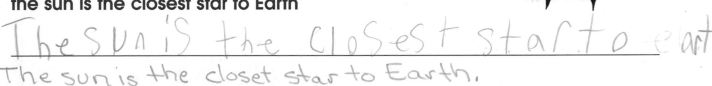

 Every sentence begins with a **capital letter.**
A **telling sentence** *ends with a* **period (.).**
An **asking sentence** *ends with a* **question mark (?).**

Rewrite each sentence correctly.

1. the sun is the closest star to Earth

The sun is the closest star to earth.

The sun is the closet star to Earth.

2. the sun is not the brightest star

The sun isnot the brightest star.

3. what is the temperature of the sun

What is the temperature of the sun?

4. the sun is a ball of hot gas

The sun is a ball of hot gas,

5. how large is the sun

How large is the sun?

6. will the sun ever burn out

Will the sun ever burn out?

 On another piece of paper, write a sentence with two mistakes. Ask a friend to circle the mistakes.

Camp Fiddlestick

 A telling sentence is called a **statement**. An asking sentence is called a **question**.
Now ask yourself:

How do sentences begin? How do statements end? How do questions end?

Write three statements and three questions about the picture.

Statements:

1. _____

2. _____

3. _____

Questions:

1. _____

2. _____

3. _____

 Sing "Where is Thumbkin?" to yourself. Count the number of questions and statements in the song.

Scholastic Professional Books

A Happy Camper

Complete:
Every sentence begins with a _____.
A statement ends with a _____.
A question ends with a _____.

Uh oh! Dalton was in a hurry when he wrote this letter. Help him find 10 mistakes. Circle them.

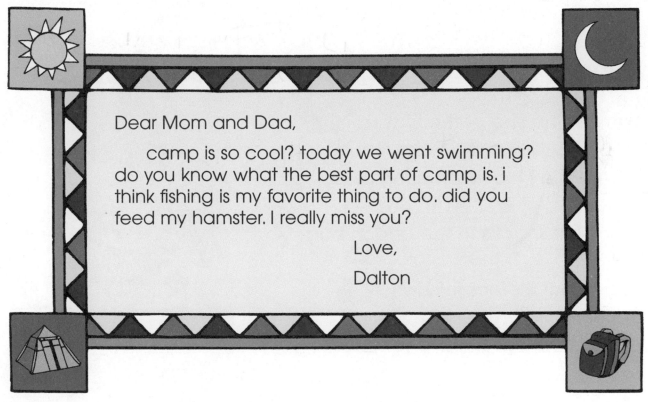

Dear Mom and Dad,

camp is so cool? today we went swimming? do you know what the best part of camp is. i think fishing is my favorite thing to do. did you feed my hamster. I really miss you?

Love,

Dalton

Now choose two questions and two statements from Dalton's letter. Rewrite each correctly.

1. _____

2. _____

3. _____

4. _____

 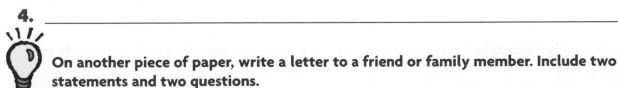 **On another piece of paper, write a letter to a friend or family member. Include two statements and two questions.**

A Day at the Beach

 *A sentence that shows strong feeling or excitement is called an **exclamation**. It ends with an **exclamation point** (!). For example: Look at that shark!*

Finish each sentence by putting a period, a question mark, or an exclamation point in the shell at the end.

1. I wonder if Jamie will be at the beach today

2. Did you bring the beach ball

3. Look at the size of the waves

4. Where did I leave my sunglasses

5. Mom put snacks in the beach bag

6. Watch out for that jellyfish

7. Do you want to build a sandcastle

8. The sun is bright today

9. Did you see that sailboat

10. Don't step on that starfish

11. It is windy near the seashore

12. Should we put up an umbrella

💡 **Read these sentences: I see a sand crab. I see a sand crab! How does your voice change?**

Seashore Sentences

Complete:

A _____ ends with a period.

A _____ ends with a question mark.

An _____ ends with an exclamation point.

Write a statement (S), a question (Q), and an exclamation (E) about each picture.

S _____

_____

Q _____

_____

E _____

_____

S _____

_____

Q _____

_____

E _____

_____

 On another piece of paper, write a statement, a question, and an exclamation about a cartoon in the newspaper.

Building Blocks

 A good sentence has a part that tells who or what the sentence is about. This is called the **subject**.

Make a list of possible subjects to complete each sentence.

_____ jumped the fence.	_____ is too full.
1. _____	1. _____
2. _____	2. _____
3. _____	3. _____

 A good sentence has a part that tells what happens. This is called the **action**.

Make a list of possible actions to complete each sentence.

We _____ on the playground.	The cowboy _____ on his horse.
1. _____	1. _____
2. _____	2. _____
3. _____	3. _____

 On another piece of paper, make a list of five subjects you would like to write about.

Scholastic Professional Books

Keep Building!

 Some sentences have a part that tells where or when the action is happening.

For each sentence, make a list of possible endings that tell where or when the action happens.

The wind blew _____.

1. _____

2. _____

3. _____

The baby tripped _____.

1. _____

2. _____

3. _____

Complete each sentence.

1. _____ made us laugh last night.

2. The door leads _____.

3. The crowd _____ at the circus.

4. The paint bucket spilled _____.

5. _____ was never seen again.

6. The firefighter _____ into the fire truck.

Get Your Ticket!

Write a sentence to match each picture. Be sure to include a subject, an action, and a part that tells where or when.

1. A boy climbs a tree in his backyard.

2. _____

3. _____

 Find a cartoon in the newspaper. Use the pictures to write a sentence on another piece of paper. Be sure to include a subject, an action, and a part that tells where or when.

Slide Show

A sentence is more interesting when it includes a subject, an action, and a part that tells where or when.

Write three sentences and draw pictures to match.

subject	action	where or when

1. _____

subject	action	where or when

2. _____

subject	action	where or when

3. _____

 Switch the sentence parts around to make three silly sentences! Write the sentences on another piece of paper.

Mystery Bags

Describing words *help you imagine how something looks, feels, smells, sounds, or tastes.*

Make a list of words that describe the object in each bag below.

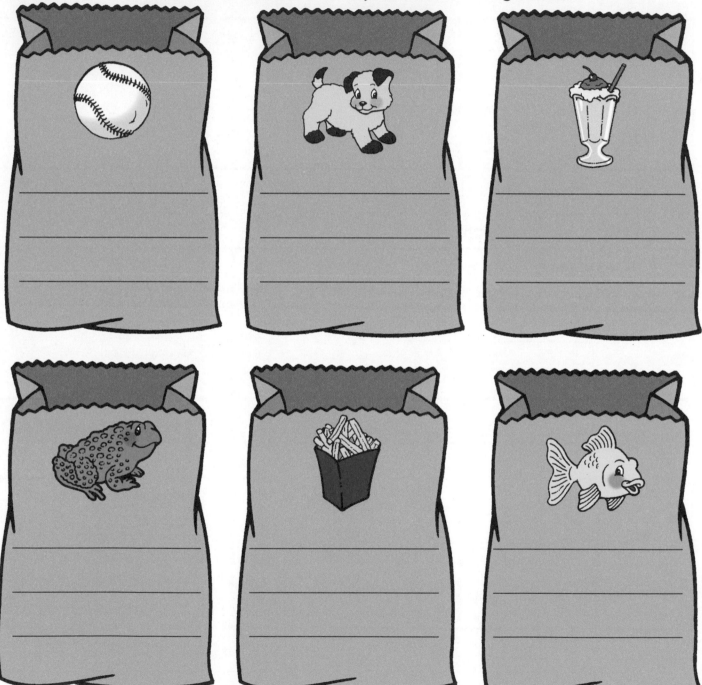

Use a paper sack to make a real mystery bag. Place an object in the bag and give describing clues to someone at home. Can he or she guess the mystery object?

Scholastic Professional Books

Country Roads

 A good sentence uses describing words to help the reader "paint a picture" in his or her mind.

Add a describing word from the list to finish each sentence.

1. The _____ chicken laid

   _____ eggs in her nest.

2. The _____ barn

   keeps the _____

   animals warm at night.

3. _____ carrots grow in

   the _____ garden.

4. Two _____ pigs sleep in

   the _____ pen.

5. The _____ cows drink

   from the _____ pond.

6. A _____ scarecrow

   frightens the _____ birds.

wooden

sunny

lazy

black

three

orange

thirsty

cold

shallow

muddy

funny

fat

 On another piece of paper, write three sentences describing your favorite place to visit.

It's in the Bag

Describing words *make a sentence more interesting.*

Add a describing word to each sentence.

1. My friend's _____ dog has fleas!

2. The _____ popcorn is in the big bowl.

3. How did the _____ worm get on the sidewalk?

4. The _____ ocean waves crashed against the rocks.

5. The _____ ball broke a window at school!

6. My _____ skin itched from poison ivy.

7. The two _____ squirrels chased each other up the tree.

8. The _____ sand felt good on my feet.

9. Are the _____ apples ready to be picked?

10. The _____ ball was hard to catch.

11. Is the _____ salamander hiding under the rock?

12. The _____ snow cone melted quickly.

 Ask someone at home to make a mystery bag and give you clues about the object inside.

Scholastic Professional Books

City Streets

 A good sentence uses describing words.

Write a statement (S), a question (Q), and an exclamation (E) about the picture. Use each of the following describing words:

fast   busy   crowded

S _____

_____

Q _____

_____

E _____

_____

 Describe a "mystery object" to a friend. Can he or she guess what you are describing?

Football Frenzy

A sentence is more interesting when it gives exact information.

Replace each 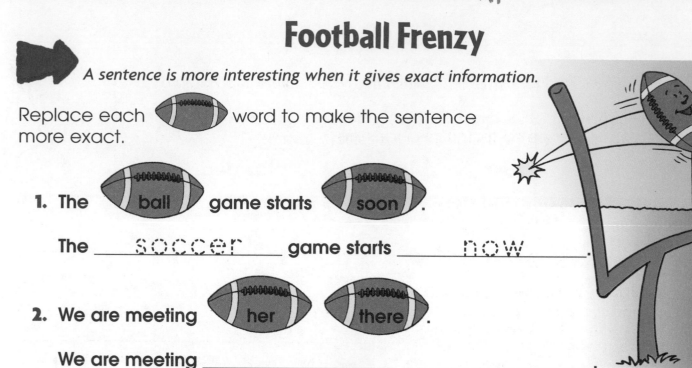 word to make the sentence more exact.

1. The ball game starts soon .

   The _____soccer_____ game starts _____now_____ .

2. We are meeting her there .

   We are meeting _____ _____ .

3. Let's eat this and that before the game.

   Let's eat _____ and _____ before

   the game.

4. I hope they score some points.

   I hope _____ score _____ points.

5. They were also there .

   _____ were also _____ .

6. 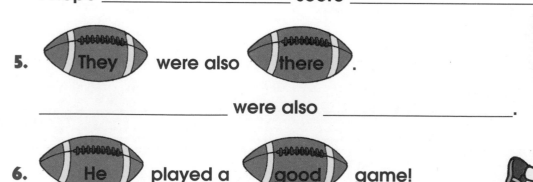 He played a good game!

   _____ played a _____ game!

Scholastic Professional Books

Take Me Out to the Ball Game

 A sentence is more interesting when it gives complete information.

Finish each sentence so that it answers the  question.

1. The players get to the stadium  when.

_____

2. The team is excited because  why.

_____

3. The fans arrive in  what.

_____

4. Flags are flying  where.

_____

5. A man sings the "Star-Spangled Banner"  when.

_____

6. The fans cheer for  whom.

_____

7. The ball is hit  where.

_____

 On another piece of paper, write a sentence about your favorite game. Be sure to tell who plays the game with you.

Scholastic Professional Books

Cake and Ice Cream

 Two sentences that share the same subject can be combined to make one sentence by using the word **and**.

Rewrite the sentences by combining their endings.

1. The party was fun.
The party was exciting.

The party was fun and exciting.

2. We blew up orange balloons.
We blew up red balloons.

_____

3. We ate cake.
We ate ice cream.

_____

4. The cake frosting was green.
The cake frosting was yellow.

_____

5. We made a bookmark.
We made a clay pot.

_____

6. We brought games.
We brought prizes.

_____

Salt and Pepper

 Two sentences that share the same ending can also be combined to make one sentence.

Rewrite the sentences by combining their subjects.

1. These peanuts are salty!
These pretzels are salty!

These peanuts and pretzels are salty!

2. The first graders eat lunch at noon.
The second graders eat lunch at noon.

_____

3. Where is the salt?
Where is the pepper?

_____

4. The napkins are on the table.
The forks are on the table.

_____

5. Are the muffins in the oven?
Are the cookies in the oven?

_____

6. Michael bought lunch today.
Stephen bought lunch today.

_____

Scholastic Professional Books

Great Gardening Tips

Sentences can also be combined to make them more interesting. Key words can help put two sentences together.

I will plan my garden. I am waiting for spring.

I will plan my garden while I am waiting for spring.

Combine the two sentences using the key word. Write a new sentence.

1. Fill a cup with water. Add some flower seeds.  and

_____

2. This will soften the seeds. They are hard.  because

_____

3. Fill a cup with dirt. The seeds soak in water.  while

_____

4. Bury the seeds in the cup. The dirt covers them. until

_____

5. Add water to the plant. Do not add too much.  but

_____

6. Set the cup in the sun. The plant will grow.  so

_____

Growing Sentences

Sentences can be combined to make them more interesting.

Write a combined sentence of your own. Use the given key word to help you.

1. while   I watch TV while my mom makes lunch,

2. until   _____

   _____

3. because _____

   _____

4. but   _____

   _____

5. or   _____

   _____

6. and   _____

   _____

 On another piece of paper, write a combined sentence of your own using one of these key words: *after, before, during.*

Scholastic Professional Books

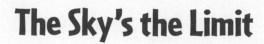
The Sky's the Limit

 Some sentences include a list. A **comma** *(,) is used to separate each item in the list.*

For example: Mrs. Jones asked the class to work on pages two, three, and four.

Fill in the blanks to make a list in each sentence. Watch for commas!

1. I ate _____, _____,

and _____ for breakfast.

2. We stayed with Grandma on _____,

_____, and _____ nights.

3. I found _____, _____,

and _____ in my party bag.

4. The boys played _____,

_____, and _____

at summer camp.

5. The _____, _____,

and _____ ate the corn we scattered.

6. The pigs built their houses using _____,

_____, and _____.

 **Cut a balloon out of paper. On one side, list
three objects that fly. On the other side,
write a sentence that lists these objects.**

Scholastic Professional Books

Up, Up, and Away

 *Some sentences include a list. A **comma** (,) is used to separate each item in the list.*

Write a sentence that includes a list of the words that are given.

**coat
hat
gloves**

1. _____

_____

2. _____

_____

**spelling
reading
math**

**bread
peanut butter
jelly**

3. _____

_____

4. _____

_____

**birds
flowers
butterflies**

 On another piece of paper, write a sentence that lists colors or shapes of balloons.

Out of This World

 After you write a sentence, go back and look for mistakes. This is called **proofreading** *your work.*

Use the proofreading marks to correct the two mistakes in each sentence.

<u>mars</u> = **Make a capital letter.**   (?) = **Add a question mark.**   (!) = **Add an exclamation point.**

(.) = **Add a period.**   (,) = **Add a comma.**   [ ] = **Add a word. (Write a describing word in the box.)**

1. Sometimes I can see mars Jupiter, and Saturn with my telescope.

[ ]

2. There are ∧ stars in our galaxy .

[ ]

3. comets are ∧ pieces of ice and rock.

[ ]

4. The sun is really a ∧ star

5. is there life on any other planet

[ ]

6. Look at that ∧ shooting star

7. can you imagine traveling in space

[ ]

8. i think I saw a ∧ alien.

On another piece of paper, write two sentences about space with two mistakes in each. Ask someone at home to proofread your sentences. Is he or she correct?

Smart About Saturn

 Be sure to proofread your work.

Matthew's science report has nine mistakes. Use proofreading marks to correct his work. Then rewrite the report. Add at least two describing words to the report.

**Saturn
by Matthew**

Saturn is famous for the rings that surround it? its rings are made of ice, rock and dirt. The rings circle around the planet! Saturn is made of gas? saturn's gases are lighter than water That means Saturn would float if you put it into a tub of water Saturn has at least 17 moons

_____

_____

_____

_____

_____

On another piece of paper, write a short report about your favorite planet. Be sure to proofread it when you are done.

Name _____

Banana-Rama

Color the word that is missing from each sentence.

1. We _____ a spelling test yesterday.   taked   took

2. There _____ frost on the ground.   was   were

3. Tommy _____ the Statue of Liberty.   seen   saw

4. How _____ elephants are at the zoo?   much   many

5. Claire _____ her lizard to school.   brought   brang

6. Have you _____ my dog?   seen   saw

7. Alyssa _____ a new pair of skates.   gots   has

8. You _____ supposed to finish your work.   are   is

9. We _____ standing near a snake!   were   was

10. They _____ a pig in the mud.   seen   saw

11. We _____ our winter boots.   wore   weared

12. Is she _____ to come over?   gonna   going

13. _____ your cat climb trees?   Do   Does

14. Rosie _____ cookies to the bake sale.   brang   brought

An Apple a Day

Find the word that is incorrect in each sentence. Draw an apple around it and write the correct word on the line.

1. Laura brang a snack to camp. _____

2. I seen the sea lion show at the zoo. _____

3. Drew gots a dinosaur collection. _____

4. Mara taked her dog for a walk. _____

5. We is going to see the movie. _____

6. Jason runned to the playground. _____

7. How many pennies do you got? _____

8. The kids was having fun. _____

9. Did you saw the soccer game? _____

10. How much do that cost? _____

11. Kelly brang her cat to school! _____

12. I does my homework after school. _____

Eat an apple. Then on another piece of paper, write a statement, a question, and an exclamation describing the apple. Be sure each sentence uses correct words.

Stories of Nature

 Sentences should be written in the correct order to tell a story.

Finish the stories by writing a sentence about each of the last two pictures.

First: Two birds build a nest.

Next: _____

Last: _____

First: A flower bud grows.

Next: _____

Last: _____

Scholastic Professional Books

Nestled in a Nest

Write a sentence about each picture to make your own story.

_____

_____

_____

_____

_____

_____

_____

_____

_____

_____

_____

_____

 Read your story to a friend.

Stories on Parade

*Stories have a **beginning** (B), a **middle** (M), and an **end** (E).*

Write a middle sentence that tells what happens next. Then write an ending
sentence that tells what happens last.

B During the parade, five funny clowns jumped out of a purple bus.

M Next, _____

E Last, _____

B A big balloon got loose in the wind.

M Next, _____

E Last, _____

B A group of horses stopped right in front of us.

M Next, _____

E Last, _____

B Some clowns were riding motorcycles.

M Next, _____

E Last, _____

**On another piece of paper, draw a picture of a parade that shows what is happening in the
stories you wrote.**

Scholastic Professional Books

An Original Story

Choose a story idea from the list. Then write a beginning, middle, and ending sentence to make a story of your own. Color a picture to match each part.

The Best Birthday Ever   **King for a Day**

My Dog's Dream   **The Magic Rock**

First: _____

_____

_____

_____

B

Next: _____

_____

_____

_____

M

Last: _____

_____

_____

_____

E

 Staple three pieces of paper together to make a book. Write another story and draw a picture for each part.

Once Upon a Time

*The **setting** of a story tells when or where it is happening.*

Imagine that you are writing a story for each picture below. How will you describe the setting? Write a sentence describing each setting.

| setting | → | characters | → | problem | → | solution |

It was a hot morning in the desert.

On another piece of paper, describe the setting of your favorite movie.

Scholastic Professional Books

All Kinds of Characters

 The people or animals in a story are called **characters.**

Some characters are likable and others are not. Write a describing sentence about each character. Be sure to give each character a name.

setting	→	characters	→	problem	→	solution

_____

_____

_____

_____

_____

_____

_____

_____

On another piece of paper, make a list of four people you know well. Write three words that describe each of them. Cross out the four names and write animal names instead. Now you have four characters to use in your next story!

That's a Problem!

 *To make a story exciting, one of the characters often runs into a **problem**.*

Think about each character in the sentences below. What could happen that would make a problem for that character? Write the next sentence creating a problem.

| setting | → | characters | → | problem | → | solution |

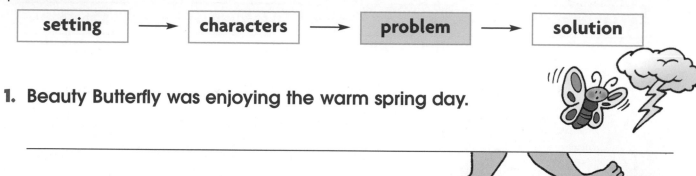

1. Beauty Butterfly was enjoying the warm spring day.

_____

2. Jesse was supposed to wear shoes outside.

_____

3. Gabby could not wait to bite into her apple.

_____

4. Ben smacked the baseball into the air.

_____

5. Barney Bass had never seen such a big worm!

_____

Scholastic Professional Books

Good Solution!

*At the end of a story, the problem is usually solved. This is called the **solution**.*

Read the beginning and middle parts of the stories below. Write an ending solution for each.

setting → characters → problem → solution

David and his dog, Spot, were best friends. They went everywhere together. At bedtime, David whistled for Spot to jump in his bed. One winter night, David whistled and whistled, but Spot did not come.

_____

_____

_____

Josh loved second grade, but he did not like recess. Josh's class was always the last one out to the playground. Every day, Josh ran to get a swing, but they were always taken.

_____

_____

_____

On another piece of paper, make a list of three problems you have faced. How did you solve each problem?

Scholastic Professional Books

The Mighty Knight

 *A **story map** helps you plan the setting, characters, problem, and solution.*

Write a sentence about each part of the map to make a story.

_____

_____

_____

_____

_____

_____

_____

_____

_____

_____

 Read your story to a friend.

Scholastic Professional Books

A Story Fit for a King

Use a story map to help plan your story before you begin writing.

Complete the map. Then use it to write a story "fit for a king."

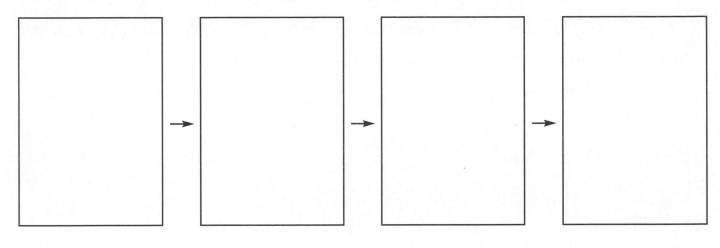

_____

_____

_____

_____

_____

_____

_____

_____

 Turn your story into a puppet show! Perform your puppet show for someone at home.

The Father of Our Country

After you finish writing, go back and look for mistakes.

Use the proofreading marks to correct eight mistakes in the letter.

m̲a̲r̲s̲ = **Make a capital letter.**   ? = **Add a question mark.**   ! = **Add an exclamation point.**

• = **Add a period.**   , = **Add a comma.**

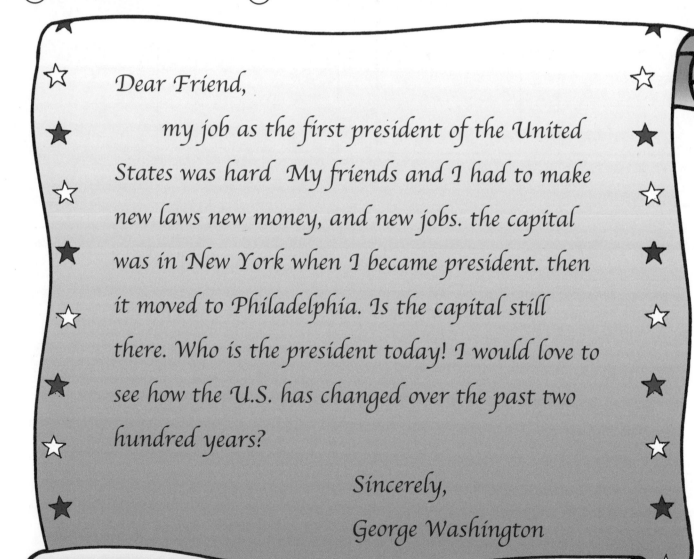

Dear Friend,

    my job as the first president of the United
States was hard My friends and I had to make
new laws new money, and new jobs. the capital
was in New York when I became president. then
it moved to Philadelphia. Is the capital still
there. Who is the president today! I would love to
see how the U.S. has changed over the past two
hundred years?

                                    Sincerely,

                                    George Washington

On another piece of paper, write a letter to today's president. The White House address is: 1600 Pennsylvania Avenue Washington, D.C. 20500.

Presidential Pen Pals

A friendly letter *has five parts: the date, greeting, body, closing, and signature.*

Use the five parts to write a letter back to George Washington. Be sure to proofread your work for mistakes.

_____
(today's date)

_____,
(greeting)

_____
(body)

_____

_____

_____

_____

_____

_____

_____

_____,
(closing)

_____
(your name)

MAPS

Looking at a Map

Have you ever been in an airplane? Did you look down on Earth? Then you know that things look different from above.

This photo was taken from an airplane. It shows a community below.

Circle YES if you see the thing in the photo.
Circle NO if you do not.

1. building	YES	NO
2. street	YES	NO
3. car	YES	NO
4. bus	YES	NO

5. What else do you see? _____

The map on this page shows the same place as the photo. A **map** is a drawing of a place from above. A map shows where things are.

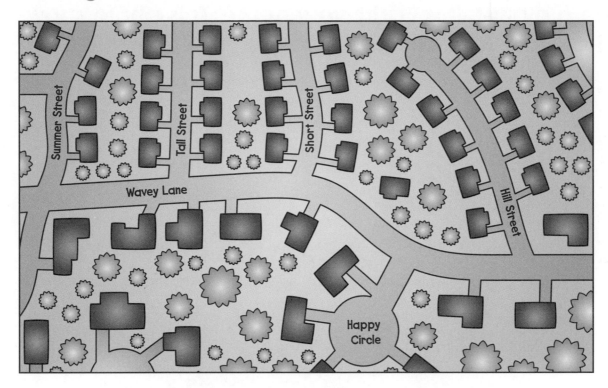

1. Find the house on the corner of Summer Street and Wavey Lane on the map. Make an X on that house.

2. Find a swimming pool in the photo.
   Draw it in the same place on the map.

3. How are the map and photo alike? _____

   _____

4. How are the map and photo different? _____

   _____

A Globe and Earth

Pretend you are in a spaceship. You look out and see a planet. It is Earth, your home. This photo shows what Earth looks like from space. Isn't it beautiful?

1. You can see only one side of Earth at a time.

   What shape is Earth? _____

2. **Does Earth have more land or water?** _____

3. **Why is part of Earth green?** _____

Have you ever played with a toy car? A toy car is a model of a real car. This picture shows a **globe**. A globe is a model of Earth. You can see that the globe and Earth are the same shape.

1. What shape is a globe? _____

2. Is the globe bigger or smaller than Earth? _____

3. What do the words on the globe tell you? _____

_____

A World Map

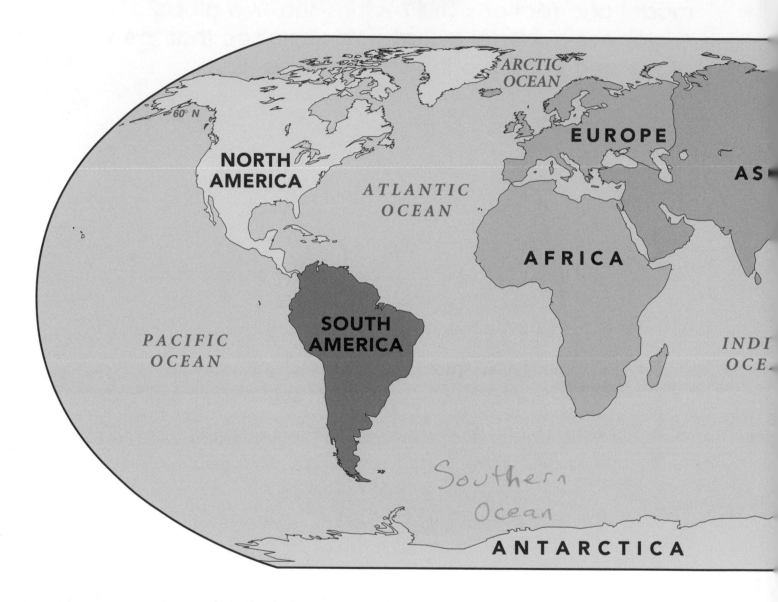

A globe is handy for finding places on Earth.
A world map can show all of Earth, too.

1. This map shows Earth's continents. A continent is a large body of land. Can you find all seven of Earth's continents? Write an **X** on each one.

Scholastic Professional Books

PACIFIC
OCEAN

AUSTRALIA

2. The map also shows Earth's oceans.

   An ocean is a large body of salt water.

   How many oceans do you see?

   _____

3. Name four continents that begin with "A."

   _____

   _____

   _____

   _____

4. Name two oceans that begin with "A."

   _____

   _____

5. How is a world map different from a globe?

   _____

   _____

A Compass Rose

This is a **compass rose**. A compass rose is a symbol that helps you read a map. The arrows on a compass rose point to the four main **directions**. They are north, south, east, and west.

North is the direction toward the North Pole.

South is the direction toward the South Pole.

When you face north, west is on the left. East is on the right.

Sometimes a compass rose has letters that stand for the direction words.

1. **N stands for** _____

2. **S stands for** _____

3. **E stands for** _____

4. **W stands for** _____

Scholastic Professional Books

Map of the World

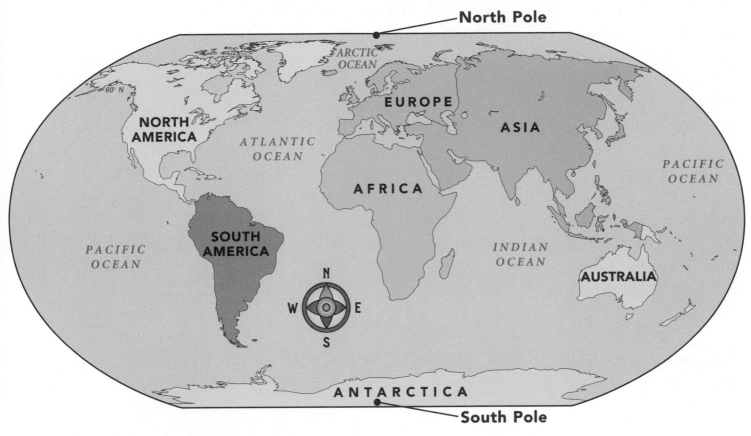

North Pole

South Pole

1. What continent is south of
   South America and Africa? _____

2. What ocean is north of
   North America and Europe? _____

3. Draw a straight line from the North Pole to the South Pole.
   Are these places east or west of your line?

   Indian Ocean _____   North America _____

   Europe _____   Australia _____

Using Directions

When you use a map, look for the compass rose.
Use the directions to tell you how to get places.

Pretend you are at this park. Use a pencil to trace the way you go.

1. Start at the gate and go east. What do you see? _____

2. Go to the swings. In which direction are they? _____

3. Next you come to a fountain.
   In which direction did you walk? _____

4. If you go north, what will you see? _____

Scholastic Professional Books

Lucy lives in Fun City. Her house is on Chuckles Street. Find Lucy's house.

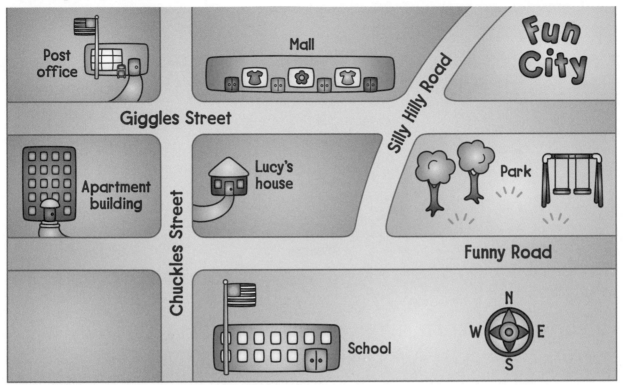

Circle the correct answers.

1. To get to the park, Lucy goes _____.
   west   east   south

2. The mall is _____ of Lucy's house.
   north   south   west

3. The post office is _____ of the mall.
   south   east   west

4. When Lucy walks to school, she heads _____.
   north   west   south

5. If Lucy walks west on Funny Road, she will be at the _____.
   park   library   apartment building

Map Symbols

A map has **symbols**. A symbol is a drawing that stands for something real. A symbol can also be a color or a pattern.

Woods

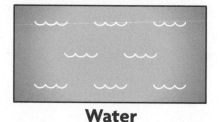
Water

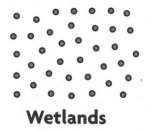
Wetlands

A map key tells what each symbol stands for. Study the map key. Find each symbol on the map. Write the number of the symbol in the correct circle on the map.

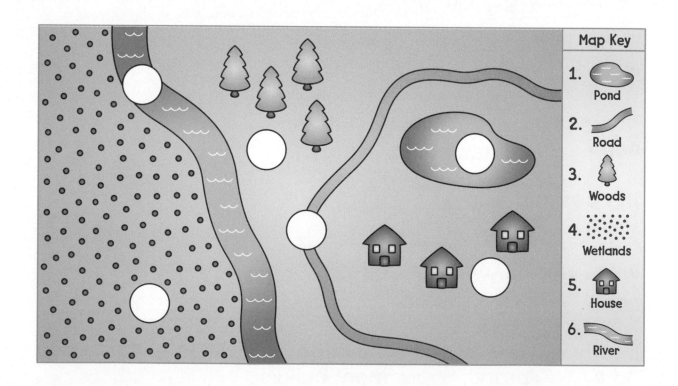

Scholastic Professional Books

Use symbols to read a map.

Use the map key and the compass rose to answer the questions.

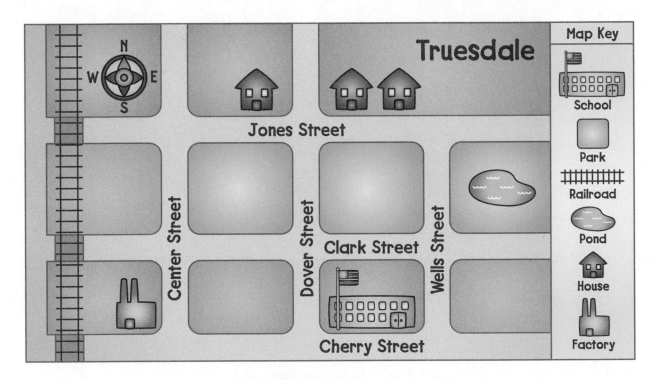

1. What does the symbol mean? _____

2. What street is north of the school? _____

3. What is just west of the factory? _____

4. What color is used to show the park? _____

5. Is the park north or south of the houses? _____

Using Map Symbols

Welcome to the zoo! You can use this map to get around.

Most zoos have maps for visitors to use.
Use the map to answer the questions.

1. What does this symbol mean? _____

2. Are the elephants on the east or west side of the zoo? _____

3. Can you get a snack at this zoo? _____

4. Are the monkeys north or south of the bears? _____

Jungle Path

Map Key

Lions

Elephants

Seals

Monkeys

Bears

Food

Snakes

Wild Way

Center
Zoo

Jungle Path

N
W E
S

5. On what road are the seals? _____

6. Does this zoo have lions? _____

7. Does this zoo have hippos? _____

8. The map key is missing a snake symbol.
   Draw a snake symbol in the map key.

9. Find the space south of the elephants.
   Add your snake symbol there.

Distance

A map can show how far it is from one place to another. This is called **distance**.

Look at these lines.

A. ▬ ▬ ▬ ▬ ▬ ▬ ▬ ▬ ▬ ▬

B. ════════

C. ●●●●●●●●●●●●●●●●

Circle YES or NO.

1. Line A is the longest line.   YES   NO

2. Line C is the shortest line.   YES   NO

3. Line B is longer than Line C.   YES   NO

4. Line C is longer than Line A.   YES   NO

5. Line B is shorter than Line A.   YES   NO

6. Line C is longer than Line B.   YES   NO

The Tang family is playing catch.
This map shows where each player is standing.

Use a ruler to help answer the questions.

1. The longest distance is between Ellen and_____ .

2. The shortest distance is between Jason and_____ .

3. Is Buddy farther from Mom or Ellen? _____ .

4. Is Dad nearer to Mom or Buddy? _____ .

5. It is almost the same distance between
   Ellen and Mom and Mom and _____ .

A Map Grid

Some maps have lines like this:
These lines form a **grid**.
A grid is a pattern
of lines that
form squares.

Each square on
a grid has a letter
and a number.
Find the letter "A"
at the side of the
map. Then find the
number 1 at the
top of the map.
The first square
in the top row is A1.
Can you find A2?

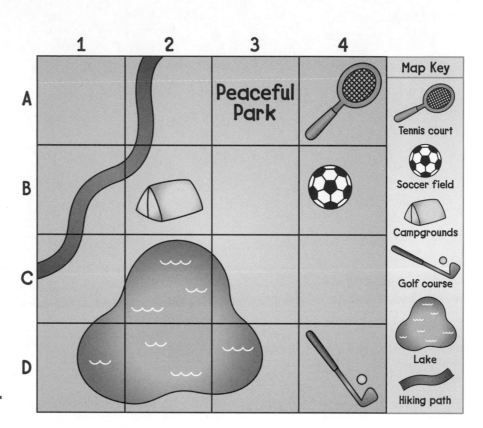

Use the grid to answer the questions.

1. What is in A4? _____

2. In what square is the soccer field? _____

3. Find D4. What can you do there? _____

4. Through what squares does the hiking path go? _____

Here is a map grid game you can play. Study the map. Then look for each square below. Write the square name under each picture.

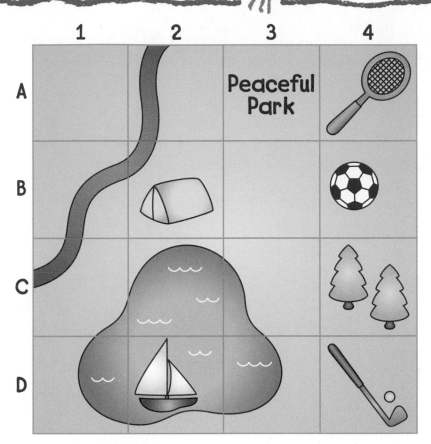

1.

_____

2.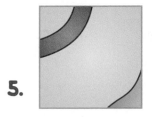

_____

3.

_____

4.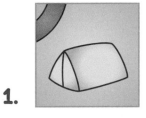

_____

5.

_____

6.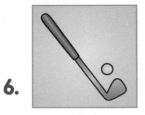

_____

Using a Map Grid

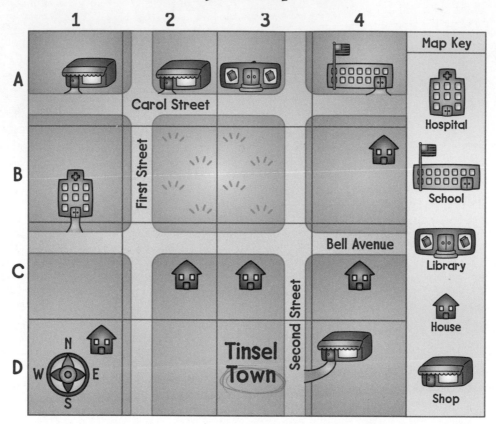

A grid helps you find places on a map. Use the grid to answer the questions.

1. In which square is the hospital? _____

2. What is in square C4? _____

3. What street runs through
   squares A2, B2, C2, and D2? _____

4. Can you shop in D1? _____

5. You want to borrow a book.
   In which square would you look? _____

This map shows the state of Ohio.

States contain many towns and cities.

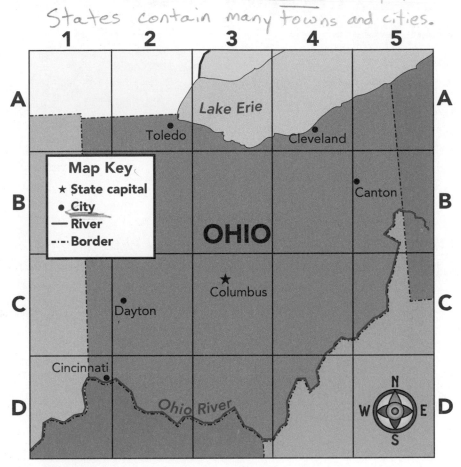

Use the grid and map key to answer the questions.

1. In what square is Cleveland? _A4_ _____

2. What city is in D1? _Cincinnati_ _____

3. What is in A3? _Lake Erie_ _____

4. In what square is Columbus? _C3_ _____

5. Name the squares that the Ohio River runs through. _D1 D2 D3 D4 C5 B5_

The United States — our Country

This is a map of the United States.

The map shows the 50 states. It also shows the capital of each state. A capital is a city where government leaders work.

The United States has a capital, too. It is Washington, D.C.

Find this symbol ————— on the map. A border shows where places begin and end. The borders on this map show the dividing lines between states.

1. **Find your state on the map. What is the capital of your state?** _Richmond_

2. **Find Oregon. What is its capital?** _Salem_

3. **Find Texas. What is its capital?** _Austin_

4. **Is Washington, D.C., in the east or west part of the country?** _east?_

MICHIGAN

MAINE

VERMONT

Augusta

Montpelier

NEW HAMPSHIRE

Concord

MASSACHUSETTS

Albany

Boston

NEW YORK

Hartford

Providence

RHODE ISLAND

CONNECTICUT

PENNSYLVANIA

Trenton

NEW JERSEY

Harrisburg

Dover

DELAWARE

Annapolis

MARYLAND

WASHINGTON, D.C.

RTH DAKOTA   MINNESOTA

Bismarck

St. Paul

WISCONSIN

Pierre

UTH DAKOTA

Madison

Lansing

EBRASKA

IOWA

Des Moines

ILLINOIS

Indianapolis

OHIO

Columbus

Lincoln

INDIANA

WEST
VIRGINIA

KANSAS

Topeka

MISSOURI

Springfield

Charleston   Richmond

VIRGINIA

Jefferson City

Frankfort

KENTUCKY

Raleigh

Nashville

NORTH CAROLINA

OKLAHOMA

Oklahoma City

ARKANSAS

TENNESSEE

Columbia

Little Rock

Atlanta

SOUTH
CAROLINA

MISSISSIPPI

GEORGIA

ALABAMA

TEXAS

Jackson

Montgomery

Baton
Rouge

Tallahassee

Austin

LOUISIANA

FLORIDA

MAP KEY

— State border
⊛ National capital
★ State capital

5. Find Montana. What state has a
   border on the west side of Montana? _Idaho_

6. Find your state. How many
   states share a border with it? _5_

Looking at a State

Have you ever been to Nebraska?
This is how Nebraska looks on a map.

Map Key
★ State capital
-·- State border
— River

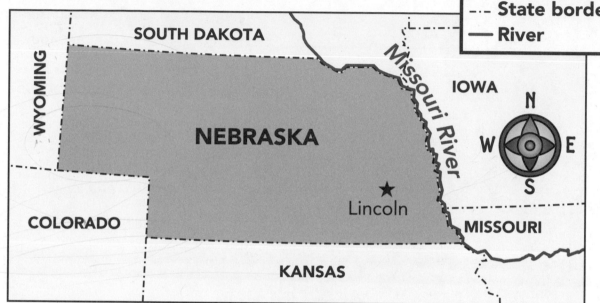

Use the map to answer the questions.

1. What is the symbol for the state capital? _____ Star

2. What is the capital of Nebraska? _____ Lincoln

3. What state is north of Nebraska? _____ South Dakota

4. What states are on the
   western border of Nebraska? _____ Wyoming, colorado

5. What forms the border
   between Nebraska and Iowa? _____ Missouri River

Scholastic Professional Books

The grid can help you find places in Nebraska.

Map Key
- ★ State capital
- ● City
- -·- State border
- — River

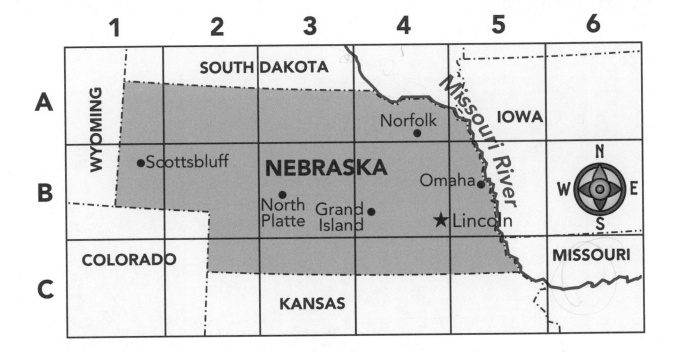

Use the map to answer the questions.

1. In what square is North Platte? ___B3_____

2. What city is in A4? __Norfolk_____

3. In what square is Nebraska's capital? __B4_____

4. Name the squares that the Missouri River runs through. __A3, A4, A5, B5, C5, C6_____

5. What state takes up most of A1? __Wyoming_____

A City Map

(Or - linz)

This map shows New Orleans.

the state of

It is the biggest city in ^Louisiana. (Loo-ee-zee-anna)
Can you find Louisiana on the map on page 277? Underline
its name on that map in red pen.

	1	2	3	4	5	6	7	
A	Tulane Avenue		Louis Armstrong Park	Esplanade Avenue		North Clairborne Avenue		**A**
B	Pontchartrain Expressway	Canal Street	North Rampart Street	French Quarter	Mississippi River	Royal Street		**B**
C		● Superdome / Union Station						**C**
D		New Orleans Convention Center				N W E S		**D**

Use the map to answer the questions.

1. **What river flows through New Orleans?** Mississippi river

2. **Why do you think people built a city on a river?** So they
   can have water

3. **Sports teams play in the Superdome.
   In what square is this building?** C 2

Many people visit New Orleans each year. The city is known for its jazz, a kind of music.

Louis Armstrong
(Loo-ee)

4. Louis Armstrong was a famous trumpet player. What place is named for him in New Orleans? _Louis Armstrong Park_

5. Find C3. What building is there? _Union Station_

6. The French Quarter is the oldest part of New Orleans. In what squares is this part of the city? _B 4_

7. Is the river east or west of the French Quarter? _east_

This means start at the French Quarter and tell me which direction I'd have to walk in to get to the river.

Small Spaces . . .

Look at the maps
on these pages.

Map 1 shows a city.
Map 2 shows a state.
Map 3 shows a country.
Are the places that these
maps show all the same size?

A city is smaller than a state.
A state is just one part of
the United States. The maps
are the same size on paper,
but they show places of
different sizes.

AUSTIN, TEXAS

Map 1

Use the maps to answer the questions.

1. **What city is shown on all three maps?** Austin

2. **In what state is this city?** Texas

3. **In what country is this city?** United States

4. **Is Texas larger or smaller than Austin?** larger

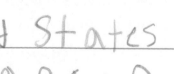
Scholastic Professional Books

Large Spaces

TEXAS

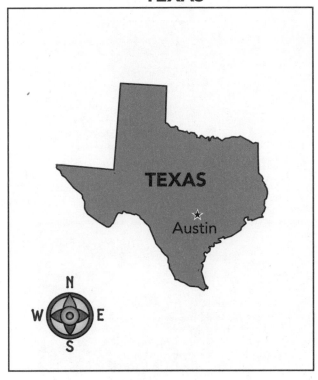

Map 2

UNITED STATES

Map 3

5. Is Austin larger or smaller than the United States? <u>Smaller</u>

6. Is the United States larger or smaller than Texas? <u>larger</u>

7. Is Texas in the north or south part of the United States? <u>South</u>

8. Which map would you use to find your way to the LBJ Library? <u>Map 1</u>

Scholastic Professional Books

Landforms

These pictures show different parts of Earth called landforms.

A landform is a shape of land such as a mountain. You can see that Earth has many different landforms.

A **plain** is flat land.

1. How is a mountain different from a plain?

   _____

2. Through what kind of landform does a river often flow?

   _____

A **valley** is low land between hills or mountains.

3. What are two ways you could get to an island?

   _____

4. Which type of land is best for farming?

   Why? _____

Scholastic Professional Books

A **mountain** is very high land.

A **hill** is land that is higher than a plain, but not as high as a mountain.

An **island** is land with water all around it.

5. Which landform is good for skiing? _____

   Why? _____

6. Which landforms can you see near your house?

   _____

   _____

Bodies of Water

Earth has different bodies of water, too.

You named four oceans on page 261.
They are the largest bodies of water on Earth.

An **ocean** is a large
body of salt water.

A **river** is a long body
of water that flows
across the land.

A **lake** is water
with land all around it.

Use the pictures to answer the questions.

1. Which body of water would
   take the longest time to cross? _____

2. What are some things
   you might do on a lake? _____

3. How are rivers and lakes different? _____

_____

Scholastic Professional Books

The picture shows different kinds of land and water.

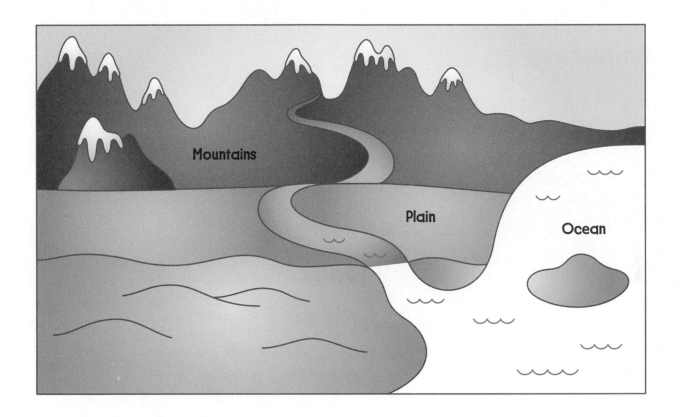

1. Find the low land between the mountains.
   Write valley on it.

2. Find the ocean. Color it blue.

3. Find land that has water all around it.
   Write the name on this land.

4. Find land that is higher than the plain, but not as high as the mountains. Add the correct label to this land.

Using a Landform Map

You are looking
at a landform map.

This map shows
where landforms
and bodies of water
are in Virginia.

OHIO

WEST
VIRGINIA

KENTUCKY

TENNESSEE

Use the map to
answer the questions.

1. What does the symbol [■] mean? _____

2. What is the symbol for plains? _____

3. Find the James River.
   Name the landforms it flows across. _____

4. Are mountains in the east or
   the west part of Virginia? _____

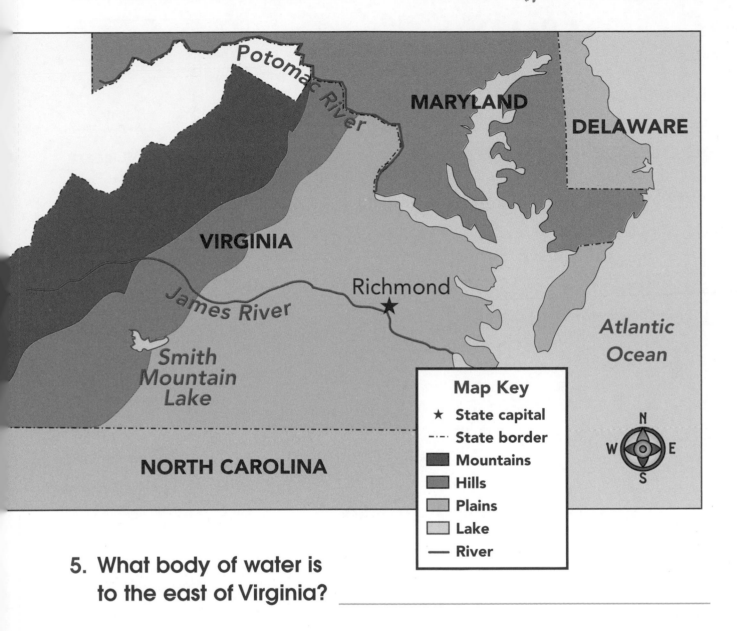

Map Key
★ State capital
- - - State border
■ Mountains
■ Hills
■ Plains
□ Lake
— River

5. **What body of water is to the east of Virginia?** _____

6. **What kind of land is near the capital of Virginia?** _____

7. **What river forms part of the border between Virginia and Maryland?** _____

8. **In which part of Virginia do you think there are more farms?** _____
   Why? _____

A Road Map

Imagine you are going on a drive through the state of Nevada. You'll need a map like this one.

A road map shows highways and other roads that you can travel on. Roads are used for transportation. Transportation is how people and things are moved from place to place.

Trucks, cars, and buses follow different routes. A route is a way to go from one place to another.

Use the map to answer the questions.

Pacific Ocean

Key
★ **State capital**
● **City**
---- **State border**
🛣 80 **Interstate**
50 **U.S. route**

1. **Find Las Vegas. What highway would you take to get to Ely?** _____

   In which direction would you travel? _____

2. **A truck leaves Reno for Elko. On which highway does it drive?** _____

3. **From Tonopath, follow Highway 95 south. What city do you reach?** _____

Scholastic Professional Books

4. If you follow Highway 15 north and east
   from Las Vegas, what states do you reach? _____

5. What highway takes you from Elko to Utah? _____

   In which direction do you travel? _____

6. What highway links Carson City with California? _____

7. What are two routes you could
   take to go from Reno to Ely? _____

_____

A Resource Map

A **natural resource** is something found in nature that people use. Water, trees, and minerals are all natural resources. A mineral is a resource found in the ground.

Coal is a mineral. People burn coal to make power for electricity.

Oil is a mineral. Plastic is made from oil.

Sand is a mineral. Sand is used to make concrete for houses and sidewalks.

1. **Name two ways that you use water.**

   _____

   _____

2. **Name something that is made from plastic.**

   _____

3. **What natural resource is used to make a wooden chair?** _____

Scholastic Professional Books

Many of Wyoming's resources are minerals.
This resource map shows where some
of Wyoming's minerals are found.

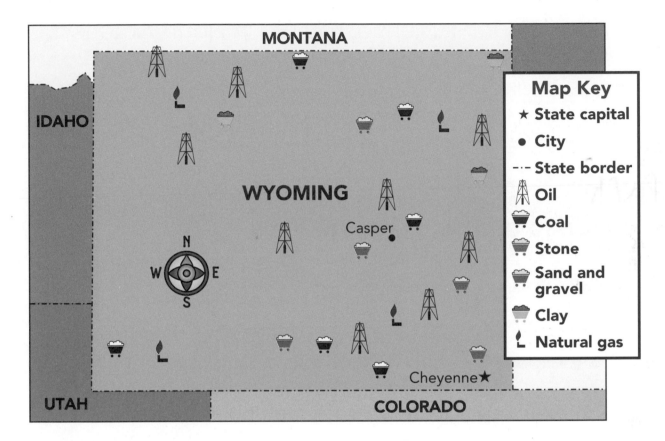

Circle YES or NO. Use the map to help you.

1. **Stone is found near Cheyenne.**   YES   NO

2. **Clay is mostly in the north part of Wyoming.**   YES   NO

3. **There is no coal in the west part of the state.**   YES   NO

4. **Most of Wyoming's oil is in the west.**   YES   NO

5. **Wyoming has more coal than gravel.**   YES   NO

North America

Can you name Earth's seven continents?

One of them is North America. You live in North America.
The United States is one country on this continent.
A country is a land and the people who live there.
Mexico and Canada are two other countries in North
America. Find them on the map on page 295.

Use the map to answer these questions.

1. What does the symbol ——————
   stand for? _____

2. What is the country south of the United States? _____

3. In which direction is Canada from the United States? _____

4. What is the capital of Mexico? _____

5. Is the Pacific Ocean to the east or
   west of North America? _____

6. What state is separated from the
   United States by Canada? _____

7. What river forms the border between
   the United States and Mexico? _____

8. Which country is larger, Canada or Mexico? _____

ARCTIC
OCEAN

Bering Strait

Bering Sea

Greenland Sea

Alaska
(U.S.)

Beaufort Sea

Greenland
(Denmark)

Gulf of Alaska

Baffin Bay

☉Nuuk

Not at same scale

Labrador Sea

Hawaii
(U.S.)

Hudson Bay

Canada

ROCKY MOUNTAINS

Mississippi River

Ottawa ☉

Washington, D.C.

ATLANTIC

OCEAN

PACIFIC

OCEAN

United States
of America

Rio Grande

Bermuda (U.K.)

Bahamas

Mexico

Gulf of Mexico

Cuba

Dominican
Republic

North America

Mexico City ☉

Haiti

Puerto
Rico (U.S.)

Jamaica

☉ National capital

∧ Mountains

Belize

—— Border

Honduras

Caribbean Sea

Guatemala

Nicaragua

El Salvador

Costa Rica

SOUTH AMERICA

Area of detail

Panama

Map Review 1

Use the map to answer the questions.

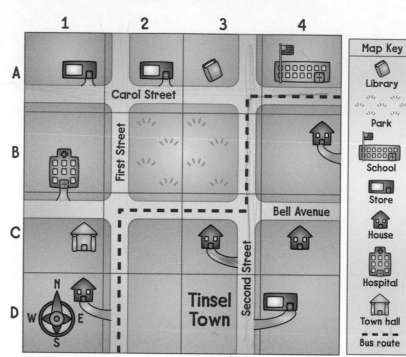

1. What does the symbol

   mean?
   Park

2. What is the symbol for library?
   book

3. What does the letter "S" mean on the compass rose? _South_

4. What is in square C1? _Town hall_

5. In which direction is the hospital from the park? _West_

6. Is the school east or west of the library? _east_

7. Amy lives on First Street. In what square is her house? _C 3_

8. Amy takes the bus to school. Name the streets that the bus route follows.

   Second street to carol street

Scholastic Professional Books

Map Review 2

Use the map to answer the questions.

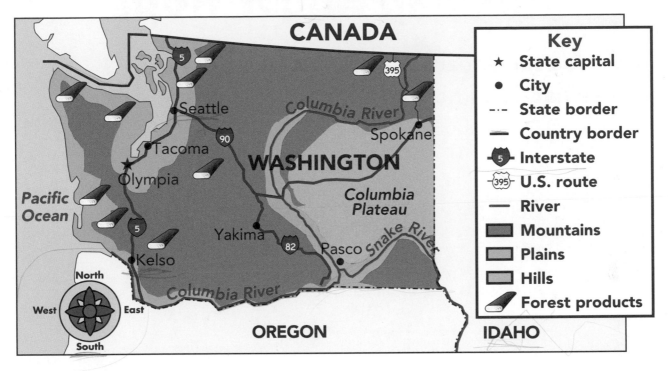

1. What does this symbol ———— mean? country border

2. What country is to the north of Washington? Canada

3. What state is east of Washington? Idaho

4. What river forms the border
   between Washington and Oregon? Columbia river

5. What is the capital of Washington? olympia

6. What resource does Washington have? Forest products

7. What highway can you take from Kelso to Seattle? 5

Thinking About Maps

You have learned a lot about maps. Use what you know to find the secret words.

1. This symbol helps you find directions.

$\underline{\hspace{0.8cm}} \underline{\hspace{0.8cm}} \underline{\hspace{0.8cm}} \underline{\hspace{0.8cm}} \underline{\hspace{0.8cm}} \underline{\hspace{0.8cm}} \underline{\hspace{0.8cm}} \underline{\hspace{0.8cm}}$

$\quad\quad\quad 1 \quad\quad\quad\quad\quad\quad\quad\quad\quad\quad\quad 4$

2. Where do you look to see what symbols mean?

$\underline{\hspace{0.8cm}} \underline{\hspace{0.8cm}} \underline{\hspace{0.8cm}} \underline{\hspace{0.8cm}}$

$\quad\quad\quad 3$

3. Land with water all around it.

$\underline{\hspace{0.8cm}} \underline{\hspace{0.8cm}} \underline{\hspace{0.8cm}} \underline{\hspace{0.8cm}} \underline{\hspace{0.8cm}}$

$\quad\quad\quad\quad 2$

4. Plains and hills are types of

$\underline{\hspace{0.8cm}} \underline{\hspace{0.8cm}} \underline{\hspace{0.8cm}} \underline{\hspace{0.8cm}} \underline{\hspace{0.8cm}} \underline{\hspace{0.8cm}}$

$\quad\quad 5 \quad\quad\quad\quad 8 \quad\quad\quad 6$

5. North America is a

$\underline{\hspace{0.8cm}} \underline{\hspace{0.8cm}} \underline{\hspace{0.8cm}} \underline{\hspace{0.8cm}} \underline{\hspace{0.8cm}} \underline{\hspace{0.8cm}} \underline{\hspace{0.8cm}}$

$\quad\quad\quad 10 \quad\quad\quad\quad\quad 7$

6. This landform is very high land.

$\underline{\hspace{0.8cm}} \underline{\hspace{0.8cm}} \underline{\hspace{0.8cm}} \underline{\hspace{0.8cm}} \underline{\hspace{0.8cm}} \underline{\hspace{0.8cm}}$

$\quad\quad\quad 9$

Now, can you figure out the secret message?

$\underline{\hspace{0.5cm}} \underline{\hspace{0.5cm}} \underline{\hspace{0.5cm}} \underline{\hspace{0.5cm}} \quad \underline{\hspace{0.5cm}} \underline{\hspace{0.5cm}} \underline{\hspace{0.5cm}} \quad \underline{\hspace{0.5cm}} \underline{\hspace{0.5cm}} \underline{\hspace{0.5cm}}$

$1 \quad 2 \quad 3 \quad 4 \quad\quad 5 \quad 6 \quad 7 \quad\quad 8 \quad 9 \quad 10$

Glossary

border
A border shows where places begin and end.

capital
A capital is a city where government leaders work. Washington, D.C., is the capital of the United States.

compass rose
A compass rose is a symbol that helps you read a map. A compass rose shows the four main directions.

continent
A continent is a large body of land. Earth has seven continents.

country
A country is a land and the people who live there. The United States is a country.

direction
A direction tells where something is. The four main directions are north, south, east, and west.

distance
Distance is how far it is from one place to another.

globe
A globe is a model of Earth.

grid
A grid is a pattern of lines that form squares.

hill
A hill is land that is higher than a plain but not as high as a mountain.

island
An island is land with water all around it.

lake
A lake is a body of water with land all around it.

landform
A landform is a shape of land such as a mountain.

Glossary

map
A map is a drawing of a place from above. A map shows where things are.

map key
A map key is a list of symbols on a map. A map key tells what each symbol means.

mountain
A mountain is very high land.

natural resource
A natural resource is something found in nature that people use. Coal is a natural resource.

ocean
An ocean is a large body of salt water. Earth has four oceans.

plain
A plain is flat land.

river
A river is a long body of water that flows across the land.

road map
A road map shows highways and other roads that people can travel on.

route
A route is a way to go from one place to another.

symbol
A symbol is a drawing that stands for something real. A symbol can also be a color or a pattern.

transportation
Transportation is how people and things are moved from place to place. Highways are used for transportation.

valley
A valley is low land between hills or mountains.

Scholastic Success With

ADDITION & SUBTRACTION

Spell It Out

Add. Complete the puzzle using number words.

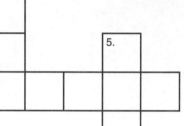
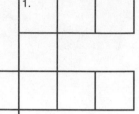

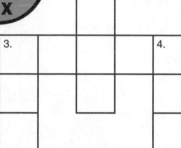

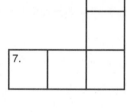

Across

1. 5 + 5 = _____

2. 3 + _____ = 7

3. 2 + _____ = 9

6. 6 + 2 = _____

7. _____ + 0 = 1

Down

1. 4 + _____ = 6

2. 2 + _____ = 7

3. _____ + 4 = 10

4. 4 + 5 = _____

5. 5 + _____ = 8

 Finish each number sentence with a number word.

five + two = _____   three + six = _____

Scholastic Professional Books

Beautiful Bouquets

Subtract. Draw petals to show the difference.

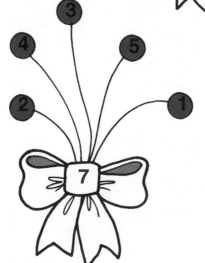

 Color the bows with an even number yellow.
Color the bows with an odd number purple.

Crazy Creatures

Add or subtract. Fill in each missing number.

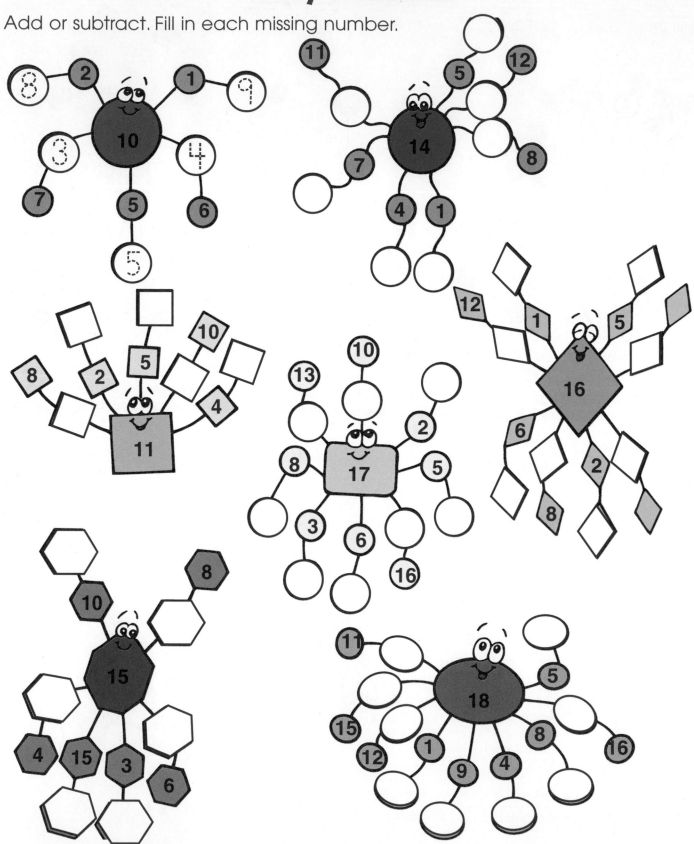

Can You See It?

Write the numbers you see with a . . .

A.  sum of **5** and difference of **1**.

B.  sum of **17** and difference of **7**.

C.  sum of **14** and difference of **2**.

D.  sum of **18** and difference of **4**.

E.  sum of **12** and difference of **2**.

F.  sum of **15** and difference of **9**.

G.  sum of **5** and difference of **3**.

H.  sum of **18** and difference of **2**.

I.  sum of **13** and difference of **5**.

J.  sum of **16** and difference of **6**.

 Make your own number glasses.
sum of _____ and
difference of _____

Scarecrow Sam

Why doesn't Scarecrow Sam tell secrets when he is near Farmer Joe's

bean patch? _____

To find out the answer, add the numbers. Circle the pumpkins that have sums of 14, and write the letters that appear inside those pumpkins in order in the boxes below.

1. 4 + 2   G
2. 7 + 7   B
3. 9 + 5   E
4. 10 + 4   A
5. 4 + 8   R
6. 6 + 8   N
7. 11 + 3   S
8. 14 + 0   T
9. 7 + 2   P
10. 13 + 1   A
11. 5 + 8   S
12. 12 + 2   L
13. 7 + 4   H
14. 5 + 9   K

You've Got Mail!

1. Solve the problems.

2. Find each number pair on the graph. Make a dot for each.

3. Connect the dots in the order that you make them.

4. What picture did you make?

_____

	Across	Up
1.	20 + 7 = _____	12 + 12 = _____
2.	12 + 3 = _____	11 + 13 = _____
3.	1 + 2 = _____	10 + 14 = _____
4.	13 + 2 = _____	10 + 5 = _____
5.	13 + 14 = _____	21 + 3 = _____
6.	23 + 4 = _____	11 + 4 = _____
7.	5 + 22 = _____	2 + 4 = _____
8.	3 + 12 = _____	1 + 5 = _____
9.	3 + 0 = _____	6 + 0 = _____
10.	2 + 1 = _____	2 + 13 = _____
11.	0 + 3 = _____	2 + 22 = _____

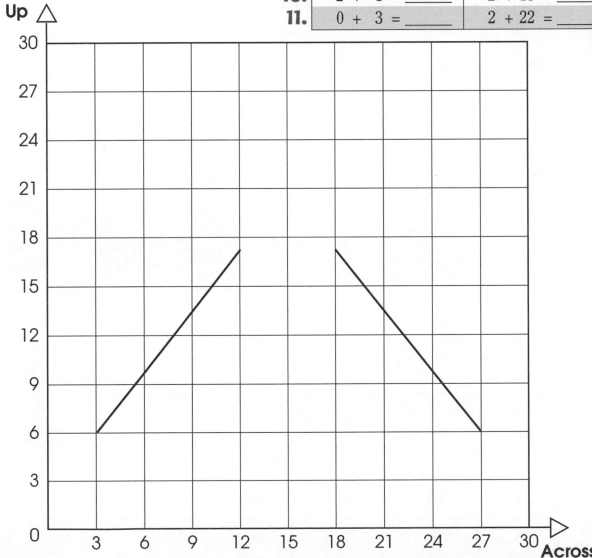

Up

Across

Counting on Good Manners

Add. Then use the code to write a letter in each oval to find the "good manner" words.

May I have some candy, please?

11 + 10	62 + 31	44 + 34	41 + 5	13 + 31	35 + 43

◯ ◯ ◯ ◯ ◯ ◯

40 + 10	43 + 24	42 + 4	54 + 25	41 + 42

◯ ◯ ◯ ◯ ◯

57 + 2	22 + 3	34 + 32

◯ ◯ ◯

Thank you!

54 + 5	21 + 4	41 + 25	21 + 11	26 + 52

◯ ◯ ◯ , ◯ ◯

50 + 30	70 + 8	50 + 43	11 + 7	15 + 10	31 + 4	17 + 61

◯ ◯ ◯ ◯ ◯ ◯ ◯

Code

18 C	21 P	25 O	32 R	35 M	44 S	46 A	50 T
59 Y	66 U	67 H	78 E	79 N	80 W	83 K	93 L

Just the Same

Add. Connect the flowers with the same sum.

| 43 | 52 |
| + 26 | + 36 |

| 18 | 23 |
| + 70 | + 22 |

| 11 | 51 |
| + 34 | + 18 |

| 62 | 14 |
| + 35 | + 11 |

| 13 | 55 |
| + 12 | + 42 |

 Make matching sums.

+	+		+	+
78	78		54	54

Planet Earth

Add.

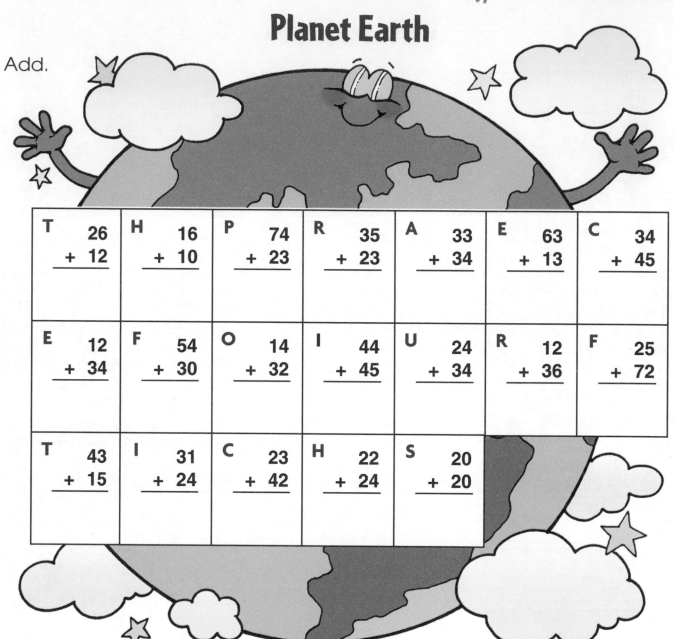

T 26 + 12	**H** 16 + 10	**P** 74 + 23	**R** 35 + 23	**A** 33 + 34	**E** 63 + 13	**C** 34 + 45
E 12 + 34	**F** 54 + 30	**O** 14 + 32	**I** 44 + 45	**U** 24 + 34	**R** 12 + 36	**F** 25 + 72
T 43 + 15	**I** 31 + 24	**C** 23 + 42	**H** 22 + 24	**S** 20 + 20		

For each sum that is an even number, write its letter below in order.

How much of the earth is covered by water?

___ ___ ___ ___ ___ — ___ ___ ___ ___ ___ ___ ___

For each sum that is an odd number, write its letter below in order.

What is the biggest ocean?

___ ___ ___ ___ ___ ___ ___ ___

Name _____

Let Freedom Ring

Add. Use the code to write words that tell about our past.

63 + 12	12 + 11	65 + 33	62 + 24	34 + 13	24 + 10	41 + 34	53 + 46

◯ ◯ ◯ ◯ ◯ ◯ ◯ ◯

40 + 46	26 + 72	23 + 10	35 + 43	21 + 43	53 + 34	22 + 10	13 + 34	64 + 14	68 + 31

◯ ◯ ◯ ◯ ◯ ◯ ◯ ◯ ◯ ◯

31 + 33	25 + 22	21 + 30	44 + 54	76 + 10	21 + 11	11 + 10

◯ ◯ ◯ ◯ ◯ ◯ ◯

40 + 11	35 + 63	44 + 20	52 + 12

◯ ◯ ◯ ◯

Code

21 Y	23 M	32 T	33 V	34 C	42 P	47 I	51 B
64 L	69 D	75 A	78 O	86 R	87 U	98 E	99 N

Name _____

Detective Work

Use the code to help Detective Dave discover the secret phone number. The first problem has been done for you.

1	2	3
4	5	6
7	8	9

1.

7 – 1 = 6

2.

__ – __ = __

3.

__ – __ = __

4.

__ – __ = __

5.

__ – __ = __

6.

__ – __ = __

7.

__ – __ = __

The phone number is:

___ ___ ___ – ___ ___ ___ ___

Scholastic Professional Books

Name _____

Chirp, Chirp!

1. Solve the problems.

2. Find each number pair on the graph. Make a dot for each.

3. Connect the dots in the order that you make them.

4. What picture did you make?

_____

	Across	Up
1.	10 − 7 = _____	10 − 8 = _____
2.	4 − 2 = _____	3 − 1 = _____
3.	7 − 5 = _____	1 − 0 = _____
4.	8 − 0 = _____	1 − 0 = _____
5.	9 − 1 = _____	8 − 6 = _____
6.	10 − 3 = _____	7 − 5 = _____
7.	10 − 2 = _____	8 − 2 = _____
8.	8 − 3 = _____	10 − 0 = _____
9.	9 − 7 = _____	7 − 1 = _____
10.	4 − 1 = _____	5 − 3 = _____
11.	9 − 2 = _____	6 − 4 = _____

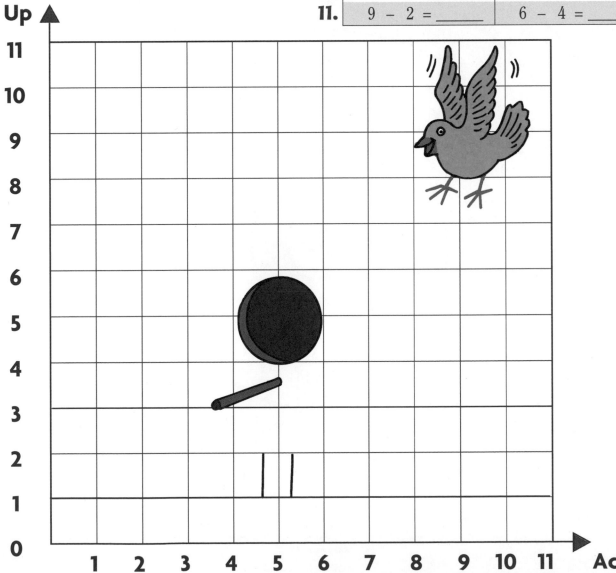

Winter Is Coming

Do the subtraction problems. Help Mr. Squirrel find his way to the tree where he is storing acorns for the winter. Make sure he doesn't cross any odd answers.

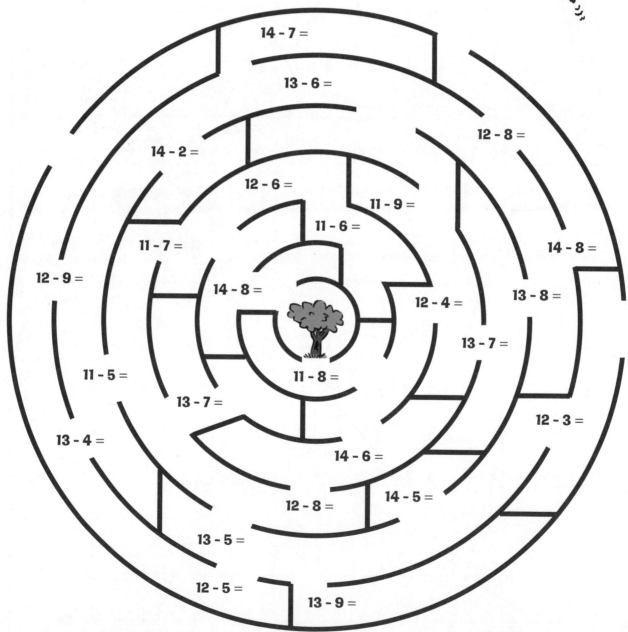

14 - 7 =

13 - 6 =

12 - 8 =

14 - 2 =

12 - 6 =

11 - 9 =

11 - 6 =

14 - 8 =

11 - 7 =

12 - 9 =

14 - 8 =

13 - 8 =

12 - 4 =

11 - 5 =

13 - 7 =

11 - 8 =

13 - 7 =

13 - 4 =

12 - 3 =

14 - 6 =

14 - 5 =

12 - 8 =

13 - 5 =

12 - 5 =

13 - 9 =

Baseball Puzzle

What animal can always be found at a baseball game?

_____

To find out, do the subtraction problems. If the answer is greater than 9, color the shapes black. If the answer is less than 10, color the shapes red.

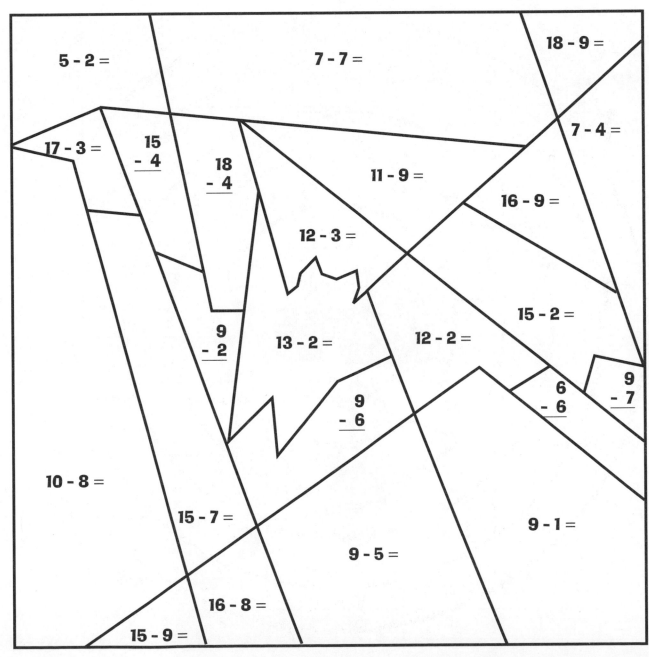

Bubble Yum!

1. Solve the problems.

2. Find each number pair on the graph. Make a dot for each.

3. Connect the dots in the order that you make them.

4. What picture did you make?

_____

	Across	**Up**
1.	27 – 23 = _____	58 – 53 = _____
2.	18 – 15 = _____	23 – 21 = _____
3.	30 – 27 = _____	29 – 28 = _____
4.	18 – 11 = _____	46 – 45 = _____
5.	58 – 51 = _____	17 – 15 = _____
6.	28 – 22 = _____	49 – 44 = _____
7.	19 – 15 = _____	77 – 72 = _____

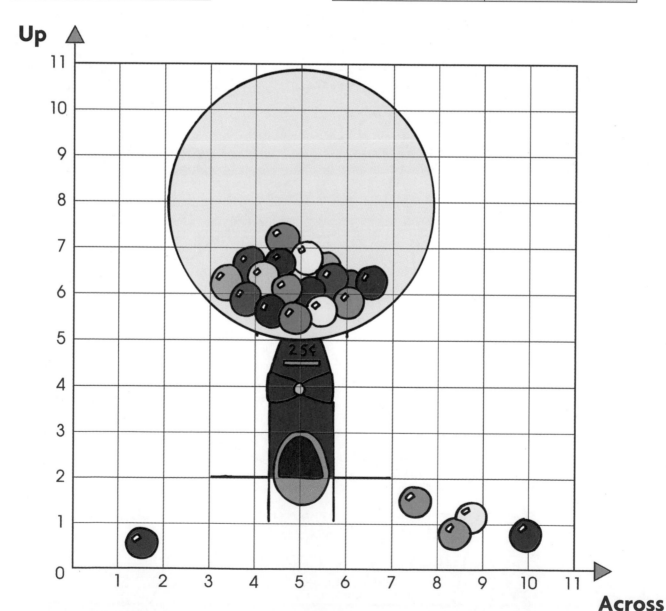

Up

Across

Super Star

Solve the problems. If the answer is between 1 and 20, color the shape red. If the answer is between 21 and 40, color the shape white. If the answer is between 41 and 90, color the shape blue. Taking It Further: Write five subtraction problems that have answers between 10 and 20.

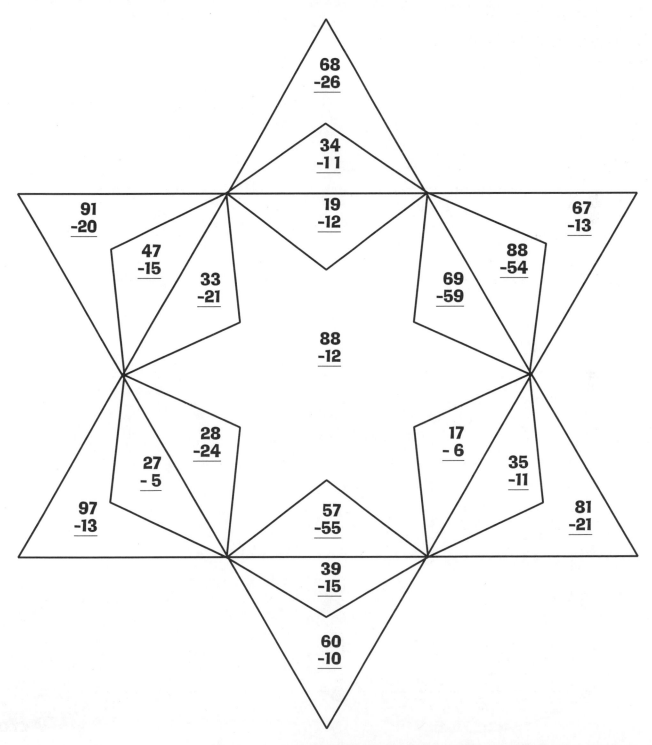

Moving West

Subtract. Follow the even sums to guide the settlers to their new home.

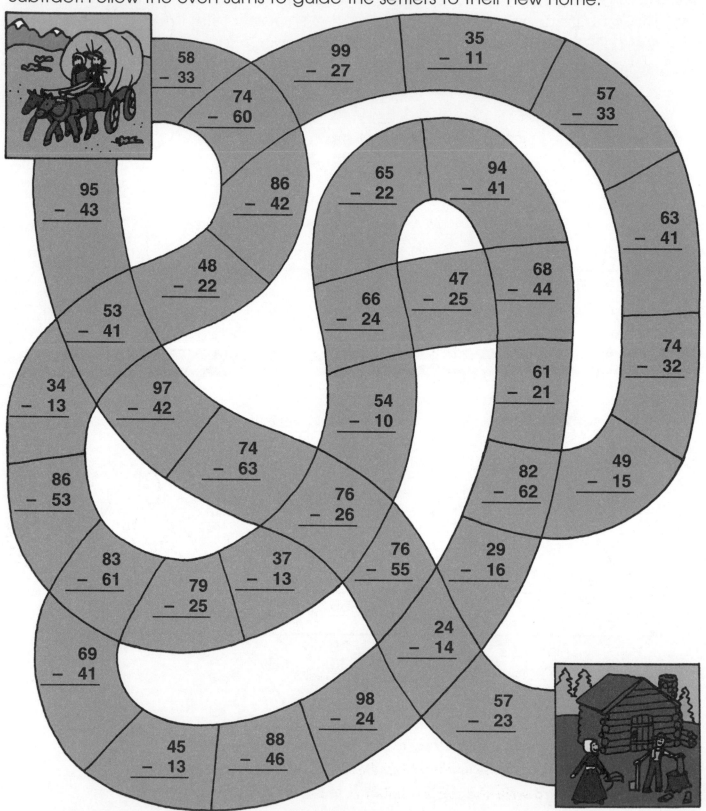

Scholastic Professional Books

Name _____

High Flying

Subtract.

$$\begin{array}{r} 96 \\ -\ 34 \\ \hline \end{array}$$

$$\begin{array}{r} 59 \\ -\ 26 \\ \hline \end{array}$$

$$\begin{array}{r} 65 \\ -\ 42 \\ \hline \end{array}$$

$$\begin{array}{r} 81 \\ -\ 51 \\ \hline \end{array}$$

$$\begin{array}{r} 43 \\ -\ 22 \\ \hline \end{array}$$

$$\begin{array}{r} 78 \\ -\ 64 \\ \hline \end{array}$$

$$\begin{array}{r} 84 \\ -\ 23 \\ \hline \end{array}$$

$$\begin{array}{r} 37 \\ -\ 15 \\ \hline \end{array}$$

$$\begin{array}{r} 92 \\ -\ 51 \\ \hline \end{array}$$

 Color the bird with the smallest number in the ones place red.

Color the bird with the smallest number in the tens place blue.

Color each bird with the same number in the ones and tens place green.

Scholastic Success With Addition & Subtraction • Grade 2   319

Weather Drops

Subtract. Using the difference in each rain drop, write the weather words in order of their differences from least to greatest by the umbrella handle. Then color your favorite kind of "weather drop" blue.

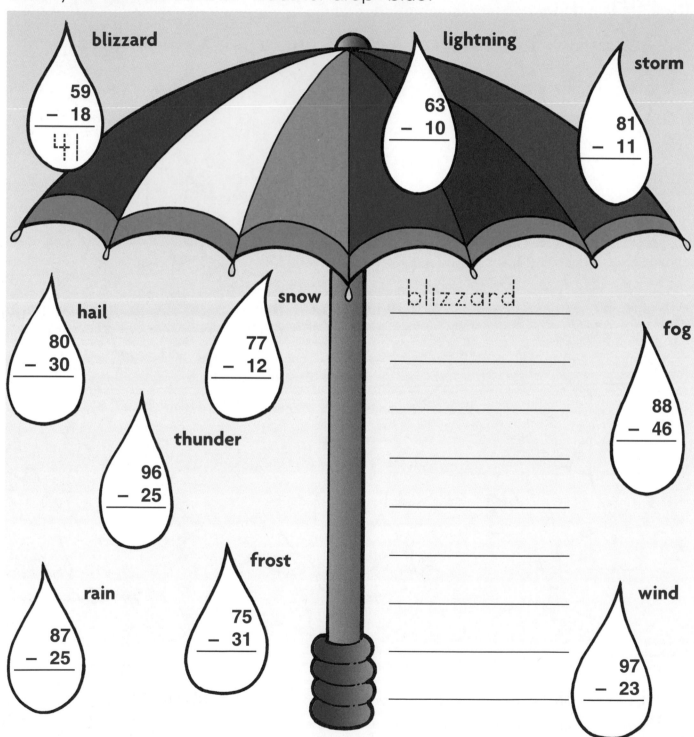

blizzard

$$59 - 18 = 41$$

lightning

$$63 - 10$$

storm

$$81 - 11$$

hail

$$80 - 30$$

snow

$$77 - 12$$

blizzard

_____

_____

_____

thunder

$$96 - 25$$

fog

$$88 - 46$$

rain

$$87 - 25$$

frost

$$75 - 31$$

_____

wind

$$97 - 23$$

_____

Scholastic Professional Books

Animal Families

Subtract.

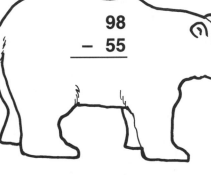

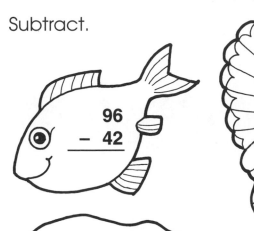

$$\begin{array}{r} 96 \\ -\ 42 \\ \hline \end{array}$$

$$\begin{array}{r} 97 \\ -\ 12 \\ \hline \end{array}$$

$$\begin{array}{r} 86 \\ -\ 43 \\ \hline \end{array}$$

$$\begin{array}{r} 99 \\ -\ 14 \\ \hline \end{array}$$

$$\begin{array}{r} 98 \\ -\ 55 \\ \hline \end{array}$$

$$\begin{array}{r} 78 \\ -\ 24 \\ \hline \end{array}$$

$$\begin{array}{r} 89 \\ -\ 22 \\ \hline \end{array}$$

$$\begin{array}{r} 77 \\ -\ 34 \\ \hline \end{array}$$

$$\begin{array}{r} 78 \\ -\ 11 \\ \hline \end{array}$$

$$\begin{array}{r} 95 \\ -\ 63 \\ \hline \end{array}$$

$$\begin{array}{r} 88 \\ -\ 56 \\ \hline \end{array}$$

Color the animals using the color code.

red	blue	purple	yellow	green
32	43	54	67	85

Triple the Fun

Add. Write the sum on each bowl.

 Color bowls with 1, 5, or 8 in the ones place yellow.
Color bowls with 0, 4, or 7 in the ones place pink.
Color bowls with 2, 6, or 9 in the ones place brown.

A Great Catch

Circle each group of 10. Write the number of tens and ones on the chart. Then write the number on the baseball glove.

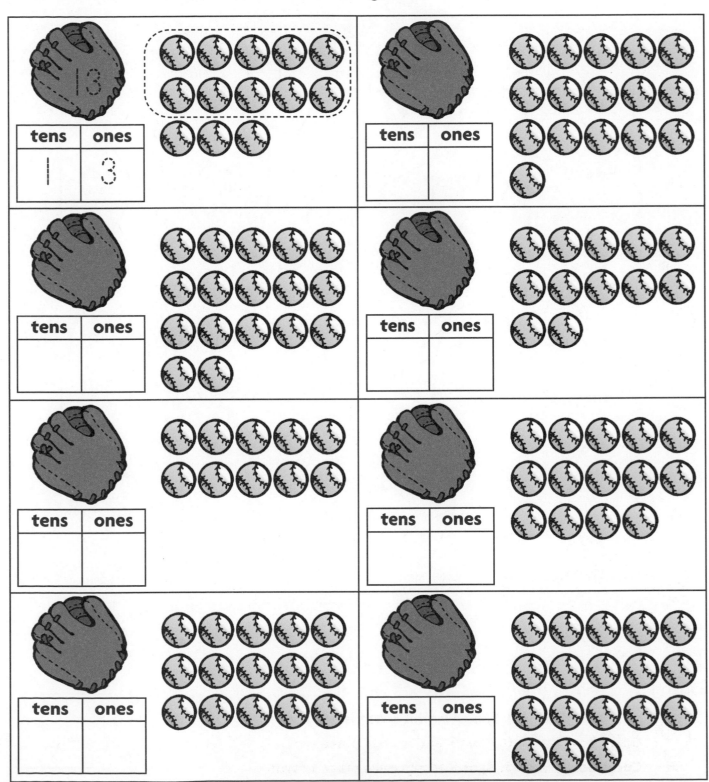

Kaleidoscope

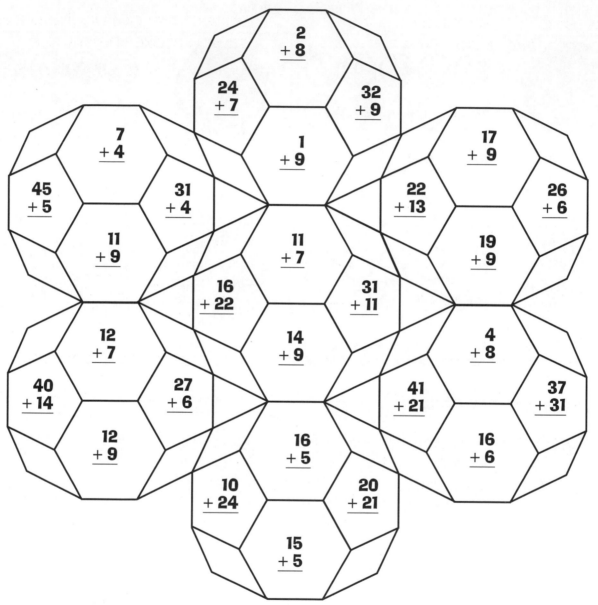

Solve the problems.

If the answer is between 1 and 30, color the shape red.

If the answer is between 31 and 99, color the shape gray.

Finish by coloring the other shapes with the colors of your choice.

Extra: Name two numbers that when added together equal 27.

_____ + _____ = _____   _____ + _____ = _____

Zoo Animal

1. Solve the problems.

2. Find each number pair on the graph. Make a dot for each.

3. Connect the dots in the order that you make them.

4. What picture did you make?

_____

	Across	Up
1.	13 + 7 = _____	12 + 4 = _____
2.	15 + 9 = _____	5 + 3 = _____
3.	11 + 9 = _____	0 + 4 = _____
4.	19 + 9 = _____	2 + 2 = _____
5.	10 + 18 = _____	11 + 5 = _____
6.	16 + 16 = _____	9 + 7 = _____
7.	28 + 8 = _____	2 + 6 = _____

	Across	Up
8.	17 + 15 = _____	1 + 3 = _____
9.	31 + 9 = _____	3 + 1 = _____
10.	8 + 32 = _____	8 + 8 = _____
11.	19 + 25 = _____	19 + 1 = _____
12.	27 + 17 = _____	18 + 14 = _____
13.	7 + 29 = _____	17 + 23 = _____
14.	18 + 6 = _____	25 + 15 = _____

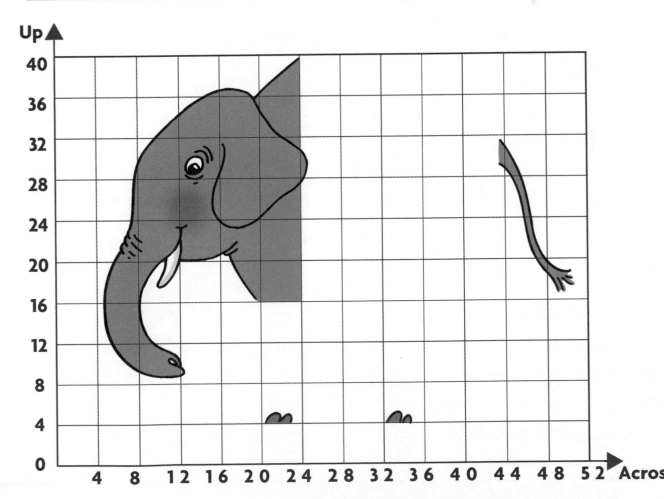

Don't Forget Your Keys

Add. Then follow the clue to find the right key. Write the sum in the key hole.

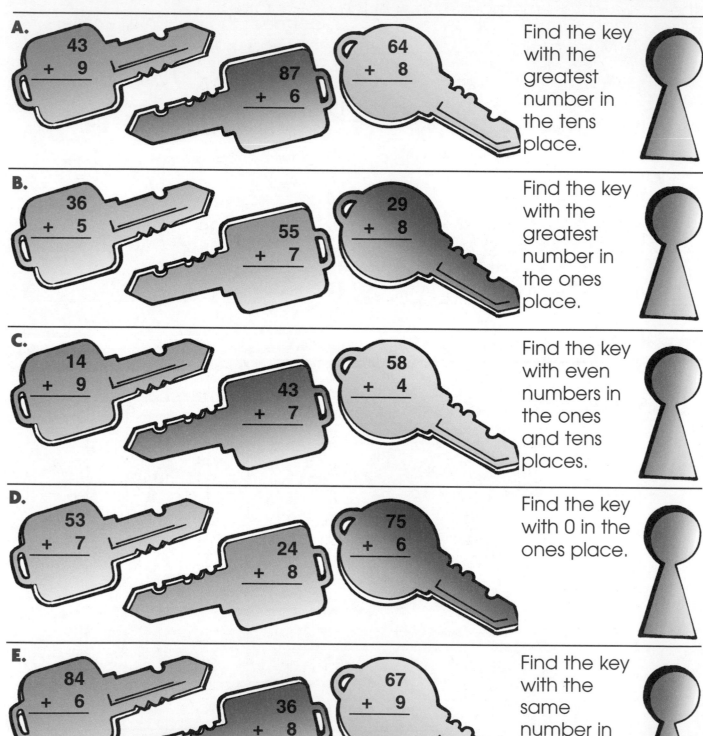

A.

43
+ 9

87
+ 6

64
+ 8

Find the key with the greatest number in the tens place.

B.

36
+ 5

55
+ 7

29
+ 8

Find the key with the greatest number in the ones place.

C.

14
+ 9

43
+ 7

58
+ 4

Find the key with even numbers in the ones and tens places.

D.

53
+ 7

24
+ 8

75
+ 6

Find the key with 0 in the ones place.

E.

84
+ 6

36
+ 8

67
+ 9

Find the key with the same number in the ones and tens places.

Treasure of a Book

Add. Then color each box with an odd sum to help the boy find his way to the book. Hint: Remember to look in the ones place.

47 + 24	74 + 19	78 + 12	15 + 37
48 + 44	31 + 59	52 + 39	29 + 57	73 + 19
63 + 18	14 + 67	57 + 16	24 + 18	63 + 29
57 + 28	27 + 47	76 + 16	72 + 18	76 + 18
32 + 19	17 + 24	55 + 38	32 + 49	

How Do We Get There?

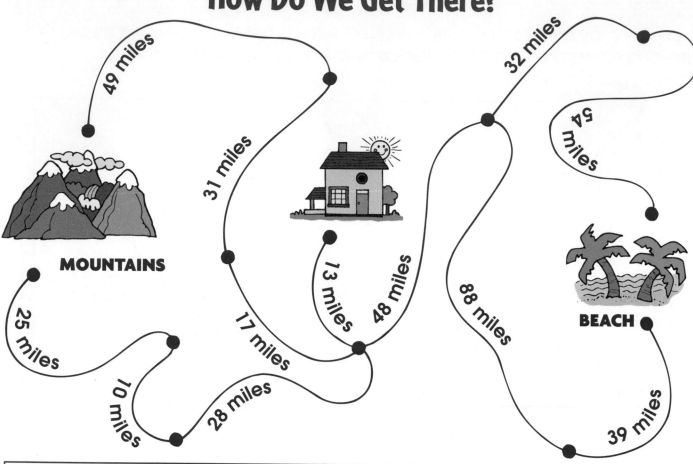

49 miles

31 miles

MOUNTAINS

25 miles

10 miles

28 miles

17 miles

13 miles

48 miles

32 miles

54 miles

88 miles

BEACH

39 miles

Add the distance of each route from the house to the beach.

Route #1	Route #2
_____	_____
_____	_____
_____	_____
+ _____	+ _____
_____ miles	_____ miles

Add the distance of each route from the house to the mountains.

Route #1	Route #2
_____	_____
_____	_____
_____	_____
+ _____	+ _____
_____ miles	_____ miles

Crossdigit Wiz

Find the sums of the three addends in the rows across and down.
The answer circles are numbered.

You can do it!

| 8 | 6 | 7 | ◯ 1. |

| 13 | 8 | 5 | ◯ 2. | | | 5 |
| 7 | 4 | 3 | ◯ 3. | | | 10 |

| | | 8 | 16 | 7 | ◯ | 20 |
| | | 9 | | | ◯ 5. |

| 30 | | 10 | | 4 | 9 | 15 | ◯ |
6.

21	7. ◯	6
7		16	5	8	◯ 8.
◯		11
9. | | ◯ 10. |

Carnival Fun

Do the problems below. Then find your answers hidden in the carnival scene and circle them. Can you find all twelve answers?

15	27	34	15	16	12
33	23	23	25	14	31
+ 27	+ 12	+ 24	+ 10	+ 14	+ 17

28	43	10	29	37	51
22	27	17	13	31	23
+ 45	+ 27	+ 18	+ 16	+ 17	+ 17

Scholastic Professional Books

Crack the Numbers

Look at the number on each chick. Write the number of tens and ones on the egg. Then trade one ten for ten ones.

35
3 tens 5 ones
2 tens
15 ones

47
____ tens ____ ones
____ tens
____ ones

82
____ tens ____ ones
____ tens
____ ones

94
____ tens ____ ones
____ tens
____ ones

61
____ tens ____ ones
____ tens
____ ones

90
____ tens ____ ones
____ tens
____ ones

Digging Up Bones

Help Daisy find a delicious bone! Subtract.
Circle the answer that goes with each bone.

> is greater than and < is less than

A.

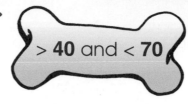
> 40 and < 70

56   94
− 8   − 5

B.

> 25 and < 55

87   53
− 8   − 7

C.

> 37 and < 82

45   81
− 9   − 5

D.

> 74 and < 96

83   68
− 6   − 9

E.

> 18 and < 49

57   23
− 9   − 9

F.

> 63 and < 87

70   75
− 9   − 7

G.

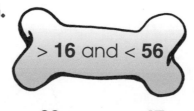
> 16 and < 56

23   47
− 9   − 8

 **Write two subtraction
problems on another
piece of paper. One
answer should match
the bone.**

> 48 and < 87

Scholastic Professional Books

First, Next, Last

Subtract. Then number the pictures in order from least to greatest.

A.

64
− 45

58
− 19

83
− 46

B.

83
− 75

24
− 18

28
− 19

C.

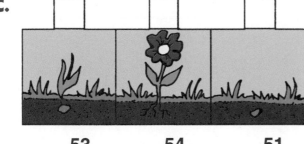

53
− 25

54
− 17

51
− 37

D.

88
− 59

91
− 53

82
− 45

E.

73
− 44

71
− 35

76
− 28

F.

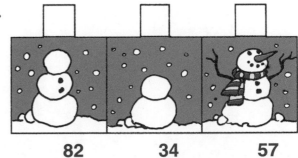

82
− 64

34
− 19

57
− 38

Purdy Bird

Purdy the Parakeet loves to look at herself in the mirror. Only one of these parakeets below really shows what Purdy looks like in the mirror. Can you find the right one? To check your answer, do the subtraction problems next to each bird. The answer for the correct bird is 24.

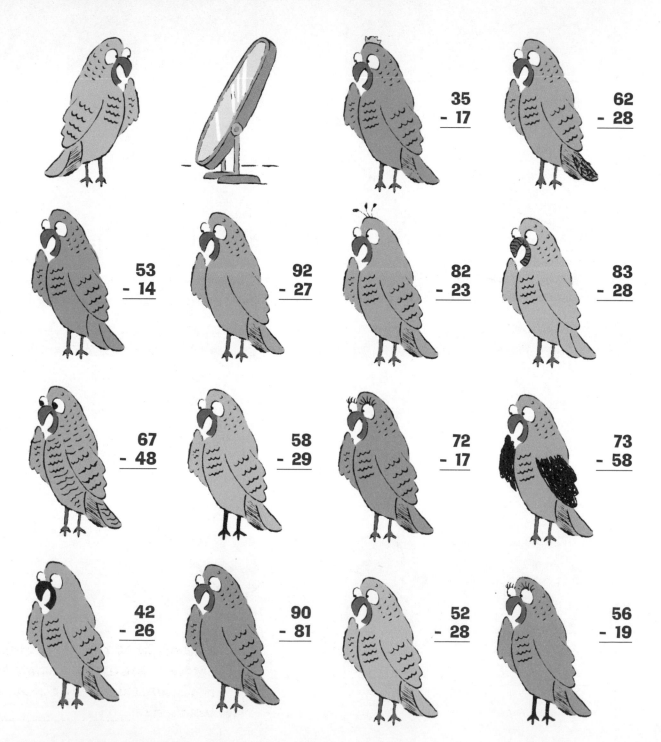

```
  35        62
- 17      - 28

  53        92        82        83
- 14      - 27      - 23      - 28

  67        58        72        73
- 48      - 29      - 17      - 58

  42        90        52        56
- 26      - 81      - 28      - 19
```

Scholastic Professional Books

Grandma's Quilt

Solve the problems. If the answer is between 1 and 50, color the shape red. If the answer is between 51 and 100, color the shape blue. Finish the design by coloring the other shapes with the colors of your choice.

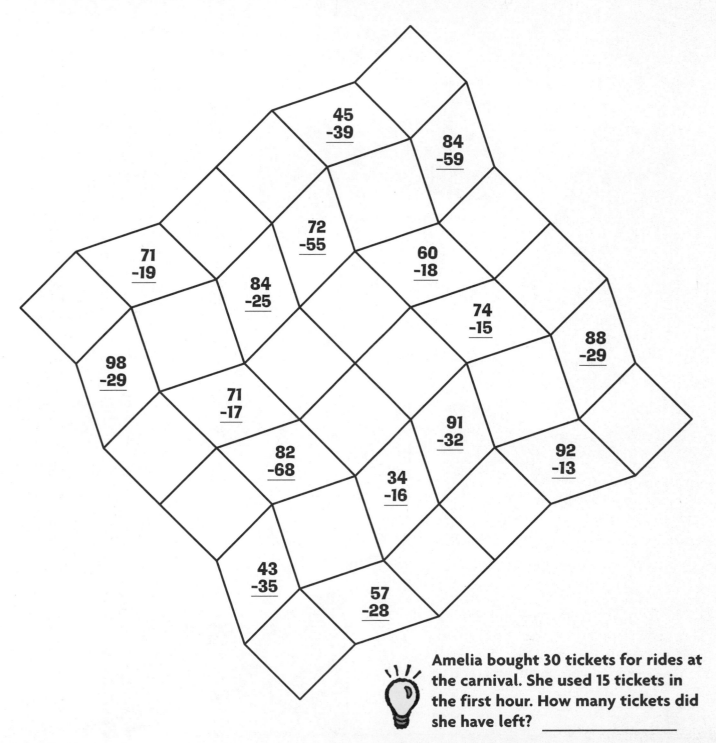

Amelia bought 30 tickets for rides at the carnival. She used 15 tickets in the first hour. How many tickets did she have left? _____

All Tied Up

Subtract. Add to check.

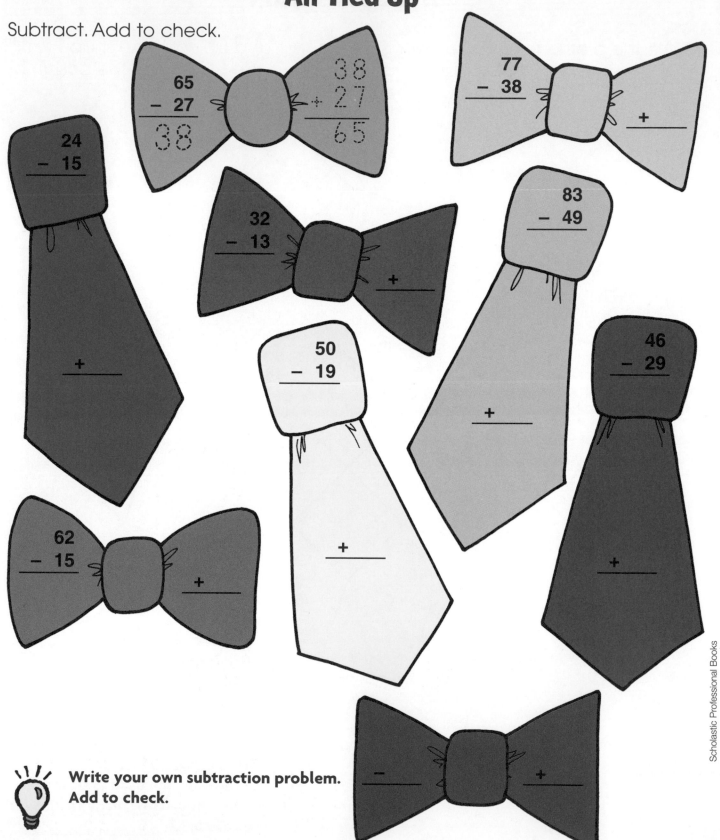

```
  65
- 27
  38
```

```
  38
+ 27
  65
```

```
  77
- 38
____
    +
```

```
  24
- 15
____
    +
```

```
  32
- 13
____
       +
```

```
  83
- 49
____
       +
```

```
  50
- 19
____
       +
```

```
  46
- 29
____
       +
```

```
  62
- 15
____
       +
```

 **Write your own subtraction problem.
Add to check.**

```
  ___
-
____
          +
```

Teenie Tiny Babies

Add or subtract.

U.	42 + 39	**L.**	53 − 48	**N.**	31 + 29	**C.**	74 − 28	**O.**	44 + 46
P.	75 − 37	**H.**	40 − 17	**K.**	27 + 36	**S.**	96 − 48	**A.**	62 − 48
G.	80 − 62	**M.**	55 + 16	**R.**	88 − 19				

Write the letter that goes with each number.

I am smaller than your
thumb when I'm born.

__ __ __ __ __ __ __ __
63 14 60 18 14 69 90 90

I am even smaller.

__ __ __ __ __
63 90 14   5 14

I am smaller than a bumblebee.

__ __ __ __ __ __ __
90 38 90 48 48 81 71

Since we are so little, we
live right next to our mothers in a safe, warm __ __ __ __ __ .
38 90 81 46 23

Day by Day

Add or subtract. Color each special date on the calendar.

July

Sun.	Mon.	Tues.	Wed.	Thur.	Fri.	Sat.
		1	2	3	4	5
6	7	8	9	10	11	12
13	14	15	16	17	18	19
20	21	22	23	24	25	26
27	28	29	30	31		

A. Camp begins one week after the second Monday. Color this date red.

B. The baseball game is two weeks before the fourth Wednesday. Color this date green.

C. The birthday party is two weeks after the second Saturday. Color this date purple.

D. The swim meet is three weeks before the fifth Tuesday. Color this date blue.

E. The trip to the zoo is one week before the third Sunday. Color this date orange.

F. The picnic is two weeks before the fifth Thursday. Color this date yellow.

G. What date is 14 days after the third Wednesday? Color this date pink.

H. What date is 18 days before the fourth Friday? Color this date brown.

Scholastic Professional Books

Name ____________________

Pizza Vote

Use the circle graph to compare the results of the pizza vote.

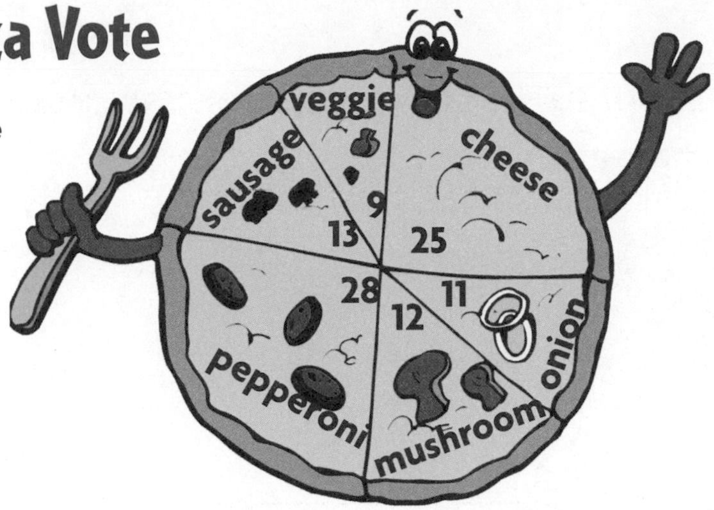

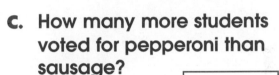

A. How many students voted for pepperoni and cheese in all?

B. How many more students voted for cheese than veggie?

C. How many more students voted for pepperoni than sausage?

D. How many students voted for mushroom and veggie altogether?

E. How many more students voted for mushroom than veggie?

F. How many students voted for sausage and pepperoni in all?

G. How many students voted for veggie, cheese, and mushroom in all?

Find the total number of students who voted.

Name _____

Adding/subtracting 2-digit numbers with regrouping

Tool Time

Find the sum of the numbers in each tool.

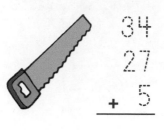
$$\begin{array}{r} 34 \\ 27 \\ +\ 5 \\ \hline \end{array}$$

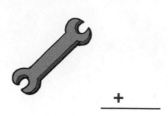 +

 +

 +

A. Write the number found in the  and .

Write the number found in the  and .

Find the sum.

B. Find the difference between the largest and smallest numbers in each tool.

 –  –   –

 On another piece of paper, find the sum of the tools altogether.
Hint: You'll be adding nine numbers.

340 Scholastic Success With Addition & Subtraction • Grade 2

Powerful Presidents

Add. Color each even sum red to learn about George Washington. Color each odd sum blue to learn about Abe Lincoln. Hint: Look in the ones place.

A. the "Father of the Country"

$$\begin{array}{r} 423 \\ + 173 \\ \hline \end{array}$$

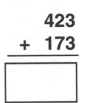

B. born in 1809 in Kentucky

$$\begin{array}{r} 384 \\ + 611 \\ \hline \end{array}$$

C. sixteenth president

$$\begin{array}{r} 325 \\ + 552 \\ \hline \end{array}$$

D. 6 feet 4 inches tall

$$\begin{array}{r} 257 \\ + 312 \\ \hline \end{array}$$

E. born in 1732 in Virginia

$$\begin{array}{r} 101 \\ + 561 \\ \hline \end{array}$$

F. studied geography

$$\begin{array}{r} 570 \\ + 408 \\ \hline \end{array}$$

G. first president

$$\begin{array}{r} 805 \\ + 163 \\ \hline \end{array}$$

H. leader in the Revolutionary War

$$\begin{array}{r} 445 \\ + 151 \\ \hline \end{array}$$

I. loved reading books

$$\begin{array}{r} 609 \\ + 290 \\ \hline \end{array}$$

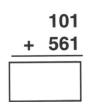

J. leader in the Civil War

$$\begin{array}{r} 314 \\ + 183 \\ \hline \end{array}$$

Hundreds of Pumpkins

Regroup tens into hundreds. Remember: 10 tens = 1 hundred. Write the number of hundreds and the number of remaining tens.

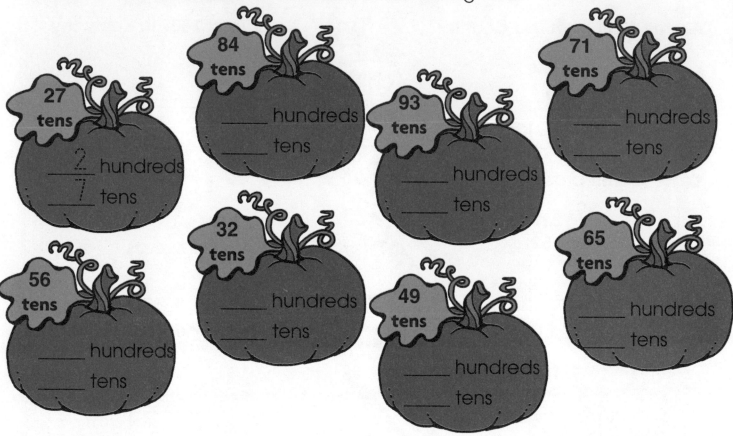

27 tens
___2___ hundreds
___7___ tens

84 tens
_____ hundreds
_____ tens

93 tens
_____ hundreds
_____ tens

71 tens
_____ hundreds
_____ tens

56 tens
_____ hundreds
_____ tens

32 tens
_____ hundreds
_____ tens

49 tens
_____ hundreds
_____ tens

65 tens
_____ hundreds
_____ tens

Write the number.

5 hundreds **7 tens** **0 ones**

8 hundreds **0 tens** **4 ones**

Scholastic Professional Books

Through the Tunnels

Add. Then trace the mole's path to the top. The mole must travel through tunnels with a zero in the sum.

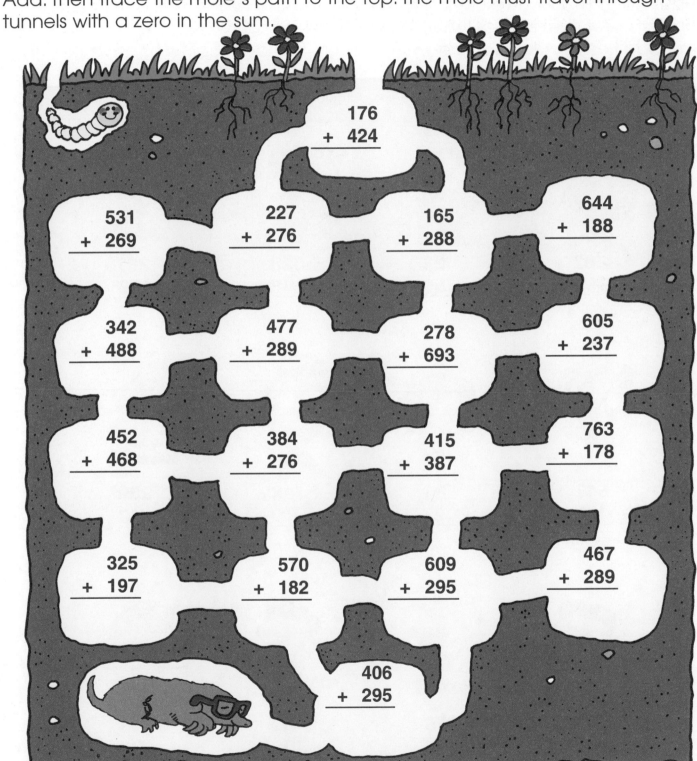

176
+ 424

531
+ 269

227
+ 276

165
+ 288

644
+ 188

342
+ 488

477
+ 289

278
+ 693

605
+ 237

452
+ 468

384
+ 276

415
+ 387

763
+ 178

325
+ 197

570
+ 182

609
+ 295

467
+ 289

406
+ 295

On another piece of paper, write three more problems that have a zero in the sum.

Tricky Twins

Sandy and Mandy are having a twin party. There are six sets of twins, but only one set of identical twins. To find the identical twins, solve the addition problems under each person. The identical twins have the same answer.

207
+ 544

126
+ 89

328
+ 348

257
+ 458

547
+ 129

624
+ 127

108
+ 107

229
+ 418

258
+ 268

379
+ 336

417
+ 109

153
+ 494

Eager Leader

Fill in the missing numbers.

```
  2 [ ] 8          4 0 [ ]
+   [ ] 5 [ ]    + 3 [ ] 5
  6   7   9        [ ] 1   8
```

```
  2 [ ] 7          3 [ ] [ ]        1 2 5
+ [ ] 5 [ ]      + 1   2   4      + [ ] [ ] [ ]
  3   9   8        [ ] 7   8        4   7   9
```

```
  1 5 [ ]
+ 3 [ ] 2
  [ ] 9 2
```

How are you doing?

```
  5 [ ] 8
+ [ ] 6 [ ]
  7   6   9
```

```
  4 [ ] [ ]        1 4 6          3 1 4
+ 2   2   0      + [ ] 3 [ ]    + [ ] [ ] [ ]
  [ ] 7   9        3   [ ] 8      4   3   7
```

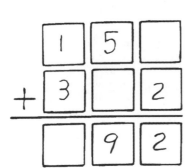
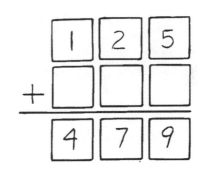

Sandwich Shop

Menu

hot dog ....$1.53   fruit salad $1.90

pbj.....................$1.49   veggies & dip ..$1.84

turkey sub..........$1.86   chips ....$ .50

hamburger........$1.72   fries.....................$ .65

juice ....$ .84   cupcake............$1.07

milk.....................$ .75   brownie.............$1.22

shake ....$1.17   cookies ....$ .86

Add.

A.

pbj

chips

milk

brownie   +
_____

B.

hamburger

fries

shake   +
_____

C.

turkey sub

veggies & dip

juice

cupcake   +
_____

D.

hot dog

fruit salad

brownie

juice   +
_____

E.

turkey sub

chips

shake   +
_____

F.

pbj

cookies

milk   +
_____

Easy as 1, 2, 3

Add to find the perimeter of each shape.

A.

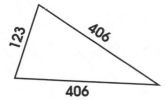

123 406 406 406

B.

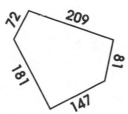

72 209 181 81 147

C.

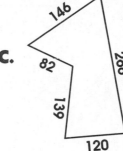

146 82 266 139 120

```
  1 2 3
  4 0 6
+ 4 0 6
```

+ _____

+ _____

D.

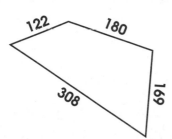

122 180 308 169

E.

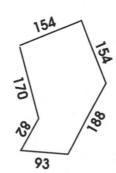

154 154 170 82 188 93

F.

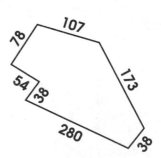

78 107 54 38 173 280 38

+ _____

+ _____

+ _____

Color each shape using the code below.

9 hundreds — orange	4 tens — red	3 ones — purple
6 hundreds — green	7 tens — yellow	8 ones — blue

Count Down

Regroup hundreds to tens. Remember: 1 hundred = 10 tens.

4 hundreds

___ tens

2 hundreds

___ tens

7 hundreds

___ tens

5 hundreds

___ tens

1 hundred

___ tens

9 hundreds

___ tens

8 hundreds

___ tens

3 hundreds

___ tens

Scholastic Professional Books

The Sun's Family

Draw a line to each matching difference to connect each planet to a fact about it.

Mars

$$\begin{array}{r} 694 \\ -\ 421 \\ \hline \end{array}$$

Saturn

$$\begin{array}{r} 935 \\ -\ 123 \\ \hline \end{array}$$

Mercury

$$\begin{array}{r} 573 \\ -\ 241 \\ \hline \end{array}$$

Pluto

$$\begin{array}{r} 937 \\ -\ 304 \\ \hline \end{array}$$

Earth

$$\begin{array}{r} 437 \\ -\ 225 \\ \hline \end{array}$$

Uranus

$$\begin{array}{r} 968 \\ -\ 413 \\ \hline \end{array}$$

$$\begin{array}{r} 397 \\ -\ 185 \\ \hline \end{array}$$ I am a ball of rock and metal but covered with soil, rock, and water.

$$\begin{array}{r} 982 \\ -\ 650 \\ \hline \end{array}$$ I am a bare, rocky ball similar to Earth's moon.

$$\begin{array}{r} 847 \\ -\ 214 \\ \hline \end{array}$$ I am usually the farthest planet from the sun.

$$\begin{array}{r} 963 \\ -\ 151 \\ \hline \end{array}$$ I am surrounded by seven flat rings made of pieces of ice.

$$\begin{array}{r} 857 \\ -\ 302 \\ \hline \end{array}$$ I am a planet with 15 moons.

$$\begin{array}{r} 596 \\ -\ 323 \\ \hline \end{array}$$ I am called the Red Planet.

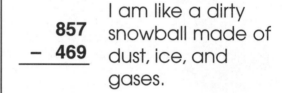

A Place in Space

Draw a line to each matching difference to connect each planet or space object to a fact about it.

 Venus
$$\begin{array}{r} 713 \\ - 171 \\ \hline \end{array}$$

 Neptune
$$\begin{array}{r} 833 \\ - 117 \\ \hline \end{array}$$

 **Jupiter**
$$\begin{array}{r} 675 \\ - 216 \\ \hline \end{array}$$

 Moon
$$\begin{array}{r} 407 \\ - 223 \\ \hline \end{array}$$

 **Comet**
$$\begin{array}{r} 514 \\ - 126 \\ \hline \end{array}$$

$$\begin{array}{r} 952 \\ - 236 \\ \hline \end{array}$$ I am a planet with days lasting only 16 hours.

$$\begin{array}{r} 857 \\ - 469 \\ \hline \end{array}$$ I am like a dirty snowball made of dust, ice, and gases.

$$\begin{array}{r} 612 \\ - 428 \\ \hline \end{array}$$ I am covered with craters.

$$\begin{array}{r} 931 \\ - 389 \\ \hline \end{array}$$ I am sizzling hot with no water.

$$\begin{array}{r} 892 \\ - 433 \\ \hline \end{array}$$ I am a giant planet with a red spot.

 Complete each pattern. Then tell someone the pattern for each set of numbers.

900, 800, 700, _____, _____, _____, _____, _____, _____

900, 700, 500, _____, _____

800, 600, 400, _____

Name _____

Tricky Zero

Subtract.

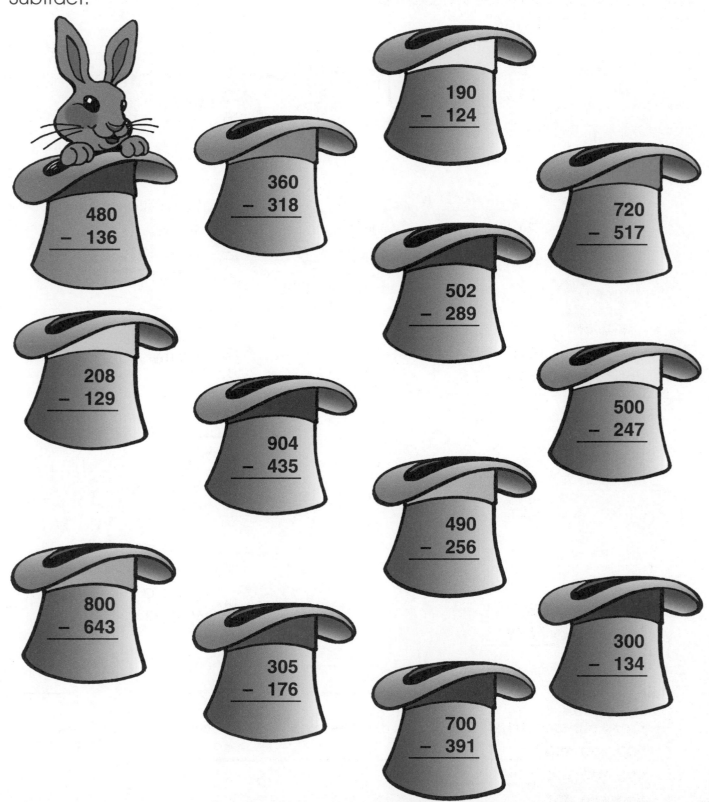

$$\begin{array}{r} 190 \\ -\ 124 \\ \hline \end{array}$$

$$\begin{array}{r} 480 \\ -\ 136 \\ \hline \end{array}$$

$$\begin{array}{r} 360 \\ -\ 318 \\ \hline \end{array}$$

$$\begin{array}{r} 720 \\ -\ 517 \\ \hline \end{array}$$

$$\begin{array}{r} 502 \\ -\ 289 \\ \hline \end{array}$$

$$\begin{array}{r} 208 \\ -\ 129 \\ \hline \end{array}$$

$$\begin{array}{r} 500 \\ -\ 247 \\ \hline \end{array}$$

$$\begin{array}{r} 904 \\ -\ 435 \\ \hline \end{array}$$

$$\begin{array}{r} 490 \\ -\ 256 \\ \hline \end{array}$$

$$\begin{array}{r} 800 \\ -\ 643 \\ \hline \end{array}$$

$$\begin{array}{r} 305 \\ -\ 176 \\ \hline \end{array}$$

$$\begin{array}{r} 300 \\ -\ 134 \\ \hline \end{array}$$

$$\begin{array}{r} 700 \\ -\ 391 \\ \hline \end{array}$$

Treasures Under the Sea

Add or subtract. Use the chart to color the picture.

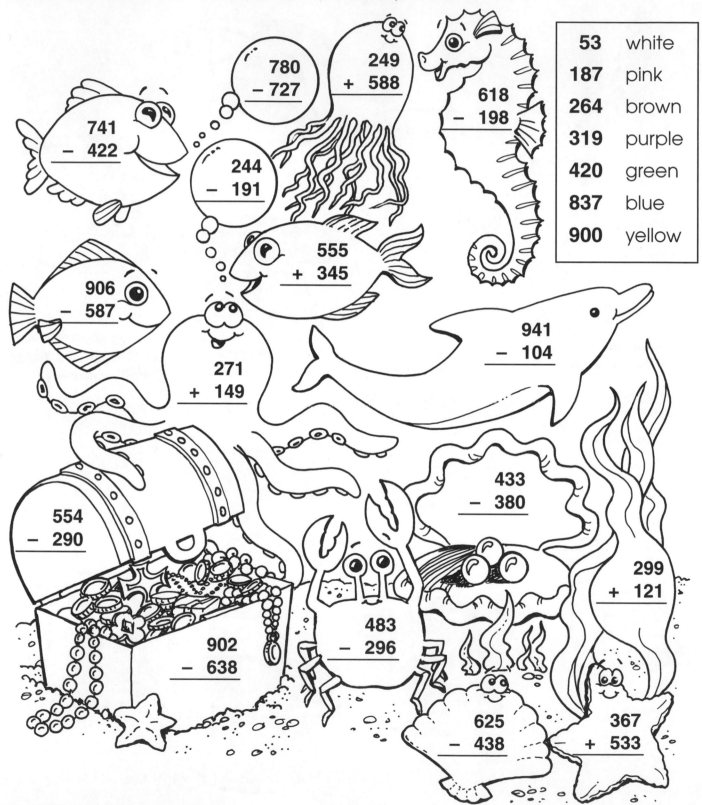

53	white
187	pink
264	brown
319	purple
420	green
837	blue
900	yellow

780 − 727

249 + 588

618 − 198

741 − 422

244 − 191

555 + 345

906 − 587

271 + 149

941 − 104

554 − 290

433 − 380

299 + 121

902 − 638

483 − 296

625 − 438

367 + 533

Name _____

Follow the Trees

Add or subtract. Then trace the bear's path to its cave. The bear follows trees with sums that have a 3 in the tens place.

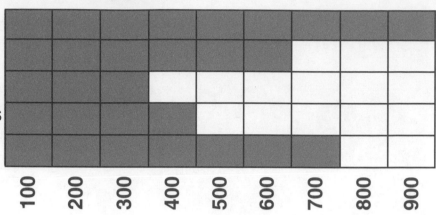
School Supplies

markers
folders
scissors
glue sticks
pencils

100 200 300 400 500 600 700 800 900

Add or subtract. Use the graph to help solve each problem.

A. Mrs. Randolph's class used 523 pencils. How many are left?

B. Mr. Kirk's class used 156 scissors. How many are left?

C. Mr. Dean's class took 248 folders. Mr. Jordan's class took 176 folders. How many did they take altogether?

How many folders are left?

D. Mrs. Fenton's class used 96 glue sticks. Mrs. McBride's class used 189 glue sticks. How many did they use altogether?

How many glue sticks are left?

E. Mrs. Barry's class needs 275 markers. Mr. Lopez's class needs 398 markers. How many do they need altogether?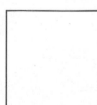

How many markers are left?

Movie Madness

Add or subtract to solve.

A. 168 people are in line to buy tickets. 159 seats are available in the theater. How many people will not get a ticket to the movie?

B. 427 people attended the rush hour show. 289 people attended the 7:00 show. How many attended both shows altogether?

C. 507 people ordered a popcorn and a soda. 278 people ordered popcorn only. How many more people ordered a soda?

D. 319 people bought a pretzel. 299 people bought a box of candy. How many pretzels and candy were sold altogether?

E. There were 826 people at the movie theater on Friday. On Saturday, there were 697 people. How many more people were at the movie theater on Friday?

F. 258 people ordered a hot dog with mustard. 273 people ordered a hot dog with ketchup. How many hot dogs were ordered in all?

Animal Facts

Add or subtract.

T	O	L	P	A	W	I
247 + 253	463 + 440	217 + 68	639 + 207	391 + 144	459 + 492	198 + 672

P	L	I	R	I	O	A
842 − 314	504 + 475	500 − 293	457 + 364	903 − 339	107 + 147	924 − 71

N	N	R	H	A
700 − 427	903 − 34	703 − 186	258 + 553	357 + 537

Move across each row. Write the letter from each box with the correct number of hundreds.

 2 hundreds I am a cat that likes to sleep 20 hours a day.

☐☐☐☐

5 hundreds I have four toes on my front feet and three toes on my back feet.

☐☐☐☐☐

8 hundreds I am a fish with razor-sharp teeth.

☐☐☐☐☐☐

9 hundreds I can see well at night but cannot move my eyes.

☐☐☐

Name _____

Very Special Helpers

Add or subtract. Write the letter that goes with each answer in the center.

	E	L	H	F	D	A
207 + 566	814 − 245	339 + 128	540 − 166	422 − 174	615 − 230	409 + 387

772
− 484

I
635 + 199

248 834 800 569 689 796 288

596
+ 287

M
841 − 152

896 569 796 259 374 569 800

385 883 259 896 883 800

600
− 341

T
478 + 418

467 834 773 800 796 800 834 796 288

603
+ 197

P
416 + 288

704 883 467 834 259 569 689 796 288

Vacation Time

Write the name and the price of each item in the correct suitcase. Add the prices.

$.77

$7.14

$6.89

$2.10

Beach

$ _____
$ _____
$ _____
$ _____
Total $ _____

$1.23

$1.23

Mountains

$ _____
$ _____
$ _____
$ _____
Total $ _____

$1.46

$3.74

How much more does it cost to fill the mountain suitcase than the beach suitcase? Show your work on another piece of paper.

Bull's-eye

Select any problem. Add or subtract. Color the answer on the target. Repeat until you hit the bull's-eye. Then answer the remaining problems.

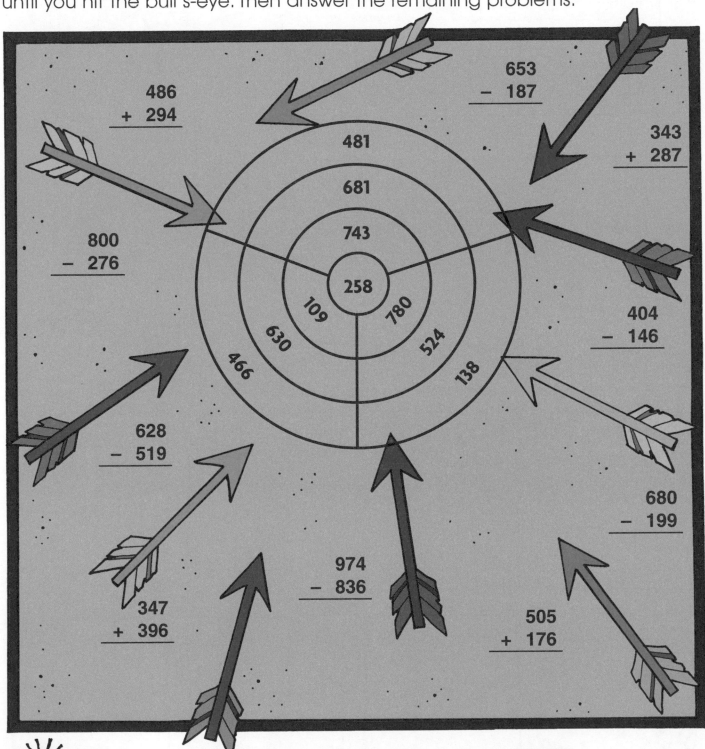

$$486 + 294$$

$$653 - 187$$

$$343 + 287$$

$$800 - 276$$

481

681

743

258

109   780

630   524

466   138

$$404 - 146$$

$$628 - 519$$

$$680 - 199$$

$$347 + 396$$

$$974 - 836$$

$$505 + 176$$

Write how many "tries" it took for you to hit the bull's-eye. [ ]

Grid Math

	A	B	C	D
3	550	636	282	963
2	189	148	579	415
1	427	751	370	804

Find the numbers on the grid. Add or subtract.

(A, 1) + (C, 3)

(B, 3) – (A, 3)

(D, 3) – (A, 2)

(B, 2) + (C, 1)

(A, 3) + (C, 1)

(D, 1) – (B, 3)

(A, 2) + (B, 1)

(C, 2) – (C, 3)

(D, 3) – (B, 2)

(D, 2) + (A, 2)

Perfect Punt

Add or subtract. Draw a line to connect each football to its goalpost.

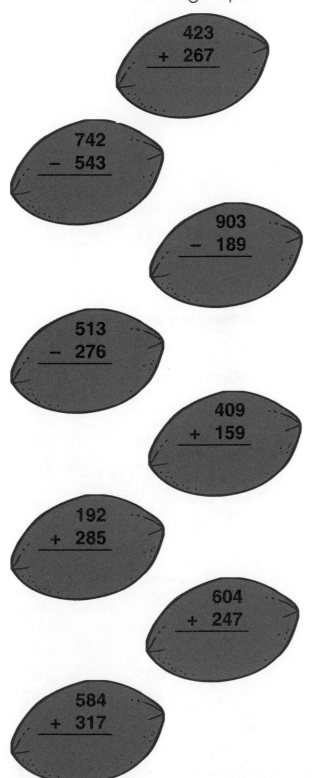

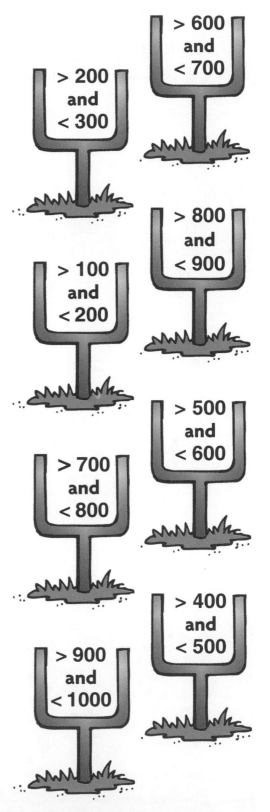

Tic-Tac-Toe

How to Play:

1. Solve the problems in the first row of a game.

2. Mark the gameboard with an X or O for the largest answer.

3. Continue to solve the problems in each row to try to get three in a row.

Game 1

X	O
374 + 263	429 + 187
154 + 199	740 − 286
643 + 208	341 + 459
973 − 784	514 − 188
291 + 263	445 + 375

Game 2

X	O
166 + 117	149 + 69
801 − 389	722 − 305
318 + 218	266 + 243
576 + 268	607 + 266
629 − 457	785 − 657

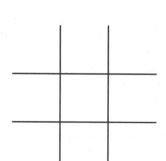

Scholastic Professional Books

Scholastic Success With

MATH

Lone Donor

This is a number line. The numbers increase as you go along the line.

Write the missing numbers.

Mystery Critter

I climb up the side of walls and never fall.

I am a fast runner and have a very long tail. Who am I? _____

To find out, connect the numbers in order from 20 to 68.

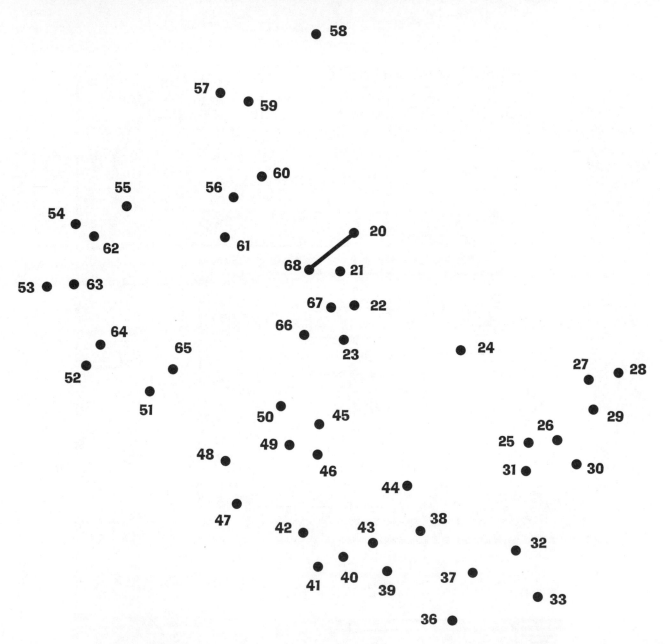

Scholastic Professional Books

Order Recorder

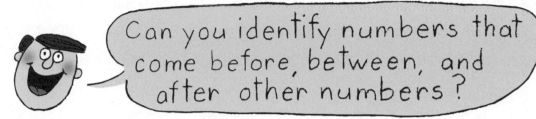

Can you identify numbers that come before, between, and after other numbers?

WRITE THE MISSING NUMBERS.

1. 64, 65, 66, ____   4. 15, ____, 17, ____, 19

2. 33, ____, ____   5. ____, ____, ____, 76

3. 41, ____, ____, 44   6. 29, 30, ____, ____, 33

WRITE WHAT COMES NEXT.

7. 2   4   6   8   ____ ____ ____

8. 3   6   9   12   ____ ____ ____

WRITE THE NUMBERS BETWEEN 82 AND 89.

9. 82 ____, ____, ____, ____, ____, ____, 89

WRITE <u>before</u> OR <u>after</u>.

10. ROOM 479 COMES _____ ROOM 478.

11. PAGE 53 COMES _____ PAGE 63.

12. 15th STREET COMES _____ 12th STREET.

13. AISLE 7 COMES _____ AISLE 12.

14. JUNE 29 COMES _____ JUNE 30.

15. EXIT 15 COMES _____ EXIT 22.

Missing Bone

McAllister the Mutt is dog-tired from walking in circles trying to find his bone. To help him find the path to the bone, move one paw print at a time in any direction except diagonally. You can only follow the tracks that have odd numbers. Draw a line to show his route.

26	11	23	19	6	13
12	5	36	9	3	7
67	17	8	14	12	4	18	16
33	38	42	34	38	16	33	35
25	18		29	39	10	20
27	44	28	50	22	15	30	56
35	54	32	48	52	21	72	41
39	37	23	57	47	43	82	70
84	62	54	90	82	46	40	66

Patterns for the Mail Carrier

Meimei the mail carrier is delivering letters. Give her some help. Fill in the missing addresses on the houses below.

Extra

What pattern do you see in the house numbers? _____

_____

_____

_____

Presidents' Day Problem

The first 18 Presidents of the United States are listed below.
They are shown in order.

1. George Washington (1789–1797)	2. John Adams (1797–1801)	3. Thomas Jefferson (1801–1809)
4. James Madison (1809–1817)	5. James Monroe (1817–1825)	6. John Quincy Adams (1825–1829)
7. Andrew Jackson (1829–1837)	8. Martin Van Buren (1837–1841)	9. William Henry Harrison (1841)
10. John Tyler (1841–1845)	11. James Knox Polk (1845–1849)	12. Zachary Taylor (1849–1850)
13. Millard Fillmore (1850–1853)	14. Franklin Pierce (1853–1857)	15. James Buchanan (1857–1861)
16. Abraham Lincoln (1861–1865)	17. Andrew Johnson (1865–1869)	18. Ulysses S. Grant (1869–1877)

1. Which President was Washington? _____**the 1st**_____

2. Which President was Lincoln? _____

3. Which President came before Lincoln? _____

4. Which President came after Lincoln? _____

5. How many Presidents were there

between Washington and Lincoln? _____

Amused Chooser

Compare numbers: > means greater than. < means less than. = means same as. Hint: The arrow points to the number that is less.

Write > < or = in the circles.

1. 11 ◯ 21   5. 59 ◯ 59

2. 56 ◯ 72   6. 38 ◯ 17

3. 47 ◯ 47   7. 526 ◯ 527

4. 64 ◯ 10   8. 159 ◯ 42

Fill in the blanks with numbers.

9. _____ < _____   13 _____ = _____

10. _____ < _____   14. _____ < _____

11. _____ > _____   15. _____ = _____

12. _____ < _____   16. _____ = _____

Write the numbers from greatest to least.

17. 37 54 61 73 _____

18. 22 96 43 24 _____

19. 79 78 69 51 _____

20. 15 27 51 37 _____

Riddle Fun

What wears shoes, sandals, and boots, but has no feet?

A ___ ___ ___ ___ ___ ___ ___ ___

To find out, write each number in standard form. Then look for the numbers in the puzzle and circle them. They are written up, down, and backward. When you have circled all the numbers given, the letters in the blocks left uncircled spell the answer to the riddle. The first number has been circled for you.

4	3	2	1	9	9	5
B	A	R	K	S	I	G
8	1	7	1	7	5	6
R	M	Y	S	O	D	T
8	5	1	8	9	1	4
D	W	E	T	E	S	S
1	6	2	5	3	3	9
W	P	C	X	A	Z	P
4	9	7	7	0	7	0
L	J	F	S	R	M	L
8	3	6	9	2	0	9
H	F	Y	K	T	E	Q

8 ones 1 ten 5 hundreds =	518	5 ones 1 ten 3 hundreds =		6 ones 7 tens 2 hundreds =		3 ones 9 tens 6 hundreds =	
7 ones 3 tens 1 hundred =		4 ones 6 tens 5 hundreds =		9 ones 0 tens 9 hundreds =		1 one 1 ten 8 hundreds =	
9 ones 0 tens 2 hundreds =		7 ones 1 ten 7 hundreds =		6 ones 3 tens 8 hundreds =		1 one 2 tens 3 hundreds =	
8 ones 8 tens 4 hundreds =		7 ones 5 tens 8 hundreds =		2 ones 3 tens 4 hundreds =		7 ones 0 tens 7 hundreds =	

Scholastic Professional Books

Pattern Learner

A pattern is a repeated arrangement of numbers, shapes, or lines in a row. Continue the patterns below.

1. 324, 435, 546, _657, 768, 879_

2. ■ ◯ △ ■ ◯ [student writing]

3. [shape patterns]

4. [square patterns]

5. [stick figure patterns]

6. [flower patterns]

7. A C E G I K [student writing]

8. 11:05, 11:10, 11:15, _11:20 11:25 11:30_

9. ☀ ★ 🌙 ☀ [student writing]

Scholastic Professional Books

Shape Tricks

Danny's class was learning about shapes. He noticed that you could draw a line across one shape to make two shapes. Draw a line through each shape below to make two new shapes. (Pattern blocks may help you.)

1. Make a square and a triangle.

2. Make two triangles.

3. Make two rectangles.

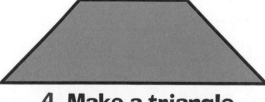

4. Make a triangle and a diamond.

5. Cut this twice to make 3 triangles.

Picking Out Patterns

On the 100th day of school, everyone in Pat's class picked out patterns on the 100 Chart. Look at the chart below.

1	2	3	4	5	6	7	8	9	10
11	12	13	14	15	16	17	18	19	20
21	22	23	24	25	26	27	28	29	30
31	32	33	34	35	36	37	38	39	40
41	42	43	44	45	46	47	48	49	50
51	52	53	54	55	56	57	58	59	60
61	62	63	64	65	66	67	68	69	70
71	72	73	74	75	76	77	78	79	80
81	82	83	84	85	86	87	88	89	90
91	92	93	94	95	96	97	98	99	100

Find and finish the pattern starting with 2, 12, 22

_____

Find and finish the pattern starting with 100, 90, 80

_____

Find and finish the pattern starting with 97, 87, 77

_____

Find and finish the pattern starting with 11, 22, 33

_____

Shape Study

A heptagon has 7 sides. On a heptagon, all the sides are the same length.

Connect the dots in the geoboards below to make other shapes with 7 sides.

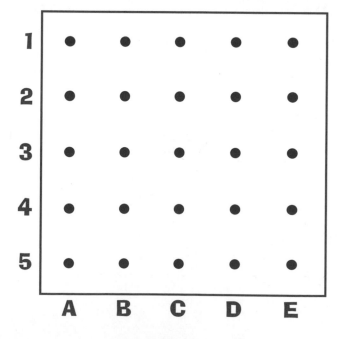

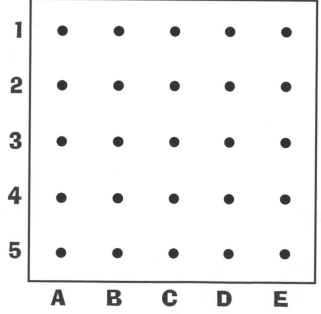

Shape Gaper

FLAT SHAPES HAVE LENGTH AND WIDTH.

A
SQUARE

B
CIRCLE

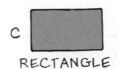
C
RECTANGLE

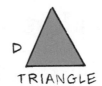
D
TRIANGLE

SOLID SHAPES HAVE LENGTH AND WIDTH AND DEPTH.

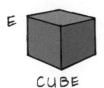
E
CUBE

F
SPHERE

G
CYLINDER

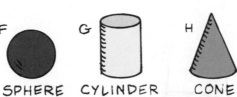
H
CONE

I
RECTANGULAR PRISM

J
PYRAMID

MATCH THE SHAPES WITH THESE OBJECTS. USE THE LETTERS ABOVE.

A.

1.	BALL
2.	WASTEBASKET
3.	RING
4.	POSTAGE STAMP
5.	BIRDHOUSE
6.	CRAYON BOX
7.	ICE CUBE
8.	APOLLO SPACECRAFT
9.	TRASH BARREL
10.	JAR
11.	ENVELOPE

B.

1.	COMPACT DISC
2.	AN ORANGE
3.	A PENNANT
4.	A BUILDING
5.	FISH BOWL
6.	CHILD'S BLOCK
7.	CHECKERS (GAME)
8.	A SAIL ON A SMALL BOAT
9.	CEREAL BOX
10.	PLANET EARTH
11	STICK OF BUTTER

C.

1.	ROAD MARKER
2.	FLAG
3.	SHEET OF PAPER
4.	FLASHLIGHT
5.	SOUP CAN
6.	POSTER
7.	BASEBALL
8.	TRAIN CAR
9.	A DIME
10.	PHOTOGRAPH
11.	WORLD GLOBE

Rocket Riddle

What did the rocket say when it left the party?

What To Do

To find the answer to the riddle, solve the multiplication problems. Then match each product with a letter in the Key below. Write the correct letters on the blanks below.

1   5 x 1 = _____

2   8 x 1 = _____

3   11 x 1 = _____

4   26 x 1 = _____

5   3 x 2 = _____

6   5 x 2 = _____

7   6 x 2 = _____

8   8 x 2 = _____

9   9 x 2 = _____

10   12 x 2 = _____

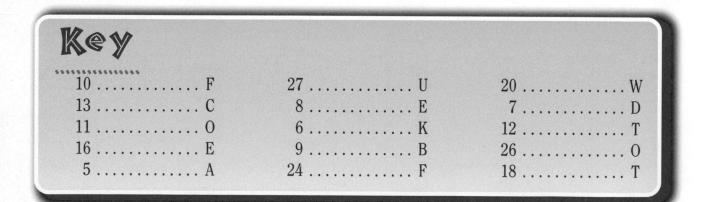

Key

10 . . . . F	27 . . . . U	20 . . . . W
13 C	8 . . . . E	7 . . . . D
11 . . . . O	6 . . . . K	12 . . . . T
16 . . . . E	9 . . . . B	26 . . . . O
5 . . . . A	24 . . . . F	18 . . . . T

Riddle Answer: "TIM ___ ___ ___   ___ ___ ___ ___   ___ ___ ___ ."

  (8) (7) (3)   (9) (1) (5) (2)   (4) (6) (10)

Wise Owls

What did the owl say when someone knocked on its door?

What To Do

To find the answer to the riddle, solve the multiplication problems. Then match each product with a letter in the Key below. Write the correct letters on the blanks below.

1 5 x 3 = _____

2 2 x 3 = _____

3 8 x 3 = _____

4 4 x 3 = _____

5 9 x 3 = _____

6 6 x 3 = _____

7 10 x 3 = _____

8 12 x 3 = _____

9 11 x 3 = _____

10 0 x 3 = _____

Key

30 . . . . O	8 . . . . K	42 . . . . N
11 . . . . A	15 . . . . O	24 . . . . T
36 . . . . H	0 I	33 . . . . O
18 I	27 . . . . O	6 . . . . Q
32 . . . . F	6 . . . . S	12 . . . . W

Riddle Answer: " ___ ___ ___ ___ ___ ___   ___ ___   ___ ___ ?"

4 **8** **5** **9** **1** **7**   **10** **2**   **6** **3**

Jack's Beanstalk

**Jack's class was growing bean plants.
After 1 week, Jack's was the tallest.
Measure Jack's plant below. Record its height: _____
After 2 weeks, Jack's plant had doubled in height.
How tall was it now? _____**

Draw a picture to show how tall the plant grew.

Measure your drawing to make sure it is the correct height.

2 weeks.

After 3 weeks, Jack's plant was still growing!

How tall would it be now? _____

Explain your answer. _____

_____

Scholastic Professional Books

Candy Boxes

Steve works in a candy store. He puts candy into boxes. Each box has 10 spaces. Steve has 32 candies. Try to draw 32 candies in the boxes below. Write the number of candies in each box on the line. Write the number of any leftover candy at the bottom of the page.

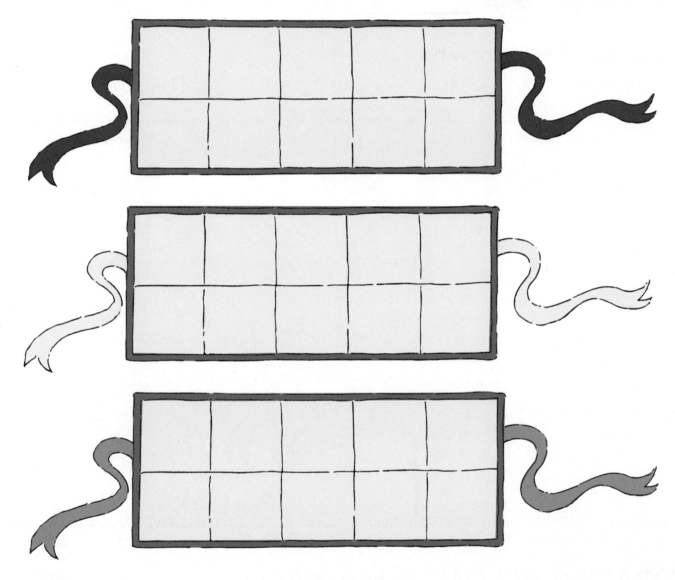

Extra

Leftover candies: _____

Creature Categories

Nick's class took a field trip to the beach. When they looked in the tide pools, they saw a lot of animals. Group the animals they saw. Color the animals in each group the same color.

Write a word or phrase that explains how you grouped them.

Group #1 _____

Group #2 _____

Group #3 _____

Scholastic Professional Books

Coin-Toss Addition

Toss 8 coins. Write "**H**" for heads or "**T**" for tails
in the circles below to show your toss. Then write
the addition equation. Write the number of "heads"
first. We did the first one for you. Try it three times.

(**H**) (**H**) (**H**) (**H**) (**T**) (**T**) (**T**) (**T**)

Equation: _____ **4 + 4 = 8** _____

Equation: _____

Equation: _____

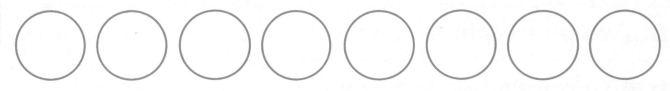

Equation: _____

Clear Reader

Write each sentence using numbers and symbols.

1. Four plus five is nine.	
2. Eleven minus six is five.	
3. Nine plus seven is sixteen.	
4. Four plus eight is twelve.	
5. Three minus two is one.	
6. Seven plus seven is fourteen.	
7. Fifteen minus ten is five.	
8. Two plus eight is ten.	
9. Five minus two is three.	

Scholastic Professional Books

Time to Get Up!

Twenty animals were hibernating near Sleepy Pond.
5 of them woke up. Color 5 animals below.

How many are still sleeping? _____

A week later, 7 more woke up. Color 7 other animals.

How many are still sleeping? _____

Pizza Party

Garth's class is having a pizza party. They made a diagram to show which pizzas they would like. Draw an X in each circle to show how many classmates wanted each kind of pizza.

- 5 wanted cheese pizza.
- 10 wanted pepperoni pizza.
- 3 wanted sausage pizza.
- 2 wanted both cheese and pepperoni pizza.

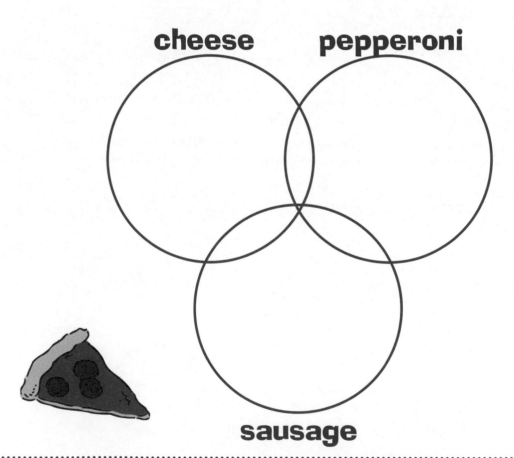

cheese   **pepperoni**

sausage

What can you learn by looking at this diagram? Write your ideas:

_____

_____

Prime Timer

WRITE THE TIME 3 WAYS.

example: ← 1:15
15 minutes after 1
45 minutes to 2

1. _____   2. _____

____ minutes after ____   ____ minutes after ____

____ minutes to ____   ____ minutes to ____

3. _____   4. _____

____ minutes after ____   ____ minutes after ____

____ minutes to ____   ____ minutes to ____

5. _____   6. _____

____ minutes after ____   ____ minutes after ____

____ minutes to ____   ____ minutes to ____

Just Snacks

Use the menu on page 389 to answer the
following questions.

1. Which snack costs the most?

   _____

   How much do they cost?

   _____

2. Which sweet costs the least? _____

   How much does it cost? _____

3. Henry spends 50¢ on a snack.

   What does he buy? _____

4. Gina orders a drink. She spends 15¢.

   Which drink does she order? _____

5. Dan orders popcorn and a cookie.

   How much does he pay? _____

6. Pat buys a cup of soup and a sip of milk.

   How much does she spend? _____

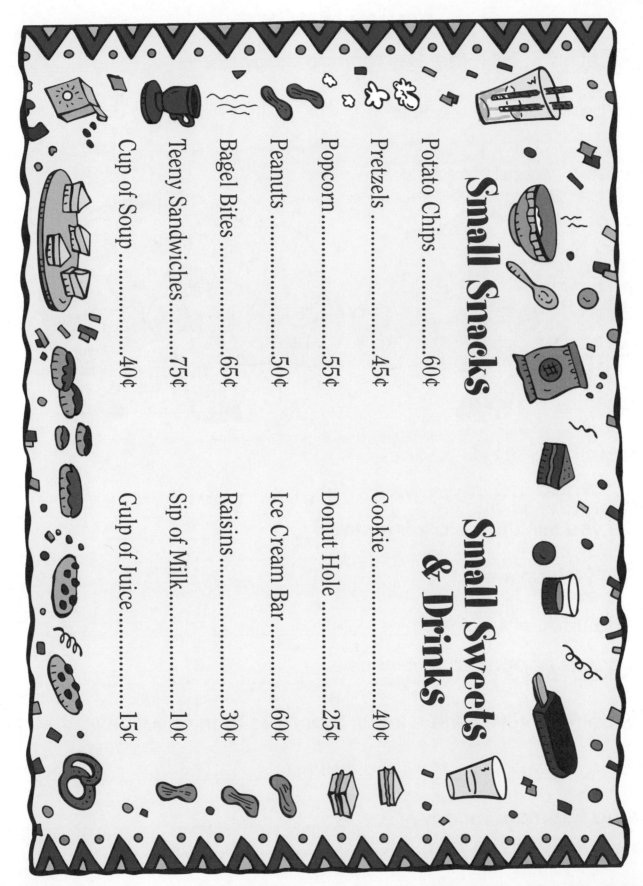

Small Snacks

Potato Chips ....60¢

Pretzels ....45¢

Popcorn ....55¢

Peanuts ....50¢

Bagel Bites ....65¢

Teeny Sandwiches ....75¢

Cup of Soup ....40¢

Small Sweets & Drinks

Cookie ....40¢

Donut Hole ....25¢

Ice Cream Bar ....60¢

Raisins ....30¢

Sip of Milk ....10¢

Gulp of Juice ....15¢

Money Matters

Alex asked his little brother Billy to trade piggy banks.

Alex's bank has these coins: **Billy's has these coins:**

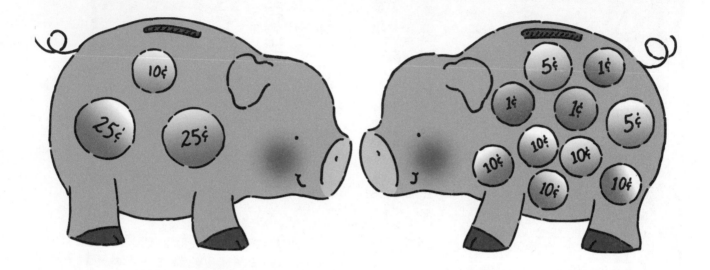

Do you think this is a fair trade? _____

Test your answer:

Add up Alex's coins: _____

Add up Billy's coins: _____

Write the totals in this Greater Than/Less Than equation:

_____ > _____

Who has more money? _____

Best Estimator

LENGTH CAN BE MEASURED IN INCHES (IN.), FEET (FT.), YARDS (YD.), AND MILES (MI.). 12 IN. = 1 FT. 5280 FT. = 1 MILE.

UNDERLINE THE MORE SENSIBLE MEASURE.

How many inches to Boston, Sir?

BUS STOP

1. HEIGHT OF A BOOKCASE
    INCHES   FEET

2. WIDTH OF YOUR BACKYARD
    YARDS   MILES

3. LENGTH OF A RIVER
    MILES   YARDS

4. WIDTH OF A DESK
    INCHES   FEET

5. LENGTH OF YOUR ARM
    FEET   INCHES

6. LENGTH OF A COMB
    INCHES   FEET

7. LENGTH OF A FOOTBALL FIELD
    INCHES   YARDS

8. DISTANCE FROM EARTH TO MOON
    MILES   YARDS

9. DEPTH OF A SWIMMING POOL
    FEET   INCHES

10. TUBE OF TOOTHPASTE
    INCHES   FEET

11. HEIGHT OF A REFRIGERATOR
    INCHES   FEET

12. WIDTH OF A BEDROOM
    FEET   INCHES

13. DISTANCE BETWEEN 2 CITIES
    YARDS   MILES

14. LENGTH OF A DOLLAR
    INCHES   FEET

15. LENGTH OF AN AUTOMOBILE
    INCHES   FEET

December Weather

In December, Mrs. Monroe's class drew the weather on a calendar. Each kind of weather has a picture:

| sunny | cloudy | rainy | snowy |

Look at the calendar. Answer the questions below.

December

SUN.	MON.	TUES.	WED.	THURS.	FRI.	SAT
	1 cloudy	2 cloudy	3 sunny	4 cloudy	5 rainy	6 snowy
7 rainy	8 snowy	9 snowy	10 sunny	11 sunny	12 cloudy	13 sunny
14 cloudy	15 sunny	16 sunny	17 snowy	18 sunny	19 cloudy	20 rainy
21 rainy	22 cloudy	23 sunny	24 sunny	25 rainy	26 snowy	27 sunny
28 snowy	29 cloudy	30 sunny	31 sunny			

How many sunny days did they have? _____

How many cloudy days did they have? _____

How many rainy days did they have? _____

How many snowy days did they have? _____

Which kind of weather did they have the most? _____

Measuring Perimeter

Use the inch side of a ruler and measure each side of each triangle. Write the inches in the spaces below. Then add up all the sides to find the perimeter, or distance around each triangle.

____ + ____ + ____ = ____ inches

____ + ____ + ____ = ____ inches

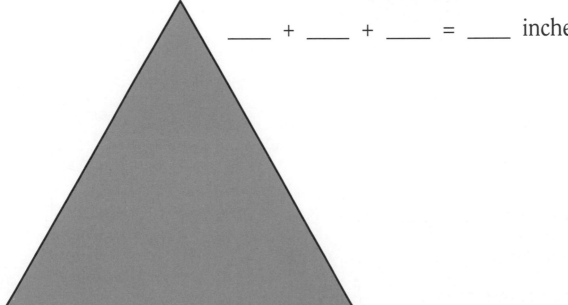

____ + ____ + ____ = ____ inches

Night-Light

1. Find each number pair on the graph. Make a dot for each.
2. Connect the dots in the order that you make them.
3. What picture did you make?

_____

	Across	Up
1.	6	11
2.	5	7
3.	1	7
4.	4	5
5.	3	0
6.	6	3
7.	9	0
8.	8	5
9.	11	7
10.	7	7
11.	6	11

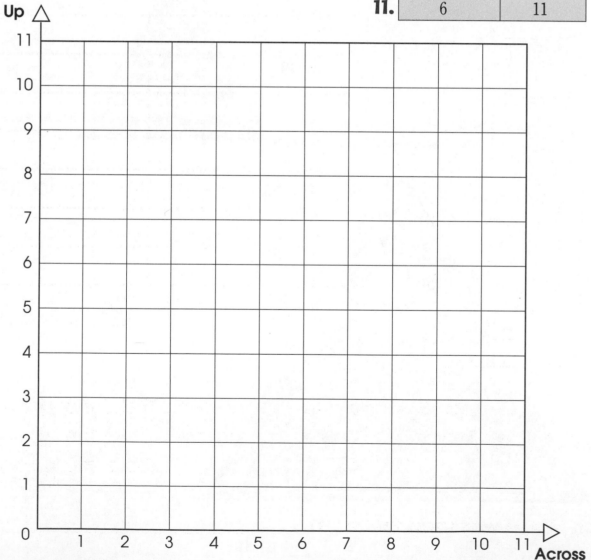

Scholastic Professional Books

Great Graphing

The picture was made with 7 different shapes. How many of each shape was used? Color in the shapes, following the instructions. Then color in the boxes on the chart, 1 box for each shape used.

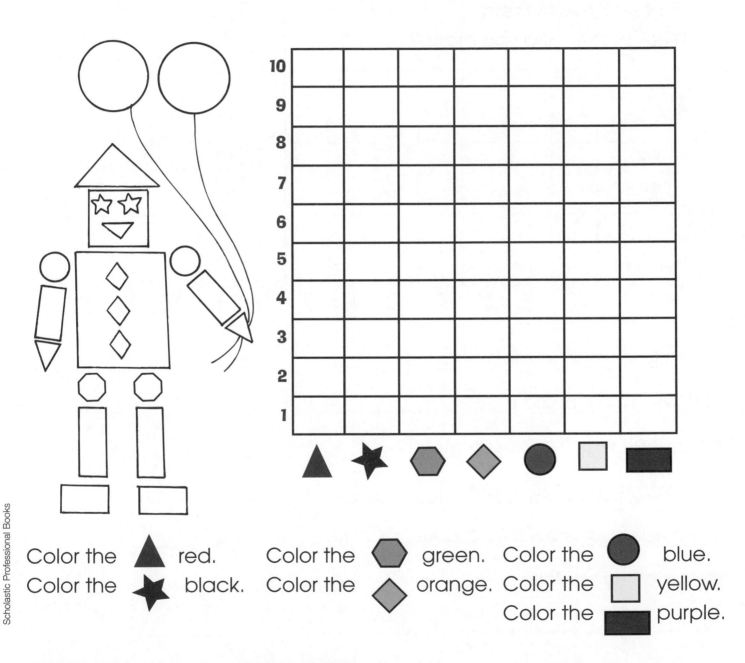

Color the ▲ red.   Color the ⬡ green.   Color the ⬤ blue.

Color the ★ black.   Color the ◆ orange.   Color the ☐ yellow.

Color the ▬ purple.

Which shape was used the most? _____

Fruit Graph

Ask 12 friends which of these four fruits they like most. Fill in the graph to find out. Color one box on the graph for each vote.

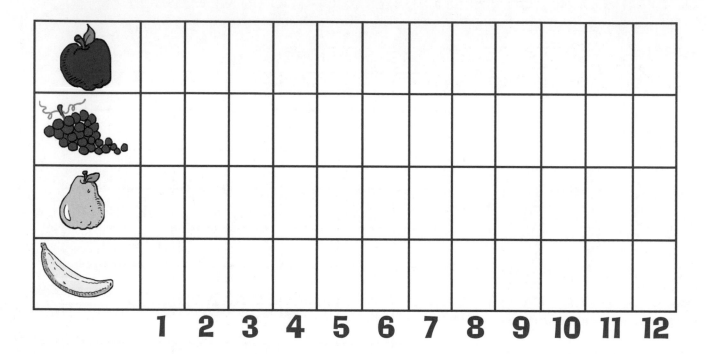

Which fruit was the most popular? _____

How many votes did it get? _____

Which fruit was the least popular? _____

How many votes did it get? _____

If two fruits got the same amount of votes, they "tied."

Write any ties below.

_____ and _____

_____ and _____

Chester's Cakes and Pies

Fill in the blanks. Chester Chipmunk was cutting cakes and pies.
Bobby Bear said, "Some aren't cut in half. When you cut something in
half, there are _____ pieces and both of the pieces are the
same _____."
Here is how Chester cut the cakes and pies.
Circle the desserts that are cut in half correctly.

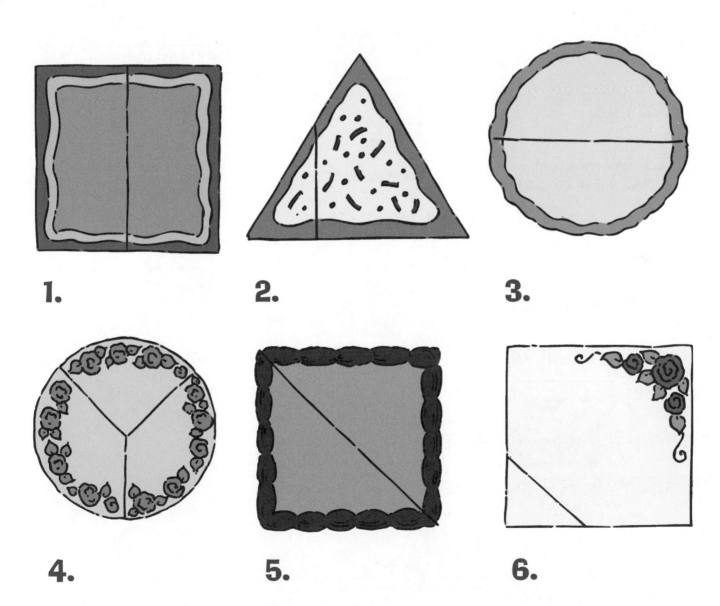

1.   2.   3.

4.   5.   6.

Part Timer

Determine fractions of a whole. Check √ your answers.

1. HOW MUCH JUICE IS LEFT?

$\frac{1}{2}$
$\frac{1}{4}$
$\frac{1}{3}$

2. HOW MUCH PIZZA IS GONE?
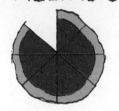
$\frac{1}{2}$
$\frac{1}{3}$
$\frac{1}{8}$

3. HOW MUCH HAS BEEN EATEN?
$\frac{1}{3}$
$\frac{1}{6}$
$\frac{1}{4}$

4. HOW MUCH IS GONE?

$\frac{1}{4}$
$\frac{1}{2}$
$\frac{1}{8}$

5. HOW MUCH IS LACED?
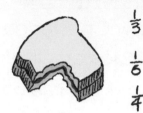
$\frac{1}{2}$
$\frac{1}{3}$
$\frac{1}{4}$

6. HOW MUCH TONIC IS LEFT?
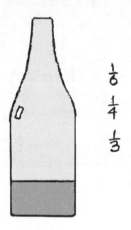
$\frac{1}{6}$
$\frac{1}{4}$
$\frac{1}{3}$

7. HOW MUCH WATER IS LEFT?

$\frac{3}{4}$
$\frac{1}{2}$
$\frac{1}{4}$

8. HOW MUCH HAS BEEN CUT OFF?

$\frac{1}{2}$ $\frac{1}{4}$
$\frac{1}{3}$

9. HOW MUCH WATER REMAINS?

$\frac{3}{4}$ $\frac{1}{2}$ $\frac{1}{4}$

10. HOW MUCH LEAF HAS BEEN EATEN?

$\frac{1}{4}$
$\frac{1}{6}$
$\frac{2}{3}$

11. HOW MUCH BREAD IS UNCUT?
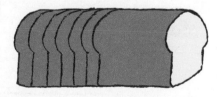
$\frac{1}{4}$ $\frac{1}{3}$ $\frac{1}{2}$

Scholastic Professional Books

Fraction Fun

Something that is split in 2 equal parts is divided in "half."

These two shapes are divided in half.

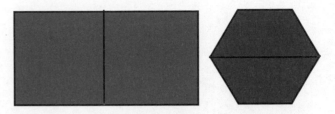

A fraction has a number on the top: ⟶ **1**

A fraction has a number on the bottom, too: ⟶ **2**

The top number tells the "fraction," or parts, of the whole.

The bottom number tells the number of parts in the whole.

Draw a line to match the picture with a fraction.

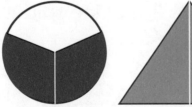

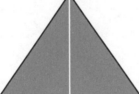

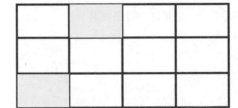

$$\frac{2}{2} \qquad \frac{2}{12} \qquad \frac{2}{3}$$

The top number in these fractions tells you how many parts to color. Try it!

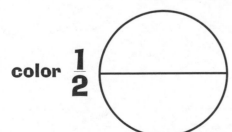

color $\frac{1}{2}$

color $\frac{2}{2}$

Fun With Fractions

A fraction has two numbers. The top number will tell you how many parts to color. The bottom number tells you how many parts there are.

Color 1/5 of the circle.   **Color 4/5 of the rectangle.**

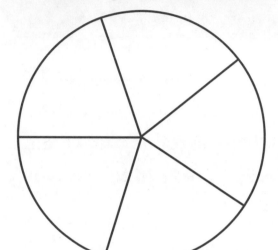   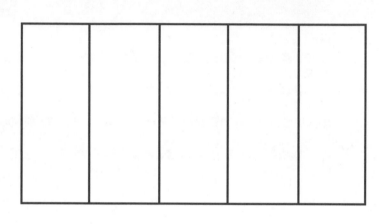

Color 3/5 of the ants.   **Color 2/5 of the spiders.**

   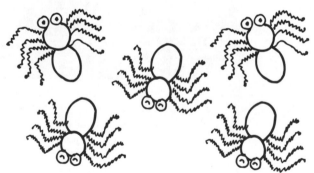

Color 0/5 of the bees.   **Color 5/5 of the worms.**

   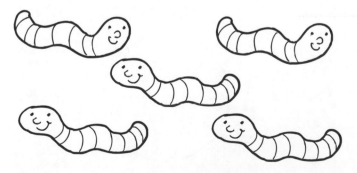

Scholastic Professional Books

More Fun With Fractions

A fraction has two numbers. The top number will tell you how many parts to color. The bottom number tells you how many total parts there are.

$\frac{10}{10}$ is the whole circle.

Color $\frac{8}{10}$ of the circle.

How much is not colored? ____

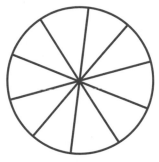

$$\frac{10}{10} - \frac{8}{10} = \underline{\quad}$$

$\frac{10}{10}$ is the whole rectangle.

Color $\frac{4}{10}$ of the rectangle.

How much is not colored? ____

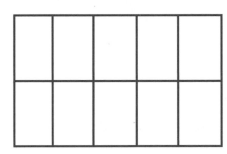

$$\frac{10}{10} - \frac{4}{10} = \underline{\quad}$$

Solve this fraction equation. Cross out the dogs to help you.

$$\frac{10}{10} - \frac{3}{10} = \underline{\quad}$$

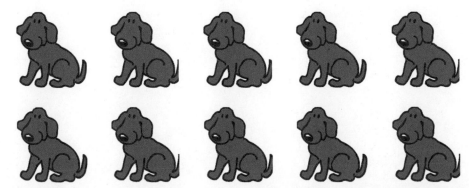

Answer Key

Reading Comprehension

Page 12
1. spots; My domino has two white spots, and yours has five. 2. sea bird; A gray seabird flew by the cruise ship. 3. A green stone; The queen had a beautiful necklace made of a green stone. 4. flute player; My sister is the best flute player in the high school band.

Page 13
Neil Armstrong was the first man to walk on the moon.

Page 14
1. IOU; 2. EZ; 3. ICU; 4. AB; 5. TP; 6. MT; 7. IV

Page 15
Police officers help people.

Page 16
On Saturday, Rachel got up early. Mom was still asleep, so Rachel made her own breakfast. She put some peanut butter in a bowl. She mixed it with a little *honey. Then she stirred in some *oatmeal, *bran flakes, and *raisins. It tasted yummy! When Mom got up, she said, "Oh, You made granola!"

Page 17
1. B; 2. U; 3. L; 4. L; 5. R ; 6. I; 7. D; 8. E; 9. R; 10. S; Bullriders

Page 18

Page 19
Make-believe: pig, goat and sheep, horses, pizza and hamburgers, mouse and table, golden eggs, crickets (The others are real.)

Page 20
Real: a woman feeding animals; a grandmother living alone; sleeping on hay in a barn; a house burning down; crying that her house burned (The rest are make-believe.)

Page 21
Children's answers will vary.

Page 22
1. Mia begged Spooky to come down. 2. Mia asked Mr. Carson for help. 3. Mr. Carson called his firefighter friends. 4. The fire truck came. 5. A firefighter climbed the ladder. 6. Spooky jumped to a tree and climbed down. 7. Mia scolded Spooky. 8. The firefighters laughed.

Page 23
Writing; Math; Recess; Social Studies; 11:00; Story Time; Science; Spelling; Music

Page 24
3, 1, 4, 2, 6, 7, 5, 8

Page 25
(Child's name) knows how to follow directions!

Page 26
Check child's picture.

Page 27
1. 50; 2. (your state); 4. 13; 6. Old Glory; 7. allegiance, America, Republic, indivisible, liberty, justice

Page 28
1. math; 2. taking out the trash; 3. playing a video game; 4. going to bed

Page 29
1. Backward Day
2. Check child's dot-to-dot picture.
3. 50, 45, 40, 35, 30, 25, 20, 15, 10, 5

Page 30
1. stealing; paid for it; 2. showed bad

manners; said "Excuse me"; 3. lying; told the truth; 4. hurt his feelings; helped him

Page 31
Each tree should be illustrated as described in the story.

Page 32
1. box shape; 2. heart shape; 3. circle shape; 4. semi-circle shape; 5. arc shape

Page 33
1. Zolak's shadow; 2. No; 3. No; He didn't see any real earthling, only his own shadow.
4.

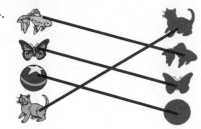

Page 34
1, 4, 6, 7, 10, 11, 14, 15, 18, 20, 21, 24, 26, teapot

Page 35
People Who Went to the Beach: Dad, Mom, Tim, and Tara

What They Did: swam, fished, built sandcastles, went sailing

Picnic Items: ham sandwiches, potato chips, apples, cookies, lemonade

Living Things They Saw on the Beach: crab, dog, starfish, sea gulls

Page 36
1. cheerful; angry; 2. away; west; 3. goat; parakeet; 4. mud; lemonade; 5. toy; arm; 6. Sarah; George; 7. spinach; pudding; 8. bicycle; crayon; 9. marble; dime

Birds 3; Desserts 7; Bad Feelings 1; Boys' Names 6; Money 9; School Supplies 8; Directions 2; Body Parts 5; Drinks 4

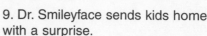

Page 37
Answers will vary.

Page 38
1. He learned to fly. 2. All of a sudden something wonderful happened. 3. afraid; 4. proud

Page 39
(Accept any reasonable answers.)
1. The home team wins the game. 2. The brownies will burn. 3. She will have a flat tire. 4. It will rain. 5. Mom will fall. 6. The boat will sink.

Page 40
Child should draw pictures that show these conclusions: Rita became a rabbit again. Diana became a duck again.

Page 41
Ryan—giant tortoise, 3-toed sloth
Both—albino alligator
Jessica—giraffe, owl

Page 42
Both had twenty dollars to spend. Joey bought sweets. Harry bought breakfast food.

Page 43
both, Kendra, Lacey, Lacey, both, Lacey, Lacey, Kendra, Lacey, Kendra, Lacey

Page 44

flowers   bales
boll   yarn
gin   fabric

Things made of cotton: shirt, pillow, sock, shorts, towel.
not made of cotton: scissors, pitcher, trumpet, cake

Page 45
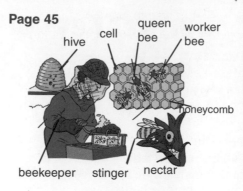
hive   cell   queen bee   worker bee
honeycomb
beekeeper   stinger   nectar

Page 46
- plains
- buffalo
- jerky
- tepee
- canoe
- buckskin clothing
- chief
- headdress

Child should put an X on the pictures of the computer, the helicopter, and the car. Other pictures should be circled.

Page 47
The girls got too loud, so Dad said to be quiet. The girls saw a bee land on Dad's bald head, so Mary Beth whopped Dad on the head with a book. The car ran off the road and through a fence, which let the cows out.

Page 48
1. spewing hot lava and ash into the air; 2. for people and animals to breathe; 3. flattened trees; 4. forest fires; 5. floods and mudslides; 6. it still erupts from time to time

Page 49
1. 2
6. Dr. Smileyface makes his patients laugh. 7. The child who wrote this story is not afraid to go to the dentist. 8. Dr. Smileyface teaches kids how to take care of their teeth.

9. Dr. Smileyface sends kids home with a surprise.

Page 50
HELPING OTHERS

Page 51
1. ~~Man~~; Lady; 2. ~~hot dogs~~; chicken nuggets; 3. ~~frowns~~; smiles; 4. ~~Miss Daniels~~; Lunch Lady; 5. ~~hardware~~; shoe; 6. ~~mean~~; kind

Page 52
Children should circle <u>Jed</u>, <u>bed</u> and <u>head</u>. They should draw a box around <u>long</u> and <u>wrong</u>.
Daisy, lazy, class, pass, crazy

Page 53

Paul Bunyan

Paul Bunyan was a mighty man. He was so big, he had to use wagon wheels for buttons. Paul was a lumberjack. He owned a blue ox named Babe. Paul and Babe were so big that their tracks made 10,000 lakes in the state of Minnesota.

Paul worked with seven axmen. They were so big that they were six feet tall sitting down. All of them were named Elmer. So when Paul called "Elmer," they all came running.

The year of the two winters, it got so cold that when the axmen would speak, their words froze in midair. When it thawed in the spring, there was a terrible chatter for weeks.

One time Paul caught two giant mosquitoes and used them to drill holes in maple trees.

Paul Bunyan had a purple cow named Lucy. In the year of two winters, it got so cold that Lucy's milk turned to ice cream before it hit the pail.

The End

Page 54
Check children's work to be sure they have correctly identified stage directions.

Tests: Reading

Pages 57–60   Test 1

A. Phonic Analysis: Consonants
Sample: cat

1. window   2. geese
3. ship   4. dog   5. lamp
6. hat   7. teeth   8. truck

B. Dictation
Sample: slide
1. boat   2. under   3. come

C. Vocabulary: Picture-Word Match
Sample: girl
1. leaf   2. barn   3. moon
4. boy   5. mouse

D. High-Frequency Word Match
Sample: the
1. or   2. from   3. have
4. where   5. through

E. Grammar, Usage, and Mechanics
Sample: He ran up the hill.
1. Did you take that book home?
2. We played outside all day.
3. Mrs. Smith is our teacher this year.
4. Maria is in my class.
5. I didn't have any homework last week.

F. Story Comprehension
1. in ponds   2. Frogs
3. a frog   4. bugs

Pages 61–64   Test 2

A. Phonic Analysis: Consonants
Sample: car
1. block   2. train   3. nest 4. bat
5. fish

B. Phonic Analysis: Vowels
Sample: cheese
1. broom   2. coat 3. mouse
4. three   5. bike

C. Dictation
Sample: rain
1. shake   2. is   3. some

D. High-Frequency Word Match
Sample: where
1. off   2. very   3. know 4. could
5. something

E. Grammar, Usage, and Mechanics
Sample: He plays in the park.
1. Did you see that star? 2. We run in the yard.
3. Mr. Smith is my neighbor.

4. She moved to New York.
5. He can't come to my house today.
6. Watch out!
7. The dog chased the cat.
8. Dr. Hamilton is nice.
9. We went to Texas.

F. Story Comprehension
1. groups of whales 2. Whales
3. stay wet 4. to get air

Pages 65–68   Test 3

A. Phonic Analysis: Consonants
Sample: car
1. bed   2. clock   3. grapes
4. hand   5. tooth

B. Phonic Analysis: Vowels
Sample: boat
1. house   2. feet   3. spoon
4. train   5. kite

C. Dictation
Sample: like
1. math   2. what   3. could

D. High Frequency Word Match
Sample: there
1. about   2. should   3. those
4. knew   5. everything

E. Grammar, Usage, and Mechanics
Sample: They walk to school.
1. I ride my bike in the park.
2. Can you lift this box?
3. My friend's name is Peter Jones.
4. We live in Maine.
5. Be careful!
6. I don't want to play.
7. We played at his house.
8. She's on her way home.
9. Our family doctor is Dr. Smith.

F. Story Comprehension
1. Tornadoes   2. a tornado
3. on hot days   4. to be safe

Pages 69–72   Test 4

A. Phonic Analysis: Consonants
Sample: broom
1. flag   2. spoon   3. snake
4. ring   5. truck

B. Phonic Analysis: Vowels
Sample: bike
1. coat   2. cake   3. leaf 4. rain
5. couch

C. Phonemic Awareness
Sample: pencil —2
1. tomato—3   2. map—1
3. information—4
4. bookmark—2   5. elephant—3

D. High-Frequency Word Match
Sample: who
1. after   2. school 3. because
4. might   5. know

E. Grammar, Usage, and Mechanics
Sample: We walk to school.
1. The boys color their pictures.
2. Yesterday, I played with my friend.
3. What is in your bag?
4. Look out!
5. My dog won't run.
6. She's going to the fair.
7. My mother will buy me a new coat next week.
8. I went on a trip to Florida.
9. Dr. Lee gave me a checkup.

F. Story Comprehension
1. Tigers   2. deer and wild pigs
3. Asia   4. Answers will vary

Pages 73–76   Test 5

A. Phonic Analysis: Consonants
Sample: tree
1. chair   2. plane   3. snake
4. nest   5. fish

B. Phonic Analysis: Vowels
Sample: baby
1. house   2. goat   3. zebra
4. spider   5. book

B. Dictation
Sample: live
1. her   2. draw   3. book

D. High Frequency Word Match
1. which   2. off   3. every 4. knot
5. will   6. together

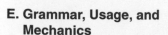

E. Grammar, Usage, and Mechanics

Sample: She ran in the park.

1. Did you read that book?
2. We swam in the lake.
3. Dr. Bell is my dentist.
4. She lives in Centerville.
5. He won't be at the soccer game.
6. Watch out!
7. The rabbit hopped to the carrot.
8. Mrs. Campbell drove the school bus.
9. We took a trip to New York.
10. I couldn't go to the park.

F. Story Comprehension

1. bird claws 2. Claws 3. to hold on to things 4. bear

Pages 77–80   Test 6

A. Phonic Analysis: Consonants

Sample: star

1. grapes 2. slide 3. branch
4. hand 5. clock

B. Phonic Analysis: Vowels

Sample: kite

1. boat 2. snake 3. pear
4. rainbow 5. cloud

C. Phonemic Awareness

Sample: apple—2

1. soup—1 2. cartwheel—2
3. television—4 4. shirt—1
5. animals—3

D. Grammar, Usage, and Mechanics

Sample: She rides a horse.

1. The children play soccer.
2. Last night, we watched a great movie.
3. Which story is yours?
4. That frog won't jump.
5. He's going to the zoo.
6. My book will come in the mail tomorrow.
7. Ms. Jones read a story to us.

E. Story Comprehension

1. Elephant Herds

2. a baby elephant
3. big and angry
4. Answers will vary

F. Story Comprehension

1. Chinese New Year
2. 15 days
3. cleaning their homes
4. Answers will vary.

Pages 81–84   Test 7

A. Phonic Analysis: Consonants

Sample: spider

1. watch 2. swan 3. plant
4. lock 5. box

B. Phonic Analysis: Vowels

Sample: baby

1. snail 2. iron 3. stove 4. ruler
5. boy

C. Phonemic Awareness

Sample: paper—2

1. elephant—3 2. ice—1
3. information—4 4. president—3
5. apple—2

D. Grammar, Usage, and Mechanics

Sample: They live in a city.

1. The farm animals eat grain.
2. Today, we will give the dog a bath.
3. Ouch! A bee stung me!
4. I can't swim in the deep water yet.
5. She's going to the library.
6. My aunt will take me to the movies tomorrow.
7. Mr. Smith fixed my bike.

E. Story Comprehension

1. Kwanzaa 2. 7 3. kind of candleholder 4. Answers will vary.

F. Reading a Graph

1. how many teeth students have lost 2. 4 students 3. 7 4. 0

Pages 85–88   Test 8

A. Phonic Analysis: Consonants

Sample: star

1. whale 2. flower 3. three
4. desk 5. zebra

B. Phonic Analysis: Vowels

Sample: foot

1. wheel 2. cloud 3. radio
4. bread 5. pie

C. Grammar, Usage, and Mechanics

Sample: We go to the park.

1. Can she run in the race?
2. They play baseball.
3. Mrs. Miller is my teacher.
4. She went on a trip to Boston.
5. He couldn't drive the car.
6. Help! There is a fire!
7. My aunt lives in Dallas, Texas.
8. "Let's eat out," said Mom.
9. The children can run around the track.

D. Story Comprehension

1. Trees Are Important 2. food
3. the fox 4. a baseball bat

E. Reading a Graph

1. what sports kids like best
2. soccer 3. 5
4. skating and baseball

Pages 89–92   Test 9

A. Phonic Analysis: Consonants

Sample: yarn

1. cheese 2. fish 3. tent
4. brush 5. clown

B. Phonic Analysis: Vowels

Sample: moon

1. house 2. feet 3. pear 4. fly
5. coin

C. Grammar, Usage, and Mechanics

Sample: We race down the hill.

1. May I go to the store?
2. He plays football every day.
3. I saw Mrs. Walker at the park.
4. I will visit my grandma in March.
5. Wow! You hit the ball hard.
6. I can't run as fast as Sam.
7. "I'm on my way," said Jane.
8. Yesterday, we rode our bikes.
9. We will soon move to Kansas.

D. Story Comprehension

1. Night Animals

2. a strong sense of smell

3. see in the dark

4. to hide from other animals

E. Reading a Graph

1. what colors students like best
   2. 6   3. red and green 4. 3

Pages 93–96   Test 10

A. Word-Match Dictation

Sample: I know the way to the playground.

1. We saw a deer in the woods.

2. Where do you want to go?

3. We got home last night.

4. I sent the letter yesterday.

5. Tim and Anna got mud on their clothes.

B. Synonyms

Sample: large

1. glad 2. quick 3. respond
4. fearless 5. furious

C. Antonyms

Sample: night

1. young 2. cold 3. dirty
4. short 5. weak

D. Grammar, Usage, and Mechanics

Sample: The boy walked home.

1. Where do you live?

2. Maria and I play soccer.

3. Our teacher is Mr. Lee.

4. We will watch a movie tomorrow.

5. Trish turned 8 years old on February 22, 2000.

6. Texas is in the South.

7. Yesterday, my mom helped me with my homework.

8. Owls don't sleep at night.

9. Jake is taller than Ed.

10. Is this your book?

11. We went for a ride in Mike's car.

E. Story and Graph Comprehension

1. twister 2. spring 3. 1996 4. 3

F. Story Comprehension

1. Hungry Spiders 2. animals

3. They eat insects that destroy crops. 4. Answers will vary.

Pages 97–100   Test 11

A. Word Match Dictation

Sample: Who won the game?

1. We built a sand castle.

2. I got mad at my brother.

3. Fill the pail with water.

4. Don't tear your jacket!

5. Did you hear the news?

B. Synonyms

Sample: center

1. kid 2. close 3. see 4. tells
5. completed

C. Antonyms

Sample: few

1. mine 2. short 3. loud 4. shrink
5. less

D. Grammar, Usage, and Mechanics

Sample: It is time for bed.

1. Did you brush your teeth?

2. Pam and I played with blocks.

3. School is over at three o'clock.

4. Today I will practice piano.

5. What do you want for your birthday?

6. Washington is where the President lives.

7. Will you push me on the swing?

8. I am finished reading this book.

9. She can ride a horse.

10. Jack's brother will turn 5 on October 28th, 2002.

11. Tim's cat has kittens.

E. Story Comprehension

1. 300 2. brain 3. living cells
4. Your Bones

F. Story Comprehension

1. They are too far away to come home each night. 2. gravity
3. sleep in a sleeping bag strapped to the walls.
4. Answers will vary.

Grammar

Page 148
1. T 2. Q 3. Q 4. T 5. T
6. Q 7. T

Page 149
1. T,
2. S,
3. D, ?
4. I, ?
5. M, .
6. Will he take the cat home?

Page 150
1. correct as is 2. The vet 3. cats.
4. correct as is 5. Do you
6. When is 7. He has 8. the vet.
9. goldfish? 10. Will you

Page 151
1. E. 2. C 3. E 4. E 5. E
6. C 7. Be yourself!
8. Don't copy other people.

Page 152
1. fear 2. excitement 3. surprise
4. anger 5. Please don't be upset!
6. Answers will vary.
7. Answers will vary.

Page 153
1. You are a great hopper!

2. The picture looks beautiful!

3. I can paint, too!

4. correct as is

5. Teach me how to hop.

6. Hop backward like this.

Page 154
1. I, . 2. M, I, ? 3. I, ! 4. C, I, ?
5. B, I, .

Telling Sentences: I sail my boat in the lake. Bill and I fly the kite.

Questions: May I have a turn? Can Kiku and I play?

Exclamations: I am so happy!

Page 155
1. T 2. C 3. T 4. C 5. Q
6. E 7. Q 8. I, Answers will vary.
9. I, Answers will vary.
10. I, Answers will vary.

Page 156
1. I have fun with my bike.
2. Can I ride to the beach?
3. I find a pretty shell.
4. correct as is
5. Get the shovel.
6. What a mess I made!

Page 157
1. boy, boat   2. brothers, park
3. girl, grandmother   4. boats, lake
5. Friends, needle, thread, sail
People: boy, brothers, girl, grandmother, friends
Places: park, lake
Things: boat, boats, needle, thread, sail

Page 158
Circled nouns: village, office, cane, pencil, doctor, boy, bed, aunt, school
People: doctor, boy, aunt
Places: village, school, office
Things: cane, pencil, bed

Page 159
1. no   2. yes   3. no   4. yes
5. place   6. person   7. person
8. thing

Page 160
1. George Ancona   2. Mexico
3. Jorgito   4. Coney Island
5. Honduras   6. Tio Mario
People: George Ancona, Jorgito, Tio Mario
Places: Mexico, Coney Island, Honduras

Page 161
1. Sue   2. California
3. Los Angeles   4. Pacific Ocean
5. Tonya   6. Sue Wong
7. Shore Road   8. Austin, Texas
Answers will vary.

Page 162
1. person   2. place   3. person
4. place   5. Emilio   6. Orlando
7. Disney World   8. Main Street

Page 163
1. runs   2. wears   3. smacks
4. holds   5. misses   6. waits

7. writes   8. helps

Page 164
1. watch   2. throws   3. opens
4. cheers   5. hits   6. runs   7. yells
8. eat

Page 165
1. action verb   2. not an action verb
3. not an action verb   4. not an action verb   5. action verb
6. action verb   7. not an action verb
8. action verb   9. action verb
10. not an action verb

Page 166
2. Crow, X   3. The water, X
6. One mouse, X

Page 167
1. a. Lin likes to play soccer.
2. b. Her friends watch her play.
3. a. They cheer for Lin.
4. a. Her mom goes to all of her games.
5. a. The coach is very proud of Lin.

Page 168
1. telling part   2. naming part
3. not the whole part   4. not the whole part   5. saw the cat go away
6. Then the bird   7. After a minute, the cat   8. walked back, too

Page 169
1. planted   2. watered   3. weeded
4. discovered   5. (blank)   6. pulled

Page 170
1. pushed   2. splashed   3. rolled
4. followed   5. washed
Answers will vary.

Page 171
1. visited   2. correct as is
3. correct as is   4. talked   5. asked
6. correct as is   7. correct as is
8. showed

Page 172
1. He, Wendell   2. She, Mother
3. They, The pigs   4. it, a board game   5. They, The pigs and Wendell   6. He, Wendell

Page 173
1. it   2. They   3. It   4. she   5. He

Page 174
1. Mrs. Fultz   2. The boy
3. The house   4. The pigs
5. He   6. they

Page 175
Exclamation: What a big mango! This tastes great!
Command: Buy me an avocado. Come over for dinner.
Question: Is that a banana? Did you find the fruit?
Telling Sentence: I want to eat dinner. I like mangoes.

Page 176
1. T   2. Q   3. T   4. C   5. E
6. C   7. Q   8. E

Page 177
1. command   2. question
3. exclamation   4. command
5. exclamation   6. telling
7. question   8. telling

Page 178
1. Two brothers can live together.
2. Hungbu will find a new home.
3. Mother will fix the house.
4. Will Sister clean the house?
5. Can the bird help them?

Page 179
1. Will I find some wood? QUESTION
2. Each of us must help. STATEMENT
3. Where are the trees? QUESTION
4. That is your pumpkin. Is that your pumpkin?
5. You can help cut the pumpkin.Can you help cut the pumpkin?

Page 180
1. Dad made eggs for breakfast.
2. He cracked open four eggs.
3. Do you like eggs?
4. Did you help him?
5. Beat eggs with a fork.
6. correct as is

Page 181
1. accordion(s) 2. brush(es)
3. clock(s), watch(es) 4. flower(s),
box(es) accordions, clocks, flowers
brushes, watches, boxes

Page 182
1. sandwiches 2. lunches
3. lunchboxes 4. dishes 5. boxes
6. dresses 7. coats 8. benches

Page 183
1. sketches 2. correct as is
3. foxes 4. correct as is 5. correct
as is 6. dresses 7. balls
8. correct as is

Page 184
1. brown, heavy 2. striped, two
3. little, six 4. brown, heavy,
striped, little 5. two, six

Page 185
1. zoo, big 2. giraffe, tall 3. girls,
two 4. spots, brown

color word: brown

size words: tall, big

number word: two

Page 186
1. red 2. yellow 3. purple 4. big
5. three 6. little 7. huge 8. Two

Page 187
1. is, now 2. are, now 3. were,
past 4. is, now 5. am, now
6. was, past

Page 188
1. is/was, one 2. is/was, one
3. were, more 4. are, more
5. was, one 6. are, more

Page 189
1. past, one
2. present, more than one
3. past, more than one
4. past, more than one
5. past, more than one
6. present, one

Page 190
1. present 2. present 3. present
4. present 5. past 6. past
7. past 8. past

Page 191
1. went 2. goes 3. does 4. did

5. Do 6. go

Page 192
1. goes 2. do 3. does 4. go
5. did 6. went 7. went 8. did

Page 193
1. "Let's go on a picnic."
2. "That's a great idea."
3. "What should we bring?"
4. "We should bring food."
5. "Yes, let's bring lots and lots of food."
6. "You're no help at all!"
7. Answers will vary.

Page 194
1. "It is raining!"
2. "What will we do today?"
3. "We could read."
4. "Maybe the sun will come out soon."
5. "But what will we do now?"
6. "Use your imagination!"
Answers will vary.

Page 195
1. "Let's make a sand castle," said Lenny.
2. "Where's the pail and shovel?" asked Sonya.
3. Sara said, "Maybe Otis can help."
4. "Do you want to dig?" asked Lenny.
5. Sonya shouted, "Get some water!"
6. "Look what we made!" cried the children.

Page 196
1. aren't, are not 2. doesn't, does
not 3. can't, cannot 4. couldn't,
could not 5. didn't, did not
6. isn't, is not 7. hadn't, had not
8. don't, do not 9. weren't, were
not

Page 197
1. couldn't 2. wasn't 3. aren't
4. can't 5. don't 6. didn't
Sentences will vary.

Page 198
1. aren't 2. isn't 3. can't
4. haven't 5. don't 6. didn't

7. couldn't 8. weren't

Page 199
1. writes 2. meets 3. ride
4. shop 5. closes 6. forget
7. locks 8. bang 9. call 10. hear

Page 200
1. play 2. hides 3. chase 4. calls
5. run 6. stand 7. closes
8. nudges 9. sleeps 10. sleep

Page 201
1. make 2. cuts 3. use 4. glow
5. hang 6. buy 7. picks 8. picks
9. wear 10. sell

Page 202
1. camp 2. likes 3. walks 4. build
5. cook 6. crawl
Sentences will vary.

Page 203
1. plays 2. play 3. runs 4. run
5. dive 6. dives 7. climb
8. climbs 9. throw 10. throw

Page 204
1. brings 2. likes 3. trade 4. eat
5. drink 6. buy 7. asks
8. wants 9. puts 10. find

Page 205
1. had; past 2. had; past 3. has;
now 4. has; now 5. has; now
6. have; now 7. have; now
8. had; past

Page 206
1. has 2. have 3. had 4. have
5. has 6. had 7. had 8. have
9. has

Page 207
1. correct as is 2. has 3. had
4. had 5. has 6. have
7. correct as is 8. correct as is

Writing

Page 210
Many of; Our teacher; The reading;
The globe; We study; Our class

Page 211
1. Art class; 2. Today we;
3. First, we; 4. The next;
5. My teacher; 6. Next week

Page 212
1. The blue whale is the largest animal in the world. 2. Even dinosaurs were not as large as the blue whale. 3. Blue whales are not part of the fish family. 4. The blue whale has no teeth. 5. Blue whales eat tiny sea creatures. 6. Blue whales have two blowholes.

Page 213
Sentences will vary.

Page 214
1. Where is the king's castle? 2. Who helped Humpty Dumpty? 3. Why did the cow jump over the moon? 4. Will the frog become a prince? 5. Could the three mice see?

Page 215
Sentences will vary.

Page 216
1. .; 2. ?; 3. ?; 4. .; 5. ?; 6. .; 7. ?; 8. .

Page 217
1. The sun is the closest star to Earth. 2. The sun is not the brightest star. 3. What is the temperature of the sun? 4. The sun is a ball of hot gas. 5. How large is the sun? 6. Will the sun ever burn out?

Page 218
Sentences will vary.

Page 219
Dear Mom and Dad,
    Camp is so cool! Today we went swimming. Do you know what the best part of camp is? I think fishing is my favorite thing to do. Did you feed my hamster? I really miss you. Love, Dalton Sentences will vary.

Page 220
1. .; 2. ?; 3. !; 4. ?; 5. .; 6. !; 7. ?; 8. .; 9. ?; 10. !; 11. .; 12. ?

Page 221
Sentences will vary.

Page 222
Sentences will vary.

Page 223
Sentences will vary.

Page 224
Sentences may vary. Possible answers: 1. A boy climbs a tree in his backyard. 2. A cat plays with fish in the living room. 3. A bunny eats a carrot in the garden.

Page 225
Sentences and pictures will vary.

Page 226
Lists of words will vary.

Page 227
Answers will vary. 1. fat, three; 2. wooden, cold; 3. Orange, sunny; 4. lazy, muddy; 5. thirsty, shallow; 6. funny, black

Page 228
Describing words will vary.

Page 229
Sentences will vary.

Page 230
Sentences will vary.

Page 231
Sentences will vary.

Page 232
1. The party was fun and exciting. 2. We blew up orange and red balloons. 3. We ate cake and ice cream. 4. The cake frosting was green and yellow. 5. We made a bookmark and a clay pot. 6. We brought games and prizes.

Page 233
1. These peanuts and pretzels are salty. 2. The first graders and second graders eat lunch at noon. 3. Where is the salt and pepper? 4. The napkins and forks are on the table. 5. Are the muffins and cookies in the oven? 6. Michael and Stephen bought lunch today.

Page 234
1. Fill a cup with water and add some flower seeds. 2. This will soften the seeds because they are hard. 3. Fill a cup with dirt while the seeds soak in water. 4. Bury the seeds in the cup until the dirt covers them. 5. Add water to the plant but do not add too much. 6. Set the cup in the sun so the plant will grow.

Page 235
Sentences will vary.

Page 236
Sentences will vary.

Page 237
Sentences will vary.

Page 238
Describing words will vary.
1. Sometimes I can see Mars, Jupiter, and Saturn with my telescope. 2. There are many stars in our galaxy. 3. Comets are large pieces of ice and rock. 4. The sun is really a huge star. 5. Is there life on any other planet? 6. Look at that beautiful shooting star! 7. Can you imagine traveling in space? 8. I think I saw a little alien.

Page 239
Describing words will vary.

Saturn is famous for the rings that surround it. Its rings are made of ice, rock, and dirt. The rings circle around the planet. Saturn is made of gas. Saturn's gases are lighter than water. That means Saturn would float if you put it into a tub of water. Saturn has a least 17 moons.

Page 240
1. took; 2. was; 3. saw; 4. many; 5. brought; 6. seen; 7. has; 8. are; 9. were; 10. saw; 11. wore; 12. going; 13. Does; 14. brought

Page 241
1. ~~brang~~, brought; 2. ~~seen~~, saw; 3. ~~gets~~, has; 4. ~~taked~~, took; 5. ~~is~~, are; 6. ~~runned~~, ran; 7. ~~get~~, have; 8. ~~was~~, were; 9. ~~saw~~, see; 10. ~~do~~, does; 11. ~~brang~~, brought; 12. ~~does~~, do

Page 242
Sentences will vary.

Page 243
Sentences will vary.

Page 244
Sentences will vary.

Page 245
Stories will vary.

Page 247
Sentences will vary.

Page 248
Sentences will vary.

Page 249
Answers will vary.

Page 250
Stories will vary.

Page 251
Stories will vary.

Page 252
Dear Friend,
    My job as the first president of the United States was hard. My friends and I had to make new laws, new money, and new jobs. The capital was in New York when I became president. Then it moved to Philadelphia. Is the capital still there? Who is the president today? I would love to see how the U.S. has changed over the past two hundred years!
Sincerely,
George Washington

Page 253
Letters will vary.

Maps

Page 256
1. yes 2. yes 3. yes 4. no
5. Answers will vary.

Page 257
3. They both show a place from above. 4. A photo has more detail.

Page 258
1. round 2. water 3. land where plants and trees grow

Page 259
1. round 2. smaller 3. the names of places

Pages 260–261
1. An x should be drawn on each continent 2. four 3. Africa, Antarctica, Asia, Australia
4. Atlantic, Arctic 5. A map is flat, but a globe is round.

Page 262
1. north 2. south 3. east 4. west

Page 263
1. Antarctica 2. Arctic Ocean
3. Indian Ocean: east; Europe: east and west; North America: west; Australia: east

Page 264
1. garden 2. south 3. west 4. ice skating rink

Page 265
1. east 2. north 3. west 4. south
5. apartment building

Page 266
Answers from left to right: 4, 6, 3, 2, 1, 5

Page 267
1. school 2. Clark Street 3. railroad
4. green 5. south

Pages 268–269
1. monkeys 2. east 3. yes 4. north
5. Circle Road 6. yes 7. no

Page 270
1. yes 2. no 3. no 4. no 5. yes
6. yes

Page 271
1. Jason 2. Buddy 3. Ellen 4. Mom
5. Buddy

Page 272
1. tennis court 2. B4 3. play golf
4. A2, B2, B1, C1

Page 273
1. B2 2. D2 3. A4 4. C4 5. C1
6. D4

Page 274
1. B1 2. a house 3. First Street
4. no 5. A3

Page 275
1. A4 2. Cincinnati 3. Lake Erie
4. C3 5. B5, C5, C4, D4, D3, D2, D1

Pages 276–277
1. Answers will vary. 2. Salem
3. Austin 4. east 5. Idaho
6. Answers will vary.

Page 27
1. star 2. Lincoln 3. South Dakota

4. Wyoming, Colorado 5. Missouri River

Page 279
1. B3 2. Norfolk 3. B4 4. A3, A4, A5, B5, C5, C6 5. Wyoming

Pages 280–281
1. Mississippi River 2. so people could travel there by boat 3. C2
4. Louis Armstrong Park 5. Union Station 6. B3, B4, B5, C3, C4
7. east

Pages 282–283
1. Austin, Texas 2. Texas 3. United States 4. larger 5. smaller 6. larger
7. south 8. Map 1: Austin, Texas

Pages 284–285
1. A mountain is much higher than a plain. 2. a valley 3. possible answers: a bridge, a boat 4. a plain; because the land is flat 5. a mountain; because the land is steep
6. Answers will vary.

Page 286
1. ocean 2. swim, fish, sail 3. a river flows, a lake is surrounded by land

Page 287
Child should write answers on map.

Pages 288–289
1. hills 2. green 3. plains, hills, mountains 4. west 5. Atlantic Ocean
6. plains 7. Potomac River 8. Answers will vary.

Pages 290–291
1. 93; north 2. 80 3. Las Vegas
4. Arizona, then Utah 5. 80; east
6. 395 7. 395 south to 50 east or 80 east to 93 south

Page 292
1. Answers will vary. 2. Answers will vary. 3. trees

Page 293
1. yes 2. yes 3. no 4. no 5. yes

Page 294
1. border 2. Mexico 3. north
4. Mexico City 5. west 6. Alaska
7. Rio Grande 8. Canada

Page 296

1. park 2. a book 3. south
4. Town hall 5. west 6. east
7. D1 8. First Street, Bell Avenue,
Second Street, Carol Street

Page 297

1. country border 2. Canada
3. Idaho 4. Columbia River
5. Olympia 6. forest products
7. 5

Page 298

1. compass rose 2. map key
3. island 4. landforms
5. continent 6. mountain
Secret Message: Maps Are Fun

Addition & Subtraction

Page 302

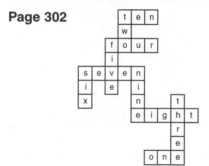

seven, nine

Page 303

Check that the child has drawn the
correct number of petals on each
flower. Bows with 4, 6, 8, and 10
should be colored yellow. Bows with
3, 5, 7, and 9 should be colored
purple.

Page 304

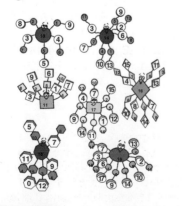

Page 305

A. 3, 2; B. 12, 5; C. 8, 6; D. 11, 7;

E. 7, 5; F. 12, 3; G. 4, 1; H. 10, 8; I. 9,
4; J. 11, 5; Answers will vary.

Page 306

Beans talk

4 + 2 = 6; 7 + 7 = 14; 9 + 5 = 14;
10 + 4 = 14; 4 + 8 = 12; 6 + 8 = 14;
11 + 3 = 14; 14 + 0 = 14; 7 + 2 = 9;
13 + 1 = 14; 5 + 8 = 13; 12 + 2 =
14; 7 + 4 = 11; 5 + 9 = 14

Page 307

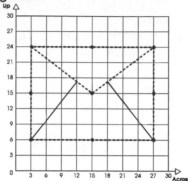

Page 308

21, 93, 78, 46, 44, 78; PLEASE
50, 67, 46, 79, 83, 59, 25, 66;
THANK YOU
59, 25, 66, 32, 78; YOU'RE
80, 78, 93, 18, 25, 35, 78;
WELCOME

Page 309

Answers will vary.

Page 310

38, 26, 97, 58, 67, 76, 79; 46, 84,
46, 89, 58, 48, 97; 58, 55, 65, 46,
40; THREE-FOURTHS, PACIFIC

Page 311

75, 23, 98, 86, 47, 34, 75, 99,
AMERICAN; 86, 98, 33, 78, 64, 87,
32, 47, 78, 99, REVOLUTION; 64,
47, 51, 98, 86, 32, 21, LIBERTY; 51,
98, 64, 64, BELL

Page 312

1. 7 − 1 = 6; 2. 9 − 2 = 7;
3. 3 − 2 = 1; 4. 8 − 4 = 4;
5. 5 − 5 = 0; 6. 6 − 1 = 5;
7. 8 − 2 = 6
The phone number is 671-4056.

Page 313

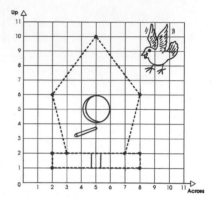

Page 314

Page 315

A bat

5 − 2 = 3; 7 − 7 = 0; 18 − 9 = 9; 17
− 3 = 14; 15 − 4 = 11; 18 − 4 = 14;
12 − 3 = 9; 11 − 9 = 2; 16 − 9 = 7;
7 − 4 = 3; 10 − 8 = 2; 15 − 7 = 8; 9
− 2 = 7; 13 − 2 = 11; 12 − 2 = 10;
15 − 2 = 13; 9 − 6 = 3; 6 − 6 = 0; 9
− 7 = 2; 15 − 9 = 6; 16 − 8 = 8;
9 − 5 = 4; 9 − 1 = 8

Page 316

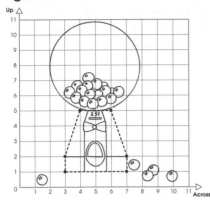

Page 317

68 - 26 = 42; 34 - 11 = 23; 91 - 20 = 71; 47 - 15 = 32; 67 - 13 = 54; 88 - 54 = 34; 19 - 12 = 7; 33 - 21 = 12; 69 - 59 = 10; 88 - 12 = 76; 28 - 24 = 4; 17 - 6 = 11; 57 - 55 = 2; 27 - 5 = 22; 97 - 13 = 84; 35 - 11 = 24; 81 - 21 = 60; 39 - 15 = 24; 60 - 10 = 50

Page 318

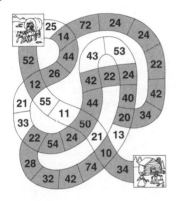

Page 319

62, 33, 23; 30, 21, 14; 61, 22, 41; The bird with the difference of 30 should be colored red. The bird with the difference of 14 should be colored blue. The birds with the differences of 22 and 33 should be colored green.

Page 320

Page 321

54, 85, 43, 85; 43, 54, 67; 43, 67, 32; 32; Check child's coloring.

Page 322

10, 12, 16; 18, 14, 19; 15, 11, 17; Bowls with 11, 15, and 18 should be colored yellow. Bowls with 10, 14, and 17 should be colored pink. Bowls with 12, 16, and 18 should be colored brown.

Page 323

Page 324

2 + 8 = 10; 24 + 7 = 31; 32 + 9 = 41; 1 + 9 = 10; 7 + 4 = 11; 45 + 5 = 50; 31 + 4 = 35; 11 + 9 = 20; 17 + 9 = 26; 22 + 13 = 35; 26 + 6 = 32; 19 + 9 = 28; 11 + 7 = 18; 16 + 22 = 38; 31 + 11 = 42; 14 + 9 = 23; 12 + 7 = 19; 40 + 14 = 54; 27 + 6 = 33; 12 + 9 = 21; 4 + 8 = 12; 41 + 21 = 62; 37 + 31 = 68; 16 + 6 = 22; 16 + 5 = 21; 10 + 24 = 34; 20 + 21 = 41; 15 + 5 = 20   Extra: Answers will vary.

Page 325

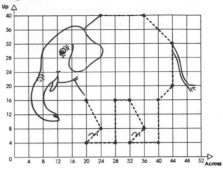

Page 326

A. 52, 93, 72, 93; B. 41, 62, 37, 37; C. 23, 50, 62, 62; D. 60, 32, 81, 60; E. 90, 44, 76, 44

Page 327

	71	93	90	52
92	90	91	86	92
81	81	73	42	92
85	74	92	90	94
51	41	93	81	

Page 328

Beach: Route #1—13 + 48 + 32 + 54 = 147 miles; Route #2—13 + 48 + 88 + 39 = 188 miles

Mountains: Route #1—13 + 17 + 31 + 49 = 110 miles; Route #2—13 + 28 + 10 + 25 = 76 miles

Page 329

1. 21; 2. 26; 3. 14; 4. 31 5. 35; 6. 28; 7. 27; 8. 29   9. 58; 10. 33

Page 330

15 + 33 + 27 = 75; 27 + 23 + 12 = 62; 34 + 23 + 24 = 81; 15 + 25 + 10 = 50; 16 + 14 + 14 = 44; 12 + 31 + 17 = 60; 28 + 22 + 45 = 95; 43 + 27 + 27 = 97; 10 + 17 + 18 = 45; 29 + 13 + 16 = 58; 37 + 31 + 17 = 85; 51 + 23 + 17 = 91

Page 331

35: 3 tens 5 ones, 2 tens 15 ones; 47: 4 tens 7 ones, 3 tens 17 ones; 82: 8 tens 2 ones, 7 tens 12 ones; 94: 9 tens 4 ones, 8 tens 14 ones; 61: 6 tens 1 one, 5 tens 11 ones; 90: 9 tens 0 ones, 8 tens 10 ones

Page 332
Boldfaced numbers should be circled.
A. **48**, 89; B. 79, **46**; C. 36, **76**; D. **77**, 59; E. **48**, 14; F. 61, **68**; G. 14, **39**; Answers will vary.

Page 333
A. 19, 39, 37; 1, 3, 2; B. 8, 6, 9; 2, 1, 3; C. 28, 37, 14; 2, 3, 1; D. 29, 38, 37; 1, 3, 2; E. 29, 36, 48; 1, 2, 3; F. 18, 15, 19; 2, 1, 3

Page 334
35 − 17 = 18; 62 − 28 = 34; 53 − 14 = 39; 92 − 27 = 65; 82 − 23 = 59; 83 − 28 = 55; 67 − 48 = 19; 58 − 29 = 29; 72 − 17 = 55; 73 − 58 = 15; 42 − 26 = 16; 90 − 81 = 9; 52 − 28 = 24; 56 − 19 = 37

Page 335
45 - 39 = 6; 84 - 59 = 25; 72 - 55 = 17; 71 - 19 = 52; 84 - 25 = 59; 60 - 18 = 42; 98 - 29 = 69; 74 - 15 = 59; 71 - 17 = 54; 88 - 29 = 59; 82 - 68 = 14; 91 - 32 = 59; 34 - 16 = 18; 92 - 13 = 79; 43 - 35 = 8; 57 - 28 = 29

She had 15 tickets left.

Page 336
65 − 27 = 38, 38 + 27 = 65; 77 − 38 = 39, 39 + 38 = 77; 24 − 15 = 9, 9 + 15 = 24; 32 − 13 = 19, 19 + 13 = 32; 83 − 49 = 34, 34 + 49 = 83; 50 − 19 = 31, 31 + 19 = 50; 46 − 29 = 17, 17 + 29 = 46; 62 − 15 = 47, 47 + 15 = 62

Answers will vary.

Page 337
U. 81; L. 5; N. 60; C. 46; O. 90; P. 38; H. 23; K. 63; S. 48; A. 14; G. 18; M. 71; R. 69; KANGAROO; KOALA; OPOSSUM; POUCH

Page 338
Check that the child has colored the appropriate spaces. A. 21; B. 9; C. 26; D. 8; E. 13; F. 17; G. 30; H. 7

Page 339
A. 28 + 25 = 53; B. 25 − 9 = 16; C. 28 − 13 = 15; D. 12 + 9 = 21; E. 12 − 9 = 3; F. 13 + 28 = 41; G. 9 + 25 + 12 = 46; 98 students

Page 340
saw: 34 + 27 + 5 = 66; wrench: 48 + 36 + 15 = 99; hammer: 43 + 15

+ 27 = 85; pliers: 39 + 34 + 15 = 88; A. 27 + 15 = 42; B. 34 − 5 = 29, 48 − 15 = 33, 43 − 15 = 28; 39 − 15 = 24; 43 + 15 + 27 + 5 + 34 + 39 + 48 + 15 + 36 = 262

Page 341
A. 596, red; B. 995, blue; C. 877, blue; D. 569, blue; E. 662, red; F. 978, red; G. 968, red; H. 596, red; I. 899, blue; J. 497, blue

Page 342
2 hundreds 7 tens, 8 hundreds 4 tens, 9 hundreds 3 tens, 7 hundreds 1 ten; 5 hundreds 6 tens, 3 hundreds 2 tens, 4 hundreds 9 tens, 6 hundreds 5 tens; 570; 804

Page 343

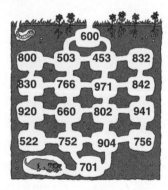

Page 344
207 + 544 = 751; 126 + 89 = 215; 328 + 348 = 676; 257 + 458 = 715; 547 + 129 = 676; 624 + 127 = 751; 108 + 107 = 215; 229 + 418 = 647; 258 + 268 = 526; 379 + 336 = 715; 417 + 109 = 526; 153 + 494 = 647

Page 345

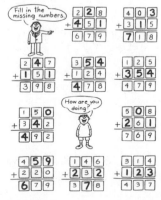

Page 346
A. $1.49 + $.50 + $.75 + $1.22 = $3.96; B. $1.72 + $.65 + $1.17 = $3.54; C. $1.86 + $1.84 + $.84 + $1.07 = $5.61; D. $1.53 + $1.90 + $1.22 + $.84 = $5.49; E. $1.86 + $.50 + $1.17 = $3.53; F. $1.49 + $.86 + $.75 = $3.10

Page 347
A. 123 + 406 + 406 = 935, orange; B. 209 + 81 + 147 + 181 + 72 = 690, green; C. 146 + 266 + 120 + 139 + 82 = 753, purple; D. 180 + 169 + 308 + 122 = 779, yellow; E. 154 + 154 + 188 + 93 + 82 + 170 = 841, red; F. 107 + 173 + 38 + 280 + 38 + 54 + 78 = 768, blue

Page 348
40 tens, 20 tens, 70 tens, 50 tens; 10 tens, 90 tens, 80 tens, 30 tens

Page 349

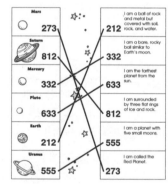

Page 350

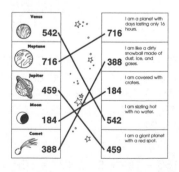

900, 800, 700, 600, 500, 400, 300, 200, 100, Subtract 100.; 900, 700, 500, 300, 100, Subtract 200.; 800, 600, 400, 200, Subtract 200.

Page 351

Page 352

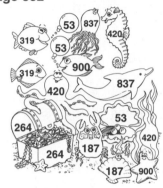

Check child's coloring.

Page 353

Page 354

A. 700 − 523 = 177; B. 300 − 156 = 144; C. 248 + 176 = 424, 600 − 424 = 176; D. 189 + 96 = 285, 400 − 285 = 115; E. 398 + 275 = 673, 900 − 673 = 227

Page 355

A. 168 − 159 = 9; B. 427 + 289 = 716; C. 507 − 278 = 229; D. 319 + 299 = 618; E. 826 − 697 = 129; F. 258 + 273 = 531

Page 356

T. 500; O. 903; L. 285; P. 846; A. 535; W. 951; I. 870; P. 528; L. 979; I. 207;

R. 821; I. 564; O. 254; A. 853; N. 273; N. 869; R. 517; H. 811; A. 894; LION, TAPIR, PIRANHA, OWL

Page 357

B. 773; E. 569; L. 467; H. 374; F. 248; D. 385; A. 796; N. 288; I. 834; O. 883; M. 689; C. 259; T. 896; R. 800; P. 704; FIREMAN, TEACHER, DOCTOR, LIBRARIAN, POLICEMAN

Page 358

sandals $2.10 + swimsuits $6.89 + sand toys $1.23 + swim ring $1.46 = $11.68

mittens $.77 + coat $7.14 + hat $1.23 + skis $3.74 = $12.88

$12.88 − $11.68 = $1.20

Page 359

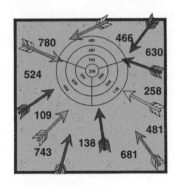

Answers will vary.

Page 360

427 + 282 = 709, 636 − 550 = 86; 963 − 189 = 774, 148 + 370 = 518, 550 + 370 = 920, 804 − 636 = 168; 189 + 751 = 940, 579 − 282 = 297, 963 − 148 = 815, 415 + 189 = 604

Page 361

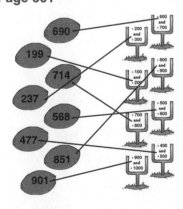

Page 362

Game 1: 637, 616; 353, 454; 851, 800; 189, 326; 554, 820

Game 2: 283, 218; 412, 417; 536, 509; 844, 873; 172, 128

Math

Page 365

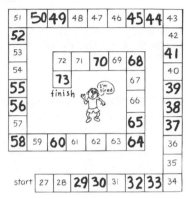

Page 366

A salamander

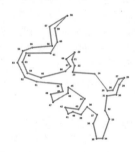

Page 367

1. 67; 2. 34, 35; 3. 42, 43; 4. 16, 18 5. 73, 74, 75; 6. 31, 32; 7. 10 12 14 16 8. 15 18 21 24; 9. 83, 84, 85, 86, 87, 88 10. after; 11. before; 12. after 13. before; 14. before; 15. before

Page 368

Students should follow these numbers:

13, 7, 3, 9, 19, 23, 11, 5, 17, 67, 33, 25, 27, 35, 39, 37, 23, 57, 47, 43, 21, 15, 39, 29

Page 369

Top side of the street: 50, 52, 54, 56 Bottom side of the street: 51, 53, 55

Extra: The even numbers are on one side of the street. The odd numbers are on the other side of the street.

Scholastic Professional Books

Page 370
1. the 1st 2. the 16th 3. James Buchanan 4. Andrew Johnson 5. 14

Page 371
1. 11 < 21; 2. 56 < 72; 3. 47 = 47; 4. 64 >10 5. 59 = 59; 6. 38 >17; 7. 526 < 527; 8. 159 > 42 9–16. Answers will vary. 17. 73 61 54 37 18. 96 43 24 22; 19. 79 78 69 51 20. 51 37 27 15

Page 372
A sidewalk. 518, 315, 276, 693, 137, 564, 909, 811, 209, 717, 836, 321, 488, 857, 432, 707

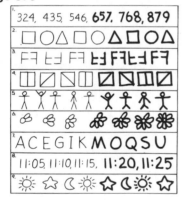

Page 373

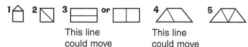

Page 374

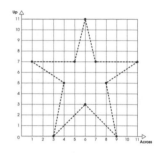

This line could move up or down.

This line could move left or right.

Page 375
1. 32, 42, 52, 62, 72, 82, 92; 2. 70, 60, 50, 40, 30, 20, 10; 3. 67, 57, 47, 37, 27, 17, 7; 4. 44, 55, 66, 77, 88, 99

Page 376
Answers will vary.

Page 377
A. 1F, 2G, 3B, 4C or A, 5E, 6I, 7E, 8H, 9G, 10G, 11C B. 1B, 2F, 3D, 4I, 5F, 6E, 7A, 8D, 9I, 10F, 11I C. 1H, 2C, 3C, 4G, 5G, 6C, 7F, 8I, 9B, 10C or A, 11F

Page 378
1. 5; 2. 8; 3. 11; 4. 26; 5. 6 6. 10; 7. 12; 8. 16; 9. 18; 10. 24

What did the rocket say when it left the party? "Time to take off."

Page 379
1. 15; 2. 6; 3. 24; 4. 12; 5. 27 6. 18; 7. 30; 8. 36; 9. 33; 10. 0

What did the owl say when someone knocked on its door? "Whoooo is it?"

Page 380
2 inches; 4 inches Two possible answers: 6 inches, because it grew 2 inches each week; or 8 inches, because it doubled in height each week

Page 381
10, 10, 10 Extra: 2

Page 382
3 groups: fish, shells, animals with multiple legs/arms

Page 383
Answers will vary.

Page 384
1. 4 + 5 = 9; 2. 11 - 6 = 5; 3. 9 + 7 = 16; 4. 4 + 8 = 12; 5. 3 - 2 = 1; 6. 7 + 7 = 14; 7. 15 - 10 = 5; 8. 2 + 8 = 10; 9. 5 - 2 = 3

Page 385
15; 8

Page 386
Extra: Answers will vary. Possible: Pepperoni is the most popular topping. Cheese is the next favorite topping. Sausage is the least favorite topping.

Page 387
1. 7:35, 35 minutes after 7, 25 minutes to 8; 2. 3:50, 50 minutes after 3, 10 minutes to 4 3. 9:15, 15 minutes after 9, 45 minutes to 10 4. 6:25, 25 minutes after 6, 35 minutes to 7; 5. 9:55, 55 minutes after 9, 5 minutes to 10 6. 2:05, 5 minutes after 2, 55 minutes to 3

Pages 388–389
1. Teeny Sandwiches; 75¢ 2. Donut Hole; 25¢ 3. Peanuts 4. Gulp of Juice 5. 95¢ 6. 50¢

Page 390
Alex's coins: 5¢ + 25¢ + 10¢ = 60¢
Billy's coins: 10¢ + 10¢ + 10¢ + 10¢ + 10¢ + 5¢ + 5¢ + 1¢ + 1¢ + 1¢ = 63¢
63¢ > 60¢ Billy has more money.

Page 391
1. feet; 2. yards; 3. miles; 4. inches; 5. inches 6. inches; 7. yards; 8. miles; 9. feet; 10. inches 11. feet; 12. feet; 13. miles; 14. inches; 15. feet

Page 392
Sunny days: 12; Cloudy days: 8; Rainy days: 5; Snowy days: 6

Page 393
1 + 1 + 1 = 3 inches; 2 + 2 + 2 = 6 inches; 4 + 4 + 4 = 12 inches

Page 394

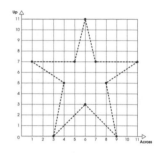

Page 395

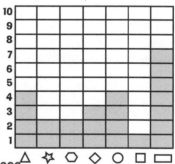

Page 396
Answers will vary.

Page 397
2, size; Correct pies: 1, 3, 5

Page 398
1. 1/2; 2. 1/8; 3. 1/4; 4. 1/4; 5. 1/2; 6. 1/6 7. 1/2; 8. 1/2; 9. 3/4; 10. 1/4; 11. 1/2

Page 399
2/2 matches triangle, 2/3 matches circle, 2/12 matches rectangle; color 1/2 circle, color the whole rectangle

Page 400
1/5 of the circle, 4/5 of the rectangle, 3 ants, 2 spiders, 0 bees, 5 worms

Page 401
2/10, 6/10, 2/10, 6/10, 7/10